Abiding in the Retreat

Previously published by the Lama Yeshe Wisdom Archive

By Lama Zopa Rinpoche
Virtue and Reality
Teachings from the Vajrasattva Retreat
Daily Purification: A Short Vajrasattva Practice
Making Life Meaningful
Teachings from the Mani Retreat
The Direct and Unmistaken Method
The Yoga of Offering Food
The Joy of Compassion
How Things Exist
The Heart of the Path
Teachings from the Medicine Buddha Retreat
Kadampa Teachings
Bodhisattva Attitude
How to Practice Dharma
The Perfect Human Rebirth
Sun of Devotion, Stream of Blessings
A Teaching on Heruka (initiates only)
A Teaching on Yamantaka (initiates only)

By Lama Yeshe
Becoming Your Own Therapist
Make Your Mind an Ocean
The Essence of Tibetan Buddhism
The Peaceful Stillness of the Silent Mind
Ego, Attachment and Liberation
Universal Love
Life, Death and After Death

By Lama Yeshe & Lama Zopa Rinpoche
Advice for Monks and Nuns
Freedom Through Understanding

Other books
Teachings from Tibet by various great lamas
The Kindness of Others by Geshe Jampa Tegchok

In association with TDL Publications
Mirror of Wisdom by Geshe Tsultim Gyeltsen
Illuminating the Path to Enlightenment by His Holiness the Dalai Lama

May whoever sees, touches, reads, remembers, or talks or thinks about these books never be reborn in unfortunate circumstances, receive only rebirths in situations conducive to the perfect practice of Dharma, meet only perfectly qualified spiritual guides, quickly develop bodhicitta and immediately attain enlightenment for the sake of all sentient beings.

⋅ ⋅ ⋅ ⋅
⋅

LAMA ZOPA RINPOCHE

Abiding in the Retreat
A Nyung Nä Commentary

Compiled and edited by Ailsa Cameron

LAMA YESHE WISDOM ARCHIVE • BOSTON
www.LamaYeshe.com

A non-profit charitable organization for the benefit of all
sentient beings and an affiliate of the Foundation for
the Preservation of the Mahayana Tradition
www.fpmt.org

First published 2017

LAMA YESHE WISDOM ARCHIVE
PO BOX 636
LINCOLN
MA 01773, USA

© Lama Thubten Zopa Rinpoche 2017

Please do not reproduce any part of this book
by any means whatsoever without our permission

Library of Congress Cataloging-in-Publication Data

Names: Thubten Zopa, Rinpoche, 1945- author. | Cameron, Ailsa.
Title: Abiding in the retreat : a nyung nä commentary / Lama Zopa Rinpoche;
compiled and edited by Ailsa Cameron.
Description: Lincoln, MA : Lama Yeshe Wisdom Archive, 2017. |
Includes bibliographical references.
Identifiers: LCCN 2017024196 | ISBN 9781891868696 (pbk.)
Subjects: LCSH: Avalokiteshvara (Buddhist deity)—Cult—Tibet Region. |
Spiritual life—Buddhism. | Buddhism—Rituals.
Classification: LCC BQ4710.A84 T573 2017 | DDC 294.3/4446—dc23

ISBN 978-1-891868-69-6

10 9 8 7 6 5 4 3 2 1

Cover photograph by Tan Seow Kheng. The new Chenrezig statue at Amitabha
Buddhist Centre, Singapore, made by Denise and Peter Griffin.
Other photos by Bill Kane, Singapore, 2016.
Designed by Gopa & Ted2 Inc.

❂ Printed in the USA with environmental mindfulness on 30% PCW recycled paper.
The following resources have been saved: 27 trees, 849 lbs. of solid waste,
12,685 gallons of water, 2,239 lbs. of greenhouse gases and 1 million
BTUs of energy. (papercalculator.org)

Please contact the LAMA YESHE WISDOM ARCHIVE
for more copies of this and our other free books.

Contents

Editor's Preface	xiii
Part One: Introduction	1
1. The Benefits of Nyung Nä Practice	3
The meaning of nyung nä	3
The benefits of nyung nä practice	4
Experiencing difficulties	8
Transforming your body	9
Don't miss the opportunity	10
2. Chenrezig	13
The story of Chenrezig	13
Manifestations of Chenrezig	16
The power of Chenrezig	20
3. Bhikshuni Lakshmi	23
4. The Nyung Nä Lineage Lamas	29
Chandra Kumara	29
Jñanabhadra	30
Peñawa of Nepal	31
Dawa Gyältsän	31
Nyiphug Chökyidrag	38
Trupa Dorje Gyälpo	43
Zhangtön Drajig	44

Jangchub Päl 46
Dewa Chän 48
Jangchub Bar 49
Modern nyung nä yogis 52
 Geshe Lama Konchog 52
 Drupa Rinpoche 54

5. **The Benefits of the Eight Mahayana Precepts** 57
When to take the Eight Mahayana Precepts 57
Receiving the lineage 60
The benefits of taking the Eight Mahayana Precepts 61
Shortening the time 63
Differences between the Mahayana and pratimoksha precepts 64
 Difference of motivation 64
 Difference of visualization 65
 Difference of ordination 66

6. **The Benefits of Reciting om mani padme hum** 67
Why everyone should recite om mani padme hum 67
The benefits of reciting om mani padme hum 69
The longest Chenrezig mantra 70
The benefits of reciting ten malas of om mani padme hum 71
Easy to become Dharma 74
Rinpoche's mother 76

7. **The Benefits of Prostrations** 83
The general benefits of prostrations 83
The ten specific benefits of prostrations 84
How to do prostrations physically 85
How to do prostrations mentally 86
Dealing with difficulties 87

8. THE BENEFITS OF OFFERINGS	89
The power of Buddha	89
Power of the object	92
Always remember the guru	93
The power of the guru	94
Dangers with the guru	97
Practicing with holy objects	99
The specific benefits of offering flowers	100
The specific benefits of offering light	101
How to make offerings	102
Dedicating the offering	103
PART TWO: THE PREPARATORY RITUAL	105
9. BRIEF MOTIVATIONS	107
1. Take the responsibility	107
2. Bodhicitta is of the utmost need	107
3. Every sentient being is your dearest one	108
4. Repaying the kindness	109
5. Numberless, kind and precious	109
6. Developing great compassion is of utmost importance	110
10. INTERMEDIATE MOTIVATION	111
1. This practice is for every sentient being	111
2. My mothers are suffering	113
3. Giving up self, cherishing others	114
4. Beginningless kindness	117
5. By myself alone	119
6. If I had great compassion	120
11. EXTENSIVE MOTIVATIONS	123
1. If I had generated bodhicitta	123
2. Freedom to practice Dharma	126

    3. Your human body is so precious   131
    4. We need to purify right now   144

12. Ablution and Lam-Rim Prayers   155
    Ablution   155
    Lam-rim prayers   156
        Calling the Guru from Afar   156
        Calling the Guru from Afar (abbreviated version)   157
        Praise and Prayer to Noble Avalokiteshvara   159
        Request to the Supreme Compassionate One   160

13. Taking the Restoring and Purifying Ordination   163
    Refuge and Bodhicitta   163
    Purifying the Place   163
    Invocation   164
    Offering Prayer   165
    Offering Cloud Mantra   165
    Extensive Power of Truth   166
    Seven-Limb Prayer   167
    Mandala Offering   168
    Visualization and Motivation   168
    Actual Ordination   169
    The Commitment Prayer to Keep the Precepts   172
    The Mantra of Pure Morality   177
    Dedication   178

14. Requests through to Invocation   181
    Requests to the Lineage Gurus   181
    Instantaneous Generation   182
    Blessing the Action Vase   183
    Blessing the Offerings   184
    Refuge and Bodhicitta   185

Generating Bodhicitta	189
Invocation of the Merit Field	190

15. The Seven-Limb Practice — 191

Limb of Prostration	192
Limb of Offering	194
Mandala Offering	202
Limb of Confession	204
The Practice of Prostrations to the Thirty-five Confession Buddhas	206
Rejoicing in Virtue	210
Rejoicing in your own merit	213
Rejoicing in the merit of ordinary sentient beings	214
Rejoicing in the merit of bodhisattvas	215
Rejoicing in the merit of buddhas	215
Rejoicing in the merit of ordinary sentient beings, bodhisattvas and buddhas together	215
Requesting to Turn the Wheel of Dharma	216
Requesting the Guru to Remain	217
Dedicating	217
The Mantra of Pure Morality	218
Prayer to Keep Pure Morality	218
Four Immeasurables	218
Departure of the Merit Field	219

Part Three: The Actual Ritual — 221

16. Meditation on the Self Generation — 223

1. The Ultimate Deity	223
A brief meditation on emptiness	224
A more elaborate meditation on emptiness	225
Meditating on the ultimate deity	227
2. The Deity of Sound	228

3. The Deity of Syllables — 228
  4. The Deity of Form — 228
  5. The Deity of Mudra — 229
  6. The Deity of Sign — 229
  Offerings to the Self Generation — 232
    Blessing the Offerings — 232
    Presenting the Offerings — 232
  Blessing the Rosary — 232
  Mantra Recitation — 233
  Padmasattva Mantra — 233

17. **Meditation on the Front Generation** — 235
  Invocation — 235
  Empowerment — 235
  Blessing the Offerings — 236
  Presenting the Offerings — 236
    Offering the twenty-five substances — 237
    Offering the seven signs of royalty — 237
    Offering the eight auspicious signs — 237
    Mandala offering — 238
  Brief Praise — 238
  Blessing the Vase Water and Reciting the Mantra — 238
  Absorption of the Exalted Wisdom Beings — 239
  The Principal Practice of Praise — 240

Part Four: The Concluding Ritual — 243

18. **The Completion Practices** — 245
  Request — 245
  Offering the Tormas — 245
    Blessing the Tormas — 246
    Offering the Torma to the Great Compassionate One and his Retinue — 247
    Praises to the Dharma Protectors — 247

Torma Offering to the Dharma Protectors and the Dakas and Dakinis	248
Torma Offering to the Local Deities	248
Offering an Ablution	249
Drying the Holy Bodies	252
Offering Divine Garments	252
Offering Ornaments	252
Offering a Vase	252
Offering a Crown	252
Request	253
Dedication	254
Purifying Errors with the Hundred-Syllable Mantra of Padmasattva	255
Inner Ablution: Taking the Vase Nectar	255
Arising as the Commitment Being	256
Dedication	256
Requesting to Reside or Depart	257
A. When the Basis of the Front Generation is a Drawn Mandala, Request the Deities to Reside Continually	257
C. When the Basis of the Front Generation is Heaps of Substances, Request the Deities to Depart	258
Verses of Auspiciousness	258
Prayer of Abiding in the Retreat	258
Expression of Auspiciousness of Abiding in the Retreat	259
Dedications	259
Lama Tsongkhapa dedication prayers	260
Author's Colophon	262
Author's Dedication	262

PART FIVE: ADDITIONAL INSTRUCTIONS — 265

19. ADDITIONAL ADVICE — 267

The yoga of sleeping	267
The final morning	267

The yoga of eating	269
The yoga of washing	272
Mantra recitation	273
Shortening sessions	273
Chenrezig great initiation	274
Tsog offering	275

APPENDIXES — 277

1. The Benefits of Cleaning — 279
2. The Meaning of *Son of the Essence* — 281
3. The Meaning of *Yidam* — 283
4. Karma Stories — 285

BIBLIOGRAPHY — 291

SUGGESTED FURTHER READING — 293

Editor's Preface

Compassion is the wish to free all living beings from suffering and its causes, and the embodiment of the compassion of all the buddhas is Chenrezig (Skt: Avalokiteshvara), the Buddha of Compassion. One of the most intensive and powerful Chenrezig practices is *nyung nä*, a two-day retreat that combines meditation on Thousand-Arm Chenrezig and recitation of Chenrezig's mantra, OM MANI PADME HUM, with prostrations, fasting and silence. *Abiding in the Retreat* is a commentary to a nyung nä *sadhana* composed by Kelzang Gyatso, the Seventh Dalai Lama,[1] according to the nyung nä lineage originating from Bhikshuni Lakshmi (Gelongma Pälmo), an Indian princess who cured herself of leprosy and achieved enlightenment through nyung nä practice.

Very little commentary to nyung nä practice is available in English. As nyung nä retreats are held each year in many FPMT[2] centers, I thought to compile a nyung nä commentary by Lama Zopa Rinpoche, Spiritual Director of the FPMT. Whenever I mentioned to Rinpoche that I was working on a nyung nä commentary, however, he would object that he had yet to give the elaborate explanation of the practice. The one time Rinpoche began such a commentary, based on Kachen Yeshe Gyältsän's extensive text, at Chenrezig Institute, Australia, in 1991, he covered only a little on nyung nä practice itself.

Because for many years I had been steadily collecting Rinpoche's teachings on Chenrezig practice in general and nyung nä practice in particu-

---

[1] See *Nyung Nä: A Nyung Nä Ritual Sadhana of the Eleven-Face Great Compassionate One in the Pälmo Tradition with the Requests to the Lineage Gurus*, by Losang Kelzang Gyatso, the Seventh Dalai Lama, translated by Lama Zopa Rinpoche and George Churinoff. In general, *Abiding in the Retreat* follows the translations in this nyung nä sadhana but sometimes uses Rinpoche's translations.
[2] The Foundation for the Preservation of the Mahayana Tradition.

lar, I was confident that I had enough material for a useful commentary to nyung nä practice. This book combines teachings given when Rinpoche participated in nyung näs at Kopan Monastery, Nepal, and Tushita Retreat Centre, India, in 1984; at Vajrapani Institute, California, in 1988; and in Taiwan in 1991; plus teachings given during an oral transmission of the nyung nä sadhana at Tushita in 2008 and during a Chenrezig great initiation in Singapore in 2009.[3] As Rinpoche had asked for stories of the nyung nä lineage lamas to be added to a new edition of *Nyung Nä* to inspire people to do the practice, I also added these stories from various other teachings.[4]

Part One: Introduction contains the benefits of nyung nä retreat and of various practices within a nyung nä (taking the Eight Mahayana Precepts,[5] reciting OM MANI PADME HUM, doing prostrations and making offerings) and the stories of Chenrezig, Bhikshuni Lakshmi and the lineage lamas. The remaining four parts (*The Preparatory Ritual*, *The Actual Ritual*, *The Concluding Ritual* and *Additional Instructions*) contain the actual instructions on how to do a nyung nä. As Rinpoche himself said, "The long motivations for the Restoring and Purifying Ordination and explanation of the benefits of doing nyung näs, taking precepts and so forth were done with the hope that you would understand that these are important practices and would wish to do them again and again in the future. Also, for you to know the way of doing nyung näs as correctly as possible."

For their contributions to this book, heartfelt thanks must go, first of all, to His Holiness Serkong Tsenshab Rinpoche, who encouraged and inspired Lama Zopa Rinpoche to preserve and spread this powerful practice. Heartfelt thanks go also to Lama Zopa Rinpoche for, as always, his amazing patience, perseverance and generosity in sharing his experiences and knowledge of nyung nä practice.

Sincere thanks also to the many people at the various FPMT centers that hosted and recorded the teachings included in this book; to Nick Ribush and the many people at LYWA for gathering, preserving and spreading these teachings; to Claire Atkins and my late parents for their generosity; to Ven. Steve Carlier for his patience and kindness in helping with Tibetan terms; to Ven. Yeshe Chodron, Ven. Thubten Munsel, Alan Marsh and

---

[3] Lama Yeshe Wisdom Archive numbers 52, 282, 623, 737, 1682 and 1761, respectively.
[4] LYWA #161, 468, 1342, 1428 and 1589. See LamaYeshe.com/archive for more information.
[5] Also called the Restoring and Purifying Ordination.

Jane Seidlitz for help with transcribing and checking some of the teachings; and Wendy Cook for copyediting the book. And special thanks to the many nyung nä participants at Chenrezig Institute who contributed to the publication of this book.

May *Abiding in the Retreat* inspire many people to do nyung näs, enrich the practice of those who do nyung näs and create the cause for Lama Zopa Rinpoche to give the elaborate nyung nä commentary.

Part One

Introduction

1. The Benefits of Nyung Nä Practice

THE MEANING OF NYUNG NÄ

NYUNG NÄ MEANS "abiding in the retreat."[1] In other words, you are retreating from negative karmas of body, speech and mind. When you hear, say or think of the word "nyung nä" don't think only of fasting, of the physical practices involved. Don't think a nyung nä is only about not eating—there is a much vaster meaning to think about.

Doing a nyung nä means your body is abiding in retreat, your speech is abiding in retreat and your mind is abiding in retreat. The essential meaning of retreat is retreat from nonvirtuous actions of body, speech and mind. Abstaining from negative karmas that harm others is the fundamental tantric practice.

Your body is in retreat from the nonvirtuous actions mentioned in the vows that you take in the Restoring and Purifying Ordination. And your body also abstains from food and drink. On the first day of a nyung nä you fast in the afternoon and on the second day you totally fast, not eating and not even drinking. You abstain from those physical activities.

You are also in retreat from the negative karmas of speech, such as chattering about subjects that increase ignorance, anger and the dissatisfied mind of attachment. On the second day of a nyung nä, by being in complete silence and saying nothing except prayers, you abstain from all negative karmas of speech.

Your mind is in retreat from the three poisonous minds—covetousness, ill will and heresy—and from the eight worldly dharmas. In particular, your mind is in retreat from ill will and anger. Cherishing others is the most important *samaya* of Chenrezig practice and the main practice

---

[1] *Nyung* does literally mean "fast," but Rinpoche prefers to translate it as "retreat" to reduce the emphasis on this physical aspect of the practice. For a glossary of terms that occur in this book please go to LamaYeshe.com/glossary.

during a nyung nä or any other Chenrezig retreat. If somebody criticizes you, you don't criticize them back. If somebody is angry with you, you don't get angry back. If somebody harms you, you don't harm them in return. If somebody beats you, you don't beat them in return. There are these four pieces of advice, but the essential point is that even if others harm you, you don't harm them in return. These are the essential samayas of Chenrezig practice, especially when you do a Chenrezig retreat. This is the meaning of the line *May I be able to abide in the samaya of Chenrezig*.[2]

You also have to live in the yoga of the three transformations. For sentient beings, you transform your body into Chenrezig's holy body; for sentient beings, you transform your speech into Chenrezig's holy speech (or another way of saying it is that you use your ordinary speech to achieve Chenrezig's holy speech); and for sentient beings, you transform your mind into Chenrezig's holy mind, which means using your ordinary mind to achieve Chenrezig's holy mind.

The benefits of nyung nä practice

Nyung nä is an unbelievably powerful practice of purification, purifying negative karmas and downfalls, and purification is the most important thing to do all the time, especially for us beginners. You can experience the heavy result of one negative karma for many lifetimes (for more on karma, see appendix 4). This is how karma works, and this is why it's so important to do purification. There are so many negative karmas that we haven't finished confessing and purifying or finished experiencing; however, all the past negative karmas we have collected during many eons can be purified in this life through a two-day nyung nä retreat.

Even though we can't live our lives without creating negative karma, purification practice helps us to experience fewer obstacles, fewer problems, now and in the future, up to enlightenment. It lessens suffering, the sufferings of samsara in general and of the three lower realms in particular. It also lessens the experience of problems in the human realm. If we could experience one fewer problem, we would. We always want our problems to be fewer. We would like not to experience even one problem in our life. Therefore, it's unbelievably important to do the practice of purification again and

---

[2] This line comes in one of the dedication verses after *Offering an Ablution*.

again. Doing a nyung nä stops our experiencing many lifetimes of sufferings and benefits us up to enlightenment.

It's generally mentioned in the teachings that doing one nyung nä purifies 40,000 eons of negative karma. However, without talking about all the other practices in a nyung nä, even reciting each of the Thirty-five Buddhas' names when doing *The Practice of Prostrations to the Thirty-five Confession Buddhas* purifies many thousands of eons of different negative karmas. For example, reciting *De zhin sheg pa me tog päl la chhag tshäl lo* (*To Tathagata Glorious Flower, I prostrate*) one time purifies 100,000 eons of negative karma. Simply reciting the names of the Thirty-five Buddhas with prostrations purifies unimaginable negative karmas.

Living in the Eight Mahayana Precepts also purifies heavy negative karmas. With each of the eight vows, we perform incredible purification and collect skies of merit, especially if we take the vows with a motivation of bodhicitta (see chapter 5 for more on the benefits of taking the Eight Mahayana Precepts).

Meditating on Chenrezig and reciting OM MANI PADME HUM are other practices that collect limitless skies of merits. And if you do them with a bodhicitta motivation, can you imagine how much merit you collect? With OM MANI PADME HUM you can purify the heavy negative karmas collected in past lives, such as the five uninterrupted negative karmas,[3] which cause you immediately after death, without the interruption of another life, to be born in the lowest hot hell, Inexhaustible Suffering, which has the heaviest suffering of samsara and which is experienced for the longest time: one intermediate eon. There is then no doubt that the ten nonvirtuous actions collected during beginningless rebirths are also purified. I'll explain more on the benefits of reciting OM MANI PADME HUM later (see chapter 6).

The essential benefits of nyung nä practice are explained at the end of the nyung nä text by Kelzang Gyatso, the Seventh Dalai Lama. The tantra *The Dharani of the Eleven-Face Arya Avalokiteshvara* says that reciting the Chenrezig mantra even one time can purify the heavy negative karma of a fully ordained person breaking all four root vows or of someone committing all five uninterrupted negative karmas. A fully ordained monk receives a root fall, or defeat, if he kills a human being, has sexual intercourse, takes

---

[3] The five are: killing father, mother or an arhat, causing blood to flow from Buddha or causing disunity among the Sangha.

what has not been given (in other words, steals) or lies about his spiritual attainments. So, a fully ordained monk who has broken all four root vows can purify them all by reciting OM MANI PADME HUM one time. The same applies to the five uninterrupted negative karmas—even these heavy negative karmas can be purified by reciting OM MANI PADME HUM just once.

It also says that if you recite the Chenrezig mantra, even cannibals and other harm-givers are hooked by the essence mantra and will generate loving kindness and compassion and be led to enlightenment.

If you chant Chenrezig's name or mantra, your life will always go up, toward enlightenment, with no turning back. You will generate virtue with regard to many hundreds of thousands times one hundred billion times ten million buddhas. In essence, all the wishes of a person who chants OM MANI PADME HUM or does Chenrezig meditation will be completely fulfilled. (Chanting OM MANI PADME HUM can have these unbelievable benefits, but it depends, of course, on how you recite the mantra.)

The Dharani of the Eleven-Face Arya Avalokiteshvara also says that if you do nyung nä practice on the fourteenth or fifteenth,[4] you purify 40,000 eons of negative karma. The duration of your stay in samsara will be shortened by 40,000 eons.

It also says that if you practice exactly according to the method, you will definitely achieve enlightenment—it's in your hands.

Also, the text *Detailed Method of Arya Avalokiteshvara with a Thousand Eyes and a Thousand Arms* says,

> On the fifteenth, if you take the eight vows,[5] wear clean clothes, and either in front of relics or a stupa that contains relics or a Buddha statue, you draw a mandala of white sandalwood and then sprinkle various flowers and offer incense and light, generate faith in Buddha and then recite the mantra 108 times, Chenrezig will be there. No matter how many times you have committed the five uninterrupted negative karmas in the past, all those will be purified. All your negative karmas of body, speech and mind will also be completely purified, and you will complete the paths and *bhumis*.

---

[4] This refers to the Tibetan lunar calendar, with the fifteenth day being the full moon.
[5] That is, the Eight Mahayana Precepts.

The text also says that since the Arya Great Compassionate One is the embodiment of the compassion of all the Victorious Ones (which means all the buddhas), it is easy for the pitiful sentient beings, who have so much suffering, to achieve Chenrezig because of the power of Chenrezig's compassion.

It's also mentioned in *White Lotus of the Holy Dharma*, a sutra text from the *Kangyur*, that the benefits of just holding in mind or reciting Chenrezig's name and doing just one prostration to Chenrezig are equal to having prostrated or made offerings to buddhas equal in number to the sand grains of sixty-two Ganges Rivers. It's just amazing!

Here, *Ganges River* means the Pacific Ocean rather than the actual Ganges River in India. The great enlightened being Pabongka explains this when talking about the benefits of bodhicitta in his own notes on teachings received from his guru, Dagpo Rinpoche. However, Ganges River, or Ganga, doesn't always refer to the Pacific Ocean. When you bless a vase, the vase water becomes the *devas'* holy water, the Ganga. The outer Ganga is the Ganges River in India, but there are also an inner and a secret Ganga, which is not water but the transcendental wisdom of nondual bliss and voidness of the Highest Yoga Tantra path. That transcendental wisdom is the quickest way to cease defilements and to achieve enlightenment. In Highest Yoga Tantra practice, merit that would otherwise take three countless great eons to collect can be collected within a few years. You are able to finish collecting all those merits by achieving clear light and the illusory body, especially the illusory body.

White Lotus of the Holy Dharma also says that when you make offerings or prostrate to Chenrezig, you collect the same amount of merit as having made offerings or prostrated to all the buddhas. With each prostration you do to Chenrezig, you collect the merit of having prostrated to all the buddhas. You collect extensive merit, skies of merit, every time you make offerings or prostrate to Chenrezig.

With nyung nä practice, you also receive the blessing of Guru Chenrezig in your heart, which makes your mind softer. When you then meditate on guru devotion, doing analytical and fixed meditation on how the guru is buddha, strong guru devotion will arise. When you meditate on renunciation, impermanence and death, compassion or bodhicitta, you will feel it strongly. You recite the words and then you feel them in your heart. Otherwise, you recite the words but your heart is like stone; there's no connection between your heart and the words. When you do the practice of nyung nä, collecting such extensive merit, doing powerful purification and receiving blessings, you feel very strong compassion for other sentient beings. It makes it easy to achieve realizations—the common realizations, the three principles of the path, and the uncommon realizations, the two stages of tantra—so it makes it easy to achieve enlightenment quickly.

It's mentioned that if you have done one nyung nä very well, when other people see you, their negative karma is purified. If you're on the top of a hill with many people down below, when they look at you, all their negative karma is purified. When you speak and your breath touches the bodies of other people, their negative karma is purified. The wind that touches your body is blessed, and when that wind then goes on to touch any being, whether human or non-human, fat or skinny, all their negative karma is purified. There are all these unimaginable benefits.

Experiencing difficulties

While doing a nyung nä, we may experience hunger, thirst, tiredness, pain and other difficulties. The more difficulties we experience during a nyung nä, the greater the purification. We should feel that all the difficulties we experience are worthwhile; that they are beneficial for us, helping us to obtain ultimate happiness. And we experience the hardships of a nyung nä retreat not only for ourselves but for the sake of the happiness of all sentient beings.

The hardships we experience in practicing Dharma, in doing a nyung nä retreat, are completely different from those generally experienced by people in the world. Look at them. Ordinary people experience hardships—difficulties of body, speech and mind—day and night, all the time. Why do they experience all these hardships day and night, working from one Sunday to the next? Check up. All the work they do and all the tiredness and other sufferings they experience are to obtain the temporary happiness of *only* this life. There is no thought of obtaining the happiness of future lives or the ultimate happiness of liberation or enlightenment. There's not even a single thought of that. All they think about is the small, temporary happiness of only this life—of a few years, a few months, a few days. That's all. You can see that their whole life from beginning to end is spent on that.

Even though they spend this life in that way, it would be different if they had some success and happiness, some peace in their mind. But, no, they don't. In fact, they experience all these great hardships to continually circle in samsara, to accomplish works that will again cause them to be born in the lower realms and experience the resultant suffering. Again they will have to be reborn in their previous home, the lower realms, and experience suffering, the result of those negative karmas.

This doesn't happen only in the West; it is also similar in the East. Even around Lawudo, the Sherpa people don't have time to practice Dharma. When you think of this, it makes you cry. When you see how sentient beings are suffering in samsara, it really makes you generate compassion.

There is a big difference in the way we experience difficulties and suffering to practice Dharma and in our reasons for doing so. The advantages that we receive from this as a Dharma practitioner and the advantages that those who don't practice Dharma receive are complete opposites. Their experiencing difficulties is completely useless. All their difficulties cause them to accumulate negative karma. There's not a single result of happiness or peace from that, just misery. The hours of hardship that we experience practicing Dharma, doing nyung nä retreat, have so much advantage, granting us both temporary and ultimate results.

Transforming your body

When you think about your body, when you look at and feel your body, it is just blood and bones and lots of other pieces wrapped in skin. There are many interesting things inside the stomach; and there's marrow inside the bones. When you look at this body, it seems kind of hopeless. When you don't think about it well, you might wonder, "How is it possible to achieve enlightenment with such a body? How can we use this body to free ourselves from samsara? How can this body, this piece of flesh, even be beneficial?" It's almost unimaginable. You feel kind of hopeless. When you think of the result, the qualities of a buddha, you almost can't mention this body. Superficially, that's how it looks.

However, it's not like that. As the great bodhisattva Shantideva said in *A Guide to the Bodhisattva's Way of Life*,

> The impure body we have taken
> Can become the priceless holy body of a Victorious One.

Therefore, you must always firmly hold what is called "bodhicitta."[6]

Our body is full of impurities, no different from a sack full of excrement covered by skin. But if we train our mind in the graduated path to enlightenment, if we practice bodhicitta, this impure body full of thirty-six impurities, which we might think is hopeless, can be transformed into something priceless. (This is without needing to talk about how this body can be transformed through tantric practices.) You could not finish describing the good qualities of a buddha's holy body even if you talked in the past, present and future. Even each pore of a buddha's holy body does great work for all sentient beings.

Your body can be transformed into the priceless holy body of a buddha and then effortlessly accomplish great work for other sentient beings. The essential cause for that is bodhicitta. Therefore, by understanding its advantages, you must always firmly hold bodhicitta; you must always remember and always practice bodhicitta. And if you have already generated bodhicitta, you should try not to lose it.

We should rejoice that with this body, through doing nyung näs, we can accumulate so many causes to be born in the Potala pure realm, where we can actually meet and receive teachings from Chenrezig and achieve Chenrezig's enlightenment.

Don't miss the opportunity

Nyung nä is a practice that is very easy to do and yet has unbelievable power. There is extraordinary benefit in doing nyung näs. Everybody should definitely attempt to do nyung nä practice, this powerful method of purification. You shouldn't regard nyung nä practice as unimportant and be careless about it. You must practice it, and from your heart you must recite OM MANI PADME HUM.

Doing this practice is an unbelievably powerful way to collect the most extensive merit and to purify the negative karmas collected during beginningless rebirths. It is a most powerful way to develop realizations, especially compassion for sentient beings. Doing Chenrezig meditation-recitation can really purify any negative karma and is the quickest way to

---

[6] Ch. 1, v. 10.

achieve enlightenment. Don't miss the opportunity to do this practice. And the harder you find it to do, the better it is, because you will purify more negative karma. As well as bringing powerful purification, however, it helps you to develop so much compassion for sentient beings.

Nyung nä practice is also very effective in healing sicknesses, even those that are difficult to cure, where other methods have been tried and haven't helped. By confessing to the guru, reciting the Chenrezig mantra and doing nyung näs, people have been cured of such sicknesses. Nyung nä is very powerful.

If you do nyung nä practice and pray to Chenrezig, everything becomes easy. Because you purify any heavy negative karma you have collected in the past, it becomes easy for you to have realizations, to go to a pure land and to achieve enlightenment. It's so easy to achieve enlightenment, without needing to undergo much hardship for many lifetimes or even eons. You don't need to put in much effort. Just by doing prayers, and especially by reciting OM MANI PADME HUM, there's no doubt that you will be able to go to a pure land.

If you make a request to Chenrezig one time, Chenrezig will then guide you in all your future lives. So there's no doubt that this will happen if you make requests to Chenrezig every day. By doing Chenrezig practice, you don't have to be reborn again and again in a suffering world and experience problems again and again. It makes it so easy to be born in a pure land and to finish all the problems of life; you won't have to experience problems again.

With Chenrezig as your special deity, if you make prayers to Chenrezig, your life becomes so easy. You accomplish whatever you want to do, whether reflecting or meditating, without much difficulty or great effort. Without doubt, if you make prayers to be born in a pure land, just with the mere prayer you will be able to be born in a pure land.

In essence, we are most fortunate beings, having the opportunity to chant OM MANI PADME HUM, meditate on Chenrezig and do nyung näs. It's so easy for us to achieve enlightenment. We don't need to collect merit for many eons; we can complete all those merits within one life, in the brief lifetime of a degenerate time. So, we must take the opportunity to recite the Compassion Buddha's mantra, OM MANI PADME HUM, as much as we can every day, and also to do as many nyung näs as possible. Our aim is to develop great compassion for sentient beings. Our main project should be to develop bodhicitta in this life. Since we need the blessing of Chenrezig for that, we need to do as much Chenrezig practice as possible.

If you can, it would be good to do one hundred nyung näs, especially at one time in a retreat of one hundred nyung näs or more, even a thousand. Of course, more is always better. Tenzin Namdrol, a Brazilian nun, has finished more than five hundred nyung näs, and is continuing nyung nä practice as she has accepted my request to do one thousand nyung näs. There are a few FPMT students who have completed more than one hundred nyung näs, including Ailsa [Cameron], who leads nyung näs quite often at Chenrezig Institute, where they have been doing eight nyung näs as a group at Saka Dawa for many years. But it's best to finish the one hundred nyung näs within one year, I think. In the future, it could be done like that.[7]

I think everybody should do at least one nyung nä each year. But if you can do more, that's very, very good as a nyung nä contains many preliminary practices. By doing nyung näs, you become a sincere, good-hearted practitioner. Since it's an intense practice, it's very helpful for realizations. Realizations come when we purify our defilements; otherwise, realizations don't happen. The more we purify, the more realizations come. It's like with a mirror: the more dirt you clean from the mirror, the more reflections come in it. Our mind is like a mirror. As we clean the mirror of our mind, it's able to give more and clearer reflections. Like that, realizations, including enlightenment, come.

It's also very good to learn how to lead a nyung nä well. I think that's a very important way to help others; many people can then learn from you.

I want to inspire you, and I want to request you to do nyung näs. It's such an incredible practice—so yum yum. To keep it very short, that's the conclusion: yum yum!

---

[7] The FPMT's Institut Vajra Yogini, France, conducts 108 nyung näs every year.

2. Chenrezig

The following stories of Chenrezig, Bhikshuni Lakshmi and some of the nyung nä lineage lamas, each of whom has an inspiring story, come from a handwritten text compiled by one of my gurus, Kyabje Gomo Rinpoche, who has now passed away. He was an incarnation of the great Indian yogi Padampa Sangye, who lived during Milarepa's time and gave the very effective teaching, *The Hundred Verses of Advice*, while he was living in Tingri, Tibet.

Gomo Rinpoche lived for many years in Mussoorie, which is close to Dharamsala, and led nyung näs and self-initiations there, leading many, many people in virtue. Along with some students, I received *chöd* initiation from Rinpoche, as well as part of a commentary on the *Six-Session Guru Yoga* and a short teaching on the *Three Principles of the Path*, many years ago at Tushita Retreat Centre[1] in Dharamsala.

I thought to mention first the story of Chenrezig, Compassion Buddha, and then that of Bhikshuni Lakshmi, the fully ordained nun and great scholar from whom the lineage of this nyung nä practice came (see chapter 3), then some of the stories of the lineage lamas who achieved Compassion Buddha (see chapter 4). While this lineage came from Chenrezig to Bhikshuni Lakshmi, there's also another nyung nä lineage that came through Nagarjuna.

The Story of Chenrezig

Gomo Rinpoche's text begins with a verse of prostration to Chenrezig:

> Your thousand arms signify a thousand wheel-turning kings;
> Your thousand eyes signify the thousand buddhas of the
>   fortunate eon;

---

[1] Now called Tushita Meditation Centre.

You manifest in whatever aspect is needed to subdue sentient beings:
To you, pure Compassionate-Eyed One, I prostrate.

The fully enlightened being, Amitabha Buddha, the Buddha of Infinite Light, had a thought to benefit transmigratory beings. From his right eye, he sent a beam of white light, which transformed into Chenrezig, and from his left eye, he sent a beam of blue light, which transformed into Tara.

In the blissful western realm called Having Lotus (Pema Chöling), there was a good-hearted wheel-turning king, King Supreme Goodness (Gyälpo Zangpo Chog), who didn't have a son. All the activities that wheel-turning king did were for Dharma. Everything, including the wealth he had, was used for Dharma.

In that blissful realm there was also a lake called Having Lotus, where lotuses grew, and every day the king would offer a flower from the lake to the Three Rare Sublime Ones.[2]

One day the servant who went to pick the lotus flower from the lake saw that a lotus stem with huge leaves the size of an eagle's wings had grown from the lake. In the center of that lotus was an unopened bud. When the servant reported what he had seen to the king, the king said, "Inside that lotus bud there will definitely be a holy nirmanakaya body that has taken spontaneous birth."[3]

King Supreme Goodness, his ministers and the rest of his entourage then went to see the lotus bud. When they opened the flower to check what was inside, they saw a sixteen-year-old youth with a radiant, white holy body adorned with the holy signs and exemplifications. He had a white scarf wrapped around his waist and an antelope skin over his left shoulder. (Antelopes are compassionate animals. It's said that when a hunter is hunting another animal, the antelope will stand in front of the animal, facing toward the hunter, to protect the threatened animal. It will actually offer itself in place of that other animal—it's an animal of compassion.)

---

[2] Buddha, Dharma and Sangha.
[3] The Tibetan term is *dzü kye*, which means entered and born. While sometimes translated as "miraculous birth," this term does not necessarily mean only a miraculous birth.

From his holy mouth, the youth was proclaiming over and over, "How pitiful[4] sentient beings in the six realms are!" He kept on repeating this.

The king and all his entourage prostrated to the youth, who was actually Chenrezig, who had manifested in this form and taken birth in the lotus. The king then spread a special cloth on the ground, asked the boy to sit on it and invited him to the palace, where he abided as a devotional holy object for the king and all his family; they used him as an object of offering in order to collect merit.

Chenrezig, in the aspect of this sixteen-year-old boy, thinking to benefit sentient beings, generated bodhicitta. He then made a request to all the buddhas and bodhisattvas of the three times,[5] saying, "I will lead each and every single sentient being to peerless full enlightenment." He then added, "Until I have brought every sentient being to enlightenment, if any thought seeking my own happiness arises, may my head crack into ten pieces like an *azarka*." (Perhaps this is some kind of fruit—the meaning is to crack into small pieces.)

When Chenrezig made this prayer, Amitabha Buddha said, "I will help you to accomplish your work for sentient beings."

Chenrezig's holy body then emitted six beams, with one beam going to each of the six realms, where it worked for sentient beings, liberating them.

Later Chenrezig went to the top of Mount Meru and looked around with his wisdom eye. Even though Chenrezig had liberated so many sentient beings from the six realms, when he looked, there still seemed to be the same number of sentient beings as before. So, he again sent beams to the six realms and liberated sentient beings. With his compassion and wisdom, Chenrezig liberated beings in this way three times, but still the sentient beings did not seem to become fewer in number.

Chenrezig then thought, "It seems that this samsara has no end. Therefore, I will abide in the blissful state of peace for myself."

Because thinking this broke his bodhicitta commitment, Chenrezig's head cracked into ten pieces. The pain was so unbearable that he screamed and wept. Amitabha then came and collected the pieces of Chenrezig's shattered head from the ground, put the pieces together and blessed them as eleven faces. (As you know, Chenrezig has a thousand arms and eyes and

---

[4] The Tibetan expression here is *nying je*, which means compassion.
[5] The three times are past, present and future.

eleven faces.) To end samsara, which is beginningless, Amitabha blessed ten of the faces in peaceful aspects to subdue sentient beings. For the sentient beings who can't be subdued by peaceful means, Amitabha blessed one face in wrathful aspect. (This is the face near the top, the one below that of Amitabha Buddha.) The different colors of the faces signify the four actions of a buddha: pacifying, increasing, controlling and wrathful.

The face of Amitabha Buddha on the very top signifies that Chenrezig achieved enlightenment by depending on the kindness of his guru, Amitabha. One reason that Amitabha Buddha is on Chenrezig's crown is to show that, even after enlightenment, Chenrezig still respects his guru. Another reason is to show that Chenrezig became enlightened in the essence of Amitabha Buddha.

To show in which essence a deity became enlightened, one of the five types of buddhas[6] is on the deity's crown. Here, for Chenrezig, it's Amitabha; for Tara, it's Amoghasiddhi or Amitabha. The crown buddha shows in which essence of the five types of buddhas you become enlightened. It also shows that you achieve enlightenment by the kindness of your guru, and even after you have achieved enlightenment, you still respect your guru.

After Amitabha Buddha had blessed him, Chenrezig thought, "I'm going to work for sentient beings until samsara ends." He then made a prayer, "To do this, may I have a thousand arms, a thousand wheel-turning kings, and a thousand eyes, the thousand buddhas of the fortunate eon." Right in the moment Chenrezig expressed this, the thousand arms and thousand eyes manifested.

This brief story is one version of how Chenrezig came to have a thousand arms and a thousand eyes.[7]

Manifestations of Chenrezig

We are always being guided by Chenrezig, who also manifests to us in human form—His Holiness the Dalai Lama, for example. While Chenrezig is a special deity karmically connected to the people of the Snow Land, Tibet, Chenrezig is now also a special deity for the whole world. His

---

[6] This was formerly translated as "five Dhyani buddhas."
[7] For other versions, see *Buddhist Fasting Practice*, pp. 8–9, and *Chenrezig: Lord of Love*, pp. 28–33.

Holiness the Dalai Lama, the actual Chenrezig, is special for the world, not only for Tibet.

Guru Shakyamuni Buddha made predictions about the Dalai Lamas being Chenrezig and about how the Dalai Lamas would particularly guide sentient beings in Tibet, bringing them refuge and spreading Dharma. Chenrezig made four prayers for the people of Tibet, but those prayers are now for everybody in the whole world, including us. And what Chenrezig prayed for in the four prayers is exactly what has been happening.

There is one story that in the past a king called Golden Rim (Ser gyi mü kyü) had a son named Unblinking Eyes (Mig me dzum). Guru Shakyamuni Buddha predicted, "You, Unblinking Eyes, will liberate sentient beings from the lower realms and from samsara. You will pacify the delusions of sentient beings. Having generated the compassionate thought, you will be called Chenrezig. You will draw many sentient beings into Dharma and bring them to enlightenment. You will achieve enlightenment and you will enlighten all sentient beings. In particular, you will become the protector, the object of refuge, the savior, of the Snow Land."

In *White Lotus Sutra*, Guru Shakyamuni Buddha tells Unblinking Eyes, "Bodhisattva Unblinking Eyes, you will spread Dharma like a shining sun in the Snow Land, this outlying land that no other buddha from the thousand buddhas of the fortunate eon has been able to benefit."

Bodhisattva Unblinking Eyes was able to spread Dharma in Tibet because in the past, in the presence of a thousand buddhas, he made prayers to be able to do that. It was due to the power of those prayers. All the incarnations of the Dalai Lama, including the present one, who as Dharma kings have preserved and spread Dharma in Tibet, are manifestations of Bodhisattva Unblinking Eyes, who made so many prayers in the presence of a thousand buddhas.

Chenrezig looks at all transmigratory beings with compassion and never gives up on any sentient being, no matter how evil they are. He is constantly looking at us sentient beings—there's not even a moment when he's not looking at us. He sees us perfectly and is concerned about us. Because he is constantly looking at us and guiding us, he is given the particular name, *Chenrezig*, which means "the one who looks with compassionate eyes."

Chenrezig also manifested to generate and spread human beings in Tibet. There may have been human beings in Tibet in the past, a long time ago, but this story happened in a particular place near Lhasa. Chenrezig manifested as a bodhisattva monkey and Tara as a female cannibal, then together they produced human beings, but the consciousnesses of their children came from the form realms. This is how human beings were first generated in Tibet.

Chenrezig then benefited those human beings by giving them food and so forth. Later, manifesting as the Dharma kings, the translators, the pandits and the ministers, Chenrezig gradually spread the Dharma in Tibet. King Songtsen Gampo and King Trisong Detsen were manifestations of Chenrezig, as were the translators, the great scholars who translated Dharma from Sanskrit into Tibetan. Showing unimaginable kindness, Chenrezig manifested in these various forms and then spread the Dharma in Tibet.

Tibetan Mahayana Buddhism, which is complete Buddhadharma, has now spread to the rest of the world, to the West and to Taiwan, Hong Kong, Malaysia, Singapore and other countries. You have to understand that we are completely in the care of and completely guided by Compassion Buddha.

That we have received a perfect human rebirth at this time is by the kindness of Chenrezig, His Holiness the Dalai Lama; and that we have met Tibetan Mahayana Buddhism, which came from India and was preserved and spread in Tibet by Chenrezig, and have the opportunity to practice and learn whatever we want about Buddhadharma is by the kindness of Chenrezig. All these incredible opportunities that we have come completely by the kindness of Guru Chenrezig, His Holiness the Dalai Lama.

The *Avatamsaka Sutra*[8] comprises six volumes of Guru Shakyamuni Buddha's teachings on bodhicitta. (It is very good to read this sutra to see how Buddha taught on bodhicitta.) It mentions,

> When the moon rises, numberless reflections appear wherever there is water in this world. That is how Chenrezig manifests. Effortlessly, naturally, Chenrezig manifests in all kinds of forms, even as medicine, a bridge or water. Chenrezig, manifesting to sentient beings in whatever form benefits them, does inconceivable work for sentient beings.

---

[8] Translated as the *Flower Ornament Scripture*.

There is only one moon, but when the moon rises in this world, any water that is uncovered, even the smallest drop of dew, has a reflection of the moon. The reflection of the one moon comes effortlessly everywhere there's water in this world; it comes in every uncovered piece of water, whether ocean, lake, river or pond.

Since Chenrezig manifests as medicine, bridges, water and other things, there is no doubt that Chenrezig manifests as the virtuous friend to guide us, to give us the opportunity to learn Dharma.

> Chenrezig manifests in the six syllables, OM MANI PADME HUM, to purify our negative karma and enable us to collect extensive merits, fulfilling all our wishes and bringing us to enlightenment in the quickest, easiest way. Chenrezig manifests even in Dharma protectors to protect us from obstacles. And Chenrezig manifests even in wealth deities to protect us from poverty.

For example, Ganapati, who protects sentient beings from poverty, is a manifestation of Chenrezig. Ganapati is a Buddhist deity,[9] with three or four different aspects.

Chenrezig also manifests as Dzambhala, the wealth-granting deity, and again there are different aspects of Dzambhala. There are various Dzambhala practices, such as making *torma* or water offerings and making wealth vases, to protect from poverty and to increase outer and inner prosperity. Outer prosperity refers to material things that we need for our practice and for benefiting sentient beings and the teaching of Buddha; inner prosperity refers to the Dharma.

The story of how Chenrezig manifested as Dzambhala is as follows. In India, near Bodhgaya, Lama Atisha saw one man dying of starvation. Lama Atisha wanted to cut flesh from his holy body to give to him, but the starving man said, "I don't want to eat it because it comes from a monk's body."

Lama Atisha then said, "You're right, especially not flesh from someone who has actualized the *arya* path." Lama Atisha, disappointed, then lay down on the ground. Suddenly white light appeared, and when Lama Atisha looked up he saw Chenrezig. He explained the situation to Chenrezig, who told him, "Don't worry. I will manifest as Dzambhala. You can then

---

[9] Ganapati is distinct from Ganesh, the elephant-face Hindu deity.

use the various methods such as offering water on Dzambhala, as well as offering tormas and making wealth vases, to relieve this man from poverty."

In these ways, Chenrezig brings happiness to us sentient beings. There's no such thing as exhaustion, discouragement or laziness in Chenrezig's working to bring happiness to us sentient beings. In every second, Chenrezig liberates numberless sentient beings.

The power of Chenrezig

Chenrezig is extremely quick to grant blessings and to guide sentient beings. Why? Because Chenrezig is the embodiment of the compassion of all the buddhas. That's why, if you pray to Chenrezig, Chenrezig is extremely quick to guide you.

As I have already mentioned, there are many different aspects of Arya Chenrezig, the Compassionate-Eyed One. I think there are even a hundred different aspects of Kuan Yin.[10] Tony Wong, whose story I will be telling soon, made a book about them. Also, many different aspects of Chenrezig are mentioned in the Chenrezig initiation text. However, among all the many aspects of Chenrezig, the Chenrezig with eleven faces, a thousand arms and a thousand eyes is said to have greater blessing, because of what the faces signify.

There are many stories about the power of Chenrezig. Tibetans have many stories, but it is the same in Singapore, Malaysia and Mainland China, where so many people pray to Compassion Buddha, often chanting the mantra for many hours. Every time I go to Singapore or Malaysia I hear stories of people recovering from sickness through Chenrezig practice. When I was in Singapore many years ago there was a student who had a needle inside her body. (I don't know how the needle got there.) She made many prayers to Compassion Buddha and chanted the long *dharani* over and over. The needle then came out—not through her going to hospital but just through chanting the mantra.

Since people have much faith in Chenrezig and do much chanting, there are a lot of stories of practitioners helping other people, as well as themselves, with healing and bringing success. Tony Wong, in Kuala Lumpur, is one example of this. The first time I went to Singapore, Dharmawati

---

[10] The female aspect of Compassion Buddha worshipped by Chinese Buddhists.

[Brechbuhl] arranged the teachings in Singapore and Malaysia. Before I went to Singapore to give teachings that first time, I had a feeling that I must go and that there would be great benefit in establishing a center there. This thought came very naturally and strongly.

I wrote to Dharmawati, an old student of Lama Yeshe and mine, and she arranged the teachings. In those past times Tony Wong received many lamas—he hosted me at least twice and also received lamas from the other traditions. Tony arranged where the lamas stayed and everything else. He also organized the blessing and healing of people and visits to various places. He was very, very kind.

Tony has now bought a place for a temple, but in those early days he didn't have anything. He just used his office also as a shrine room. When you came in the door, on one side of the office was his shrine, full of Buddha statues given to him by many lamas, and on the other side of the room was his wife's shrine, with statues of Jesus Christ, as she's a Christian.

Tony Wong has a very strong connection with Kuan Yin, the female aspect Chenrezig. His wife said that she would allow him to become Buddhist if he won the lottery. So, he won, but I don't know how much money was involved. That's how the decision was made between them.

People would come to Tony's office on Friday nights, Saturdays and Sundays. The whole place would fill up with people, with some even sitting outside on the steps. Tony kept a bottle of water in front of a picture of Kuan Yin, but I don't think there was any particular meditation of blessing the water. People would just chant the Chenrezig dharani for three or four hours. When I listened, I thought there was maybe one word in Sanskrit, but the rest I couldn't understand. I don't know what language they were using—maybe Mandarin.

Because the people had so much devotion, even though there was no particular meditation for blessing the water, I think the water was blessed. One man who had cancer was brought there one day by his wife and family; they had to help him walk as he couldn't support himself. He was given some water from the altar. The next day that man walked in by himself, without the support of his wife or any other family member. It was amazing, a kind of miraculous cure. Things like that happened many times.

That first visit I also went to Malacca as there was a student there who had met Lama Yeshe in Singapore. He later became a monk. Anyway, Tony Wong came with me in the car and started telling me his experiences with

Chenrezig. From Kuala Lumpur until we reached the house in Malacca, he continuously explained about the people he had healed. He has healed so many people—it's just unimaginable.

I'm telling you this just to give you an idea of the power of Chenrezig. Not only Tony Wong but many other people have had the experience of receiving quick guidance after praying to Chenrezig with strong devotion.

There have also been many blind people who, after reciting a number of mantras, regained their eyesight without depending on doctors. The cataract or whatever the problem was with their eyes disappeared. This happened to many people in Tibet.

Chenrezig is the special deity of not only Tibetans but also Mongolians. In Mongolia everybody, young or old, recites OM MANI PADME HUM. Everybody having the opportunity to recite OM MANI PADME HUM, which helps you generate compassion for others, is Chenrezig's holy action. If you recite OM MANI PADME HUM, Chenrezig will guide you. If you pray to Chenrezig, it is easy to purify negative karma and to have realizations. This is besides the temporary benefits in regard to the works of this life. Without need of much hardship in doing reflection and meditation, there is no doubt that with mere prayer you can be guided by Chenrezig whenever you have problems or fears. And at death time, you will easily be born in the Chenrezig pure land, Potala, or in the Amitabha pure land, Dewa Chen (Skt: Sukhavati). As I mentioned before, any heavy negative karma you have collected can be purified by reciting OM MANI PADME HUM and by doing nyung nä practice.

3. Bhikshuni Lakshmi

In Gomo Rinpoche's text, the following homage is paid to the fully ordained nun, Bhikshuni Lakshmi:

> Your holy body embodies all the past, present and future buddhas,
> Your holy speech leads all past, present and future transmigratory beings to enlightenment,
> Your holy mind simultaneously understands all the past, present and future:
> To you, glorious Pälmo, sublime guide of the past, present and future sentient beings, I prostrate.

Bhikshuni Lakshmi is the first in the lineage of this nyung nä practice. Chenrezig passed this practice to Bhikshuni Lakshmi, a fully ordained nun and a great scholar, a female pandit. (Usually you hear about male pandits, but here it's a female pandit.) She then passed the lineage to other yogis and pandits.

Bhikshuni Lakshmi was born a princess, the daughter of the king of Oddiyana (Tib: Orgyen), an area in Pakistan[1] that was previously Buddhist.

However, I think Bhikshuni Lakshmi might have been Nepalese. In the Kathmandu valley, just to the south of Kathmandu on the way to Pharping, the holy place of Padmasambhava and Vajrayogini, after you cross the mountain that is said to be the one that Manjushri cut with his sword,[2] there is a high mountain, with a long set of steps going up from the main road to the top. There you find a temple with a red Chenrezig inside, and

---

[1] Wangchen Rinpoche and Bardor Tulku Rinpoche suggest Afghanistan.
[2] Before, Kathmandu valley was a lake full of water; Manjushri cut this mountain with his sword so that the lake could easily drain.

outside the temple, on the walls of the surrounding buildings, are a lot of empty pots that people have offered, though I'm not sure why. There must be a reason, but I haven't heard the explanation of its purpose. Basically, it must be to pacify some obstacles or to fulfill some wishes. It must be for happiness—otherwise, why would people do it?

At one side of the temple, there's also a house with a large, roofed platform in front of it, like a kind of seat. It is said that it was Bhikshuni Lakshmi's family home and she lived in that house nearly a thousand years ago. (I'm not sure that she practiced there, because in the later part of her life she lived in a cave and did much recitation of OM MANI PADME HUM.) So, this is why I think Bhikshuni Lakshmi might have been Nepalese.

In any case, Bhikshuni Lakshmi was born a princess. Seeing the shortcomings of the householder's life, she took *rabjung* ordination, renouncing the householder's life. She then became expert in the five types of knowledge: logic, art, poetry, medicine and Dharma. She was also extremely strict in morality.

But due to past karma, Bhikshuni Lakshmi became sick with leprosy. Her body was in pain and her mind also experienced much suffering. She lost both her hands. Since she was unable to use her hands, she had to eat like a dog, taking food straight into her mouth.

Her family and members of the king's entourage then took her to a very isolated place, where medicinal grass grew, and left her there. In India and in many other places, when a person is deformed their family may reject them and leave them somewhere in the street.

This reminds me of something that happened in Delhi many years ago. One time we went to a park quite close to Tushita Mahayana Meditation Centre, our Delhi center. In the park, there was an old woman sitting near a tree, with her head completely wrapped in a shawl. When she saw me, she started to come toward me.

That night when we went to see her again, she was lying in the path completely covered by her shawl. She was so small that it would be easy for people to walk on her. We sent Tenzin Zopa[3] from the center to put a blanket over her. I thought to give her some food in the morning, then bring her

---

[3] Now Geshe Tenzin Zopa, the attendant of Geshe Lama Konchog and of his incarnation, Tenzin Phuntsok Rinpoche.

to Tushita, where we could make a roof over a small balcony upstairs as a place for her to stay.

When we went to see her the next morning she looked so small, sitting all hunched up, and she said, "Guru-ji." There was blood coming from her head. We discussed her situation. I wanted to take care of her and keep her at Tushita, but it seems there was a Christian place run by Mother Teresa's order that took care of such people. Tenzin Zopa then grabbed the old woman, put her in a taxi and took her to Mother Teresa's place. I heard that when she arrived there she smiled. When I next passed through Delhi I wanted to go to see her but it didn't happen. It seems that she might have gotten better. I think the woman's family, instead of looking after her, just dropped her there in the road.

When Bhikshuni Lakshmi's family abandoned her there in that isolated place, she cried and cried. She then had a dream of King Indrabhuti, one of the eighty-four mahasiddhas and the special disciple to whom Buddha gave the Guhyasamaja teaching. Buddha manifested as Vajradhara to King Indrabhuti and revealed to him the Guhyasamaja tantra; King Indrabhuti then practiced Guhyasamaja and became enlightened in one brief lifetime. It is said that everyone in the whole valley where he did all his Guhyasamaja practice achieved enlightenment; the whole valley was emptied.

In the dream King Indrabhuti predicted to Bhikshuni Lakshmi, "If you practice Chenrezig, you will quickly achieve sublime realization."

When Bhikshuni Lakshmi awoke from the dream, her pain had gone. She then recited OM MANI PADME HUM continuously, day and night. After some time, however, she got bored with the practice and her mind became depressed. In a dream she then saw Manjushri, who advised her, "Go to Pundravardhana (Li khar shing phel) and practice Chenrezig there. If you do that, after five years you will have the same realizations as Tara." Manjushri gave her a blessed pill and said, "This is for your attainment." Manjushri then disappeared. She took the pill and then woke up. All her infected wounds had completely gone, like a snake had shed its skin.

When she was going along the road to Pundravardhana, seven dakinis of the lotus family offered to help bring her there. At Pundravardhana, in front of a self-manifested statue of Chenrezig, Bhikshuni Lakshmi made a vow that she wouldn't move from her seat until she had achieved sublime realization, enlightenment. She then did nyung nä practice on one seat, eating only one meal every two days and reciting the long and short Chenrezig mantras. After she had done that for one year she was completely healed of her leprosy.

Due to the power of the loving kindness and compassion in her holy mind, she was able to gather the eight great nagas, the ten guardians and all the maras under her control, and they all promised to become Dharma protectors. The eight great nagas made a particular commitment to be protectors of the lineage of the nyung nä practice.

When Bhikshuni Lakshmi was twenty-seven years old, on the first day of Saka Dawa, the fourth Tibetan month, Tara appeared to her, and she achieved the first bodhisattva bhumi.[4] Tara predicted to her that she would be the doer of all the buddhas' activities.

On the eighth day of that month, she saw Amoghapasha (Unfailing Lasso)[5] and almost all the other Action Tantra deities and reached the eighth bhumi. The deities told her, "Bhikshuni Lakshmi, you will lead sentient beings to enlightenment through the yoga practice of Chenrezig."

In the early morning of the fifteenth day, she saw Thousand-Arm Chenrezig with all the deities and mandalas of the four classes of tantra[6] inside his holy body. She also saw numberless pure lands in the pores of Chenrezig's holy body. There are numberless pores, and in every pore she saw a buddha's pure land.

Bhikshuni Lakshmi then complained to Chenrezig, "I bore so much hardship for twelve years to achieve you—why didn't I see you before this? Why is it only now that I see you?" (The Tibetan expression is *yü*, but I don't know how to translate it precisely into English. It means something like "I did so much for you and you were ungrateful and never did what I asked you.")

Chenrezig replied, "I've always been with you, without separation, from the very first day that you began your practice of Chenrezig. But because your karmic obscurations weren't finished, you didn't see me." Chenrezig then blessed her. She then reached the tenth bhumi, and her holy body became golden in color. According to one story, her whole body totally changed: she became youthful, like a sixteen year old, and extremely beautiful.

---

[4] This means she achieved the path of seeing, the third of the five Mahayana paths.
[5] An aspect of Chenrezig.
[6] Action, Performance, Yoga and Highest Yoga Tantra.

Bhikshuni Lakshmi then engaged in tantric conduct, activities done for a few months or a year just before achievement of enlightenment. While engaging in tantric conduct, a person does all sorts of things that ordinary people might think are unreasonable or even crazy. It seems that each person has a different individual style of tantric conduct. One tantric practitioner became a butcher; another at Ganden Monastery in Tibet built a tall building for no particular reason—it wasn't a temple or a place to live.

When Bhikshuni Lakshmi engaged in tantric conduct, everybody in that area criticized her. Because she was a nun and lived near a monastery, the local people criticized her for not having pure vows.

To change the people's non-devotional thoughts toward her, on the day of a special festival of Khasarpani,[7] she went into the market, where many people had gathered. With a curved knife, she cut off her own head and put it on top of her staff (*kar sil*).[8] Holding that, she flew up into the sky and danced among the clouds. She then came down on the ground again with her head still on the staff.

The local people didn't know that Bhikshuni Lakshmi was a pure nun and had high attainments. In order to prove it to them, she said, "If it's true that I'm impure, which is what you people believe, my head won't come back to my body. If I'm pure, the head will come back." The moment she announced this to the people, her head came back and her body returned to normal.

When all the people gathered there saw this, all their non-devotional thoughts disappeared, and everybody developed incredible devotion. She brought everyone there into a state of devotion. All those people, male and female, who saw her then achieved sublime realization and went from there to the pure land of Vajrayogini (Dakpa Khachö).

Externally, Bhikshuni Lakshmi was a fully ordained nun; internally, she was Tara; and secretly, she was Vajravarahi (Dorje Phagmo). The conclusion of the whole story is that Bhikshuni Lakshmi achieved Chenrezig, the Buddha of Compassion.[9]

---

[7] A one-face, two-arm aspect of Chenrezig.
[8] One of the thirteen implements of a fully ordained nun or monk.
[9] For other versions of Bhikshuni Lakshmi's story, see *Buddhist Fasting Practice*, pp. 18–21, *Rest for the Fortunate*, pp. 5–12, and *Chenrezig: Lord of Love*, pp 99–102.

4. The Nyung Nä Lineage Lamas

Chandra Kumara

THE NYUNG NÄ PRACTICE was passed from Chenrezig to Bhikshuni Lakshmi, who then passed it to other yogis and pandits, the first of whom was Pandit Chandra Kumara (Dawa Shonnu).[10] Chandra Kumara was born in India in the Brahmin caste. He became expert in the five types of knowledge, especially in logic and Sanskrit poetry.

At one point Chandra Kumara became sick with *lung*, or wind disease, and no matter what he tried, nothing helped. He then went to see Bhikshuni Lakshmi and just by seeing her and receiving her blessings, his lung was pacified. (When you meet Tibetan Buddhism, after some time you come to know about lung. Some senior Sangha have had lung for many years, and even though they go to Burma, Sri Lanka and other places, still they don't recover.)

Bhikshuni Lakshmi told Pandit Chandra Kumara, "The reason you have wind disease is that in a past life you disturbed your guru's holy mind. Because of this, you are now experiencing this disease, but because you made confession, you have also met me in this life." She then added, "You should chant OM MANI PADME HUM and do confession practice." (Here Bhikshuni Lakshmi is giving advice as to what to do if you have lung: chant OM MANI PADME HUM and do purification, or confession, practice.)

Bhikshuni Lakshmi gave Pandit Chandra Kumara instructions on Eleven-Face Chenrezig,[11] which he practiced and then achieved *mahamudra*, the sublime realization, in that lifetime. Pandit Chandra Kumara achieved Chenrezig by receiving teachings from Bhikshuni Lakshmi.

We can relate this story to ourselves. When we have strong lung, our

---

[10] See the *Blue Annals*, Book XIV, p. 1006 ff., for more on this lineage.
[11] This is the same aspect as Thousand-Arm Chenrezig.

mind is very unhappy and disturbed. We feel very tight and have great pain in our heart. That is due to the karma of having disturbed the holy mind of the gurus, bodhisattvas or other holy beings and also of having made other people's minds unhappy. If the lung gets worse and worse, a person can become completely crazy.

This story shows how powerful and effective Chenrezig practice is and how important it is to recite OM MANI PADME HUM. Pandit Chandra Kumara tried many things, but nothing helped his lung until he did Chenrezig practice. Now you know what to do in case you already have lung or you get lung in the future.

Jñanabhadra

Pandit Jñanabhadra (Yeshe Zangpo) was born into the family of a king, but took the ordination of renunciation, renouncing the householder's life. He then became expert in the five types of knowledge, including the inner knowledge of Buddhist philosophy.

Due to past karma, huge abscesses developed on his upper body. No matter what he tried, nothing helped. Thinking the abscesses might be caused by spirit harm, he went to receive teachings on Yamantaka from a great yogi of Yamantaka, but when he tried to meditate on Yamantaka his sickness became three times worse. His whole body became swollen and covered with pus, and he was in unbearable burning pain. It was so painful that he couldn't bear anything to touch his body. When he went to bathe in a pool, the water of which was normally supposed to help heal wounds and other diseases, the water in the pool became so hot that it boiled, and he had to keep changing the water.

He then went to see many great yogis, but nobody could help him. No matter what he tried, nothing benefited him.

Jñanabhadra then had the thought to request Pandit Chandra Kumara's help. When Pandit Chandra Kumara was on his way to see Jñanabhadra, Tara appeared to Chandra Kumara and told him, "In the past Jñanabhadra degenerated his samaya with his guru, and his disease is the ripened result of that past karma. Nobody can heal him. He must pray to Bhikshuni Lakshmi."

The guru, Pandit Chandra Kumara, and the disciple, Pandit Jñanabhadra, then went together to a lake, where they invoked Bhikshuni Lakshmi and made requests to her. Bhikshuni Lakshmi then blessed Pandit Jñanabhadra, and just with this blessing, right in that moment, his disease completely disappeared. Jñanabhadra actually saw Bhikshuni Lakshmi in the form of Eleven-Face Chenrezig, and there at that lake, Bhikshuni Lakshmi, in that manifestation, gave teachings on Chenrezig to both of them.

Pandit Jñanabhadra then received elaborate teachings on the method of attaining Chenrezig from his guru, Pandit Chandra Kumara. He did nyung nä retreat for three months and meditated on Chenrezig. He then achieved sublime realization, with his body becoming the actual holy body of Chenrezig. In this way he achieved Chenrezig.

Peñawa of Nepal

Peñawa, a Nepalese yogi, is next in the lineage of this nyung nä practice. The previous lineage lamas were Indian pandits, but Pandit Peñawa was from Nepal. He was born into a king's family and became supreme among the learned ones. (It doesn't specify here in the text, but it might mean the same as before: he became expert in the five types of knowledge.)

He then received a prediction from Manjushri, who told him, "Peñawa, you should take teachings on Eleven-Face Chenrezig from Pandit Jñanabhadra. If you then recite OM MANI PADME HUM for five years, you will see Chenrezig."

After receiving this prediction, Peñawa went to India, where he received teachings on Thousand-Arm Chenrezig from Pandit Jñanabhadra. After that, he lived by begging for five years, and he then did a retreat on Chenrezig. While doing the retreat, Peñawa actually saw Chenrezig's holy face and received teachings directly from Chenrezig. He then achieved the sublime realization of Chenrezig, Chenrezig's enlightenment. He achieved the rainbow body, which means his gross body became lighter and smaller and smaller, until it disappeared. He passed away in the rainbow body and went to the pure land.

Dawa Gyältsän

The next lineage lama is bodhisattva Dawa Gyältsän, whose story is very short. Unlike with the others, there's no detailed story about how he achieved Chenrezig. However, he was very famous, and it was commonly known that he was the actual Chenrezig. There were many predictions and stories to prove this. Many learned beings and yogis, because of predictions from Chenrezig, took teachings from bodhisattva Dawa Gyältsän and had profound realizations.

In Kyirong, which is in Tibet but close to the border with Nepal, there was a Chenrezig statue called Kyirong Lokeshvara.[12] This Lokeshvara statue is now in His Holiness the Dalai Lama's palace in Dharamsala. Sometimes, in photos of His Holiness, you see this statue, which has a crown, in a glass case behind His Holiness.

This Lokeshvara statue was in Kyirong Samten Ling Monastery, which was founded by Kachen Yeshe Gyältsän, a great lama who, like the sun rising, benefited sentient beings and the teaching of Buddha in Tibet. When the Samten Ling monks escaped from Tibet, they brought the Lokeshvara statue with them and offered it to His Holiness the Dalai Lama.

It is said that this Lokeshvara statue speaks and that it was not made by humans but came spontaneously from a tree. This statue originally came from Nepal, and there are actually four Lokeshvara statues all together. A long time ago, there was a sandalwood tree growing on top of a small hill somewhere near Swayambhunath in the Kathmandu valley. This tree was always covered by beams of light, like a net; and every day a cow would come to squirt milk onto that tree.

When Akaramati, a fully ordained monk who was an embodiment of Amitabha Buddha, came from Tibet to Nepal, one day he came to the place where this tree was. He then heard a voice from the sky say, "Cut the tree." When he did that, a Chenrezig statue came out of the tree. The Chenrezig statue then spoke, saying, "I want to be in Tibet to benefit the Tibetan people."[13] This small, standing statue is now in the Potala in Tibet; it is one of the most precious statues in the Potala. You go through a door, walk up some wooden steps and there you see that Chenrezig statue. People can sponsor gold to be offered to the statue.

The voice then came again from the sky, saying, "Cut the tree again." Again, a Chenrezig statue appeared, and this one said, "I want to be in Kyirong, because many people have cold sickness. I'm going there to heal

---

[12] Lokeshvara is another name for Chenrezig.
[13] Unlike with the other statues, there was no mention of this one curing a particular disease.

them." (This is the Lokeshvara statue I have already mentioned—the one that was brought from Tibet and is in His Holiness's palace in Dharamsala.)

Again Akaramati heard the voice from the sky, saying, "Cut the tree again." Another Chenrezig statue appeared, and this one said, "I want to be in Kathmandu to heal people who have had strokes." This statue, called Jowo Jamali, is in a temple with silver doors near the center of Kathmandu. There's a large white statue of Buddha, but I think the small Lokeshvara statue might be behind it or inside the heart of that big statue. It is said that if people who have had strokes stand at the door of the temple and pray, they get healed.

Again Akaramati heard the voice, and another statue came out of the tree and said that it wanted to go to Patan to heal some other disease.

All these statues, which still exist, are not man-made but are manifestations of Chenrezig.

In the presence of the Lokeshvara statue in Kyirong, Dawa Gyältsän made requests for seven days. Chenrezig then predicted to him, "You should make charity of eyes to a hundred people. You should build one hundred temples, repair one hundred dangerous roads and offer food to one hundred fully ordained monks. If you do this, you will quickly achieve enlightenment."

Bodhisattva Dawa Gyältsän prayed to Thousand-Arm Chenrezig to be successful in all these things and Chenrezig predicted that all his wishes to help others would be successful and that he would soon achieve enlightenment.

Dawa Gyältsän then accomplished all these works. He made charity of eyes to a hundred people and helped many people who were in danger of dying to have long lives.[14] He also built one hundred temples and repaired one hundred roads. Making difficult roads easy and comfortable to travel on is regarded as a very good practice, as a good service to other sentient beings. He offered food to one hundred monks; this means he cooked and made daily offering of food. Accumulating incredible merit by doing these things, he then quickly achieved enlightenment.

---

[14] Wangchen Rinpoche explains that Dawa Gyältsän saved hundreds of people who were sentenced to death or to have their eyes gouged out.

There is an amazing story about how bodhisattva Dawa Gyältsän benefited sentient beings through nyung nä practice.

At one time bodhisattva Dawa Gyältsän went to the southern part of Tibet. One day when he went with four monks for alms in a village (he would always bring four monks so that others could accumulate more merit), they met an old sick woman, who requested him for blessings. Bodhisattva Dawa Gyältsän offered many tormas, blessed her and did many dedication prayers for her. He then told the old woman, "Your sickness is the result of your past negative karma, and now you must meditate on patience and bodhicitta." When he said that, the woman immediately felt incredible devotion to bodhisattva Dawa Gyältsän, and she burst into tears. While crying, she said, "Forget about past lives! Even in *this* life, I've created so much negative karma."

Bodhisattva Dawa Gyältsän then advised her, "If you confess every negative karma that you remember, it can be purified."

She then explained to bodhisattva Dawa Gyältsän the negative karmas she had accumulated in her life. She had been the wife of a wealthy businessman in Kyirong and had one son with him. When their son was seven years old, her husband went to Nepal on business and didn't come back for three years. The old woman said, "During that time, because I was beautiful and under the control of strong delusions, I went with another man. I had a child, a son, with him, but I killed that child. I also used up all our wealth. My other son found out what I had done."

After he discovered the situation, her son asked her, "When my father returns from Nepal, what will happen to you, mother? What will you do?" The mother got upset and shouted, "What will I do? What will I do?" She then threw a rock at her son, hitting him in the liver. He vomited blood and then died.

A local lama found out that she had killed her two sons and was talking about what had happened. When she realized that the lama knew her story, she offered him poisoned food and killed him.

Her husband then returned to Kyirong from Nepal. The wife heard their maid, who knew what had happened, whispering to her husband, telling him secretly all the terrible things that she had done, that she had killed her two children and the lama. Listening secretly, the wife also heard her husband tell the maid, "Tonight I'm going to pretend that I haven't heard all these stories about all the terrible things she has done. And tomorrow morning, I'll gouge out her eyes." The wife pretended that she didn't know anything, and her husband also acted as if he didn't know her story.

The woman was extremely scared and tried to think what she could do. She then put poison in some *chang*, or barley beer, and gave the poisoned drink to her husband, along with their eight servants. Not only did she poison and kill her husband, but also eight servants, including the maid. In the early morning, they became unable to speak and after two days, they died.

Two of her neighbors found out what she had done. Knowing that they had found out, she also poisoned and killed both of them. Their two maids also found out what had happened, so she poisoned and killed them as well.

In total, she killed sixteen people. The old woman then said, "I was scared, so after that I escaped to the southern part of Nepal." This also made life difficult for her parents. She then said, "Besides that, I didn't act honestly, did many bad things and accumulated much negative karma."

After telling bodhisattva Dawa Gyältsän the whole story, she then said, "Without talking about past lives, I have created this very heavy negative karma in this life. Please guide me with your compassion."

Bodhisattva Dawa Gyältsän thought, "This woman has created such heavy negative karma!" He cried and cried, tears pouring from his eyes. He then gave her the solution, telling her, "Arya Chenrezig promised that anybody who does one nyung nä won't go to the lower realms. For you, there's no other hope than to do nyung nä. There's no better method for you than this." This means that even though she had created heavy negative karma by killing sixteen people, she wouldn't go to the lower realms if she did one nyung nä. (Here you can see how powerful just one nyung nä is. Even though the woman had collected so much negative karma, doing one nyung nä could save her from the lower realms.)

Bodhisattva Dawa Gyältsän then gave the woman the oral transmission of the nyung nä practice, with all the mantras and prayers, and advised her to do eight nyung näs. Even the sickness she had when she met bodhisattva Dawa Gyältsän was cured due to his compassion.

We have to apply this story to ourselves. We have to understand that the advice is the same for us, no matter how much heavy negative karma we have collected. This is the solution for us and for other people who have created heavy negative karma; this is how we can be free from that karma and all its suffering results.

The old woman did the eight nyung näs in the month of Saka Dawa, the fourth Tibetan month, which has three celebrations of Guru Shakyamuni Buddha's life. Some teachings say that the eighth was the day that Guru Shakyamuni Buddha showed the action of coming out of his mother's womb. The fifteenth, or full moon, day was the day that Buddha achieved enlightenment under the bodhi tree in Bodhgaya and also the day on which he later passed away.

However, during one nyung nä the old woman felt so thirsty that she drank a little bit of chang (as part of the eight precepts, you're not supposed to have alcohol during a nyung nä). During another nyung nä, she felt so hungry that she ate two of the four offering cakes.[15] Of the eight nyung näs, she did six perfectly, living on one meal, but two of them were broken because she drank chang in one and ate two tormas in another. Not long after doing the eight nyung näs, the old woman died.

Bodhisattva Dawa Gyältsän later went to Tsang, an upper region of Tibet, to give teachings on bodhicitta. During the teaching, Tsi Mara, a worldly protector, was in the audience and said to the bodhisattva, "Show some sign that you have attainments."

Bodhisattva Dawa Gyältsän then showed the people a very clear eye in his palm, an eye that was actually looking. Everybody there saw this sign. Some people also saw bodhisattva Dawa Gyältsän in the form of Eleven-Face Chenrezig, other people saw him in the form of Four-Arm Chenrezig, and still others saw him as Two-Arm Chenrezig. Besides that, people saw him in various other aspects.

Also, because the bodhisattva showed signs of his attainments, even Tsi Mara himself generated much devotion and promised in front of Dawa Gyältsän that he would protect the yoga of Chenrezig and help people practicing nyung nä.

After that, many people generated incredible devotion to bodhisattva Dawa Gyältsän and some of them offered confession of the negative karmas they had accumulated. During that time, while other people were making confession, a fully ordained monk asked bodhisattva Dawa Gyältsän, "I heard that the old woman who killed sixteen people died last year. Where has she been reborn? Where is she now?"

Bodhisattva Dawa Gyältsän smiled at the monk and told him, "Eleven-

---

[15] Tib: *zhal zä*, the small white cakes used as the NAIVIDYA (food) offering.

Face Chenrezig's nyung nä practice has countless benefits, but such a small number of people are able to do this practice."

From his clairvoyance, bodhisattva Dawa Gyältsän then explained, "She has been born in eastern India as the son of a rich Brahmin family and has many jewel ornaments. As the result of having previously done nyung näs, she has received a human body. But because she drank chang during one nyung nä, the boy's mind is not stable; he has many ups and downs." That could be one explanation of the karmic cause of an unstable mind, a mind that easily goes up and easily gets depressed again. From this karmic story, we can learn about the past karma that can cause that. It can't be the only cause, but it could be one cause.

Bodhisattva Dawa Gyältsän continued, "And because in her past life she ate the two tormas during another nyung nä when she was supposed to be fasting, the boy has an ugly body."

He then added, "However, that boy will practice Chenrezig as his *yidam*, or mind-seal deity.[16] Arya Chenrezig has such incredible compassion that when the boy dies he will be reborn in the Blissful Realm, Sukhavati, the pure land of Amitabha Buddha." This is what bodhisattva Dawa Gyältsän told the monk.

Dawa Gyältsän then instructed that monk, "Anyone who does eight nyung näs purely, recites the Chenrezig mantra a hundred times and makes prostrations, will *definitely* be reborn in the Blissful Realm and will achieve the level of the non-returning bhumi. They will then achieve enlightenment. Doing even one nyung nä can definitely close the door to the lower realms. This Dharma is the method of attainment of all the buddhas and bodhisattvas—everybody should do this practice."

Without need to talk about all her past lives, just in that life the old woman had created so much heavy negative karma through causing so much harm to others, but because she did the eight nyung näs, instead of being reborn in the lower realms, she was born as a Brahmin boy in eastern India, and after that life she would be born in the pure land of Amitabha. Once you're born there it's impossible to be born in the lower realms, and you can also come back to this world and bring extensive benefit to sentient beings. So, doing nyung näs is such an incredibly easy way to purify heavy negative karmas and to go to a pure land.

---

[16] See appendix 3 for Rinpoche's explanation of the meaning of *yidam*.

You don't have to suffer; you don't have to keep on reincarnating in the lower realms or as a deva or a human. You don't need to do that—you can very quickly be born in a pure land. It's very important to understand how powerful Chenrezig practice—making requests to Chenrezig, reciting the mantra, doing nyung näs—is. From just this one lineage story, you can understand the incredible benefits that come from doing nyung näs.

Nyiphug Chökyidrag

The next lineage lama is Drubchog Nyiphugpa,[17] a Tibetan yogi born in the western region of Tibet called Ngari. He took vows of celibacy, and by the time he was twenty-six he was famous for being strict in moral conduct, learned and good-hearted.

In Buddhadharma, there are three qualities we should have, if possible. First, we should be strict in moral conduct. A person who is strict in moral conduct is strict in karma. If a monk lives purely in his ordination, he doesn't allow his mind to accumulate nonvirtuous actions, only virtuous actions. I don't know if "strict" is an exact translation of the Tibetan term *tsün pa*, which means a person who is strict in observing karma. *Tsün pa* means pure, having abstained from negativities. The second quality is *khe*, which means wise, or learned. The third is *zang*, which means good-hearted.

The lamas usually advise that from these three—morally strict, learned and good-hearted—the most important is to be good-hearted. Even if someone is very learned, if he's not strict in observing moral conduct, in observing karma, it's not so good. Even though he has understanding, since he doesn't practice, he doesn't receive much benefit from his understanding. It's like a person who understands Dharma but does no practice. And even if someone is learned and also strict in moral conduct, if he doesn't have a good heart, his practice won't be successful; he can't benefit other people very much if he doesn't have a good heart.

If you have a good heart, you can succeed in any wish you have in this life or in a future life. If you can't have all three qualities, the first thing you should have is a good heart; second, you should be strict in morality; and third, you should be learned.

So, by the time he was twenty-six, the great yogi of Chenrezig, Drubchog

---

[17] Nying-phug-pa in the *Blue Annals*.

Nyiphugpa, had become famous for these three qualities. He was strict in moral conduct, was very learned and had a good heart.

After some time, Tara predicted to him in a dream, "Son of the essence,[18] Chenrezig has come to the inner country called Mangyul. You must go there, and you will then accomplish both works."

In accord with Tara's prediction, Drubchog Nyiphugpa went to Mangyul, where he saw bodhisattva Dawa Gyältsän. Tara said that Chenrezig had come to Mangyul because bodhisattva Dawa Gyältsän had come there.

When he met bodhisattva Dawa Gyältsän, the great yogi Nyiphugpa made prostrations to him and then requested, "I would like to receive a teaching that has great meaning, is very easy to achieve and keeps one away from the lower realms forever." Even these great yogis have similar ideas to Westerners, especially Americans. I'm joking. Though I don't know that Americans talk about teachings that have great meaning and banish the lower realms forever.

Bodhisattva Dawa Gyältsän then gave Nyiphugpa the teachings of Eleven-Face Chenrezig. On bodhisattva Dawa Gyältsän's instructions, Nyiphugpa then went to Takri, a place with snow mountains in northern Tibet. Without anybody knowing, he spent seven years there doing nyung näs, living on five small pots of *tsampa* and taking the essence (*chu len*) pills.

After some time, sunbeams spontaneously radiated from his palms and there were many other signs that he had achieved great attainment, with complete control over the elements.

A powerful spirit called Tako promised in front of great yogi Nyiphugpa to be the protector of the teachings of Chenrezig.[19]

Later, Nyiphugpa flew up in the sky and went to a place called Nyiphug, or Sunny Cave. That is how this great yogi came to be called Nyiphugpa, which means Sunny Cave Being.

There Nyiphugpa made a statue of Shakyamuni Buddha and also built monasteries in that area. He himself transformed into all the different people—architects, builders, artists—to do the work. With many of his own transformations, he built temples, monasteries and statues. He did amazing work for sentient beings in that area.

After Nyiphugpa had done nyung näs for a while, one day at dawn he

---

[18] For Rinpoche's explanation of this term see appendix 2.
[19] As mentioned in *Torma Offering to the Local Deities*.

got severe pain in his eyes, as if they were going to fall out. While he was in pain, a white man (a manifestation of Chenrezig) appeared to him and explained, "Four hundred lives ago you were born in the southern part of India and at that time you were a fisherman with a boat. The pain in your eyes is a result of your having blinded a big fish with an oar."

At another time, Nyiphugpa's right cheek became swollen and unbearably painful. Again, the white man appeared while he was experiencing the pain and explained the karma to him: "Nine hundred lives ago you broke the right cheek of a buffalo with a stone and this is the result. That is why your right cheek is now so swollen and painful."

Because great yogis have high attainments, they experience very quickly even small karmas they have accumulated in the past. Since they have thinner obscurations, they get to experience in this life the results of their past heavy negative karma. People like us don't experience all our past negative karmas very quickly; all our karmas are invested, like money invested in a bank. We have a big collection that we will continuously experience in the future. Even after many hundreds or even thousands of lifetimes, those karmas will definitely still exist.

I'll tell you a story about Gen Jampa Wangdu, a monk friend of ours in Dharamsala. He was one of the older meditators in Dharamsala who had much experience of the path: of emptiness and of the basic lam-rim meditations. He was a semi-sadhu, with a patch of white hair on this head, and his main guru was Geshe Rabten Rinpoche. Lama Yeshe and he were in the same class in Sera Je in Tibet, but Jampa Wangdu never studied when he was in the monastery. He was very, very naughty, always wearing torn clothes with four or five patches and spending his time fighting with other monks, even wounding them. Also, he didn't go for the daily pujas and debates; instead, he was always playing or fighting. He spent many years like this.

Later on he took a *Guru Puja* commentary from His Holiness Trijang Rinpoche, His Holiness the Dalai Lama's junior tutor. Somehow that completely changed his mind, and he left the monastery with the plan to live in the caves of Kadampa geshes[20] until he died. He spent many years in the cave of Geshe Puchungwa in a place called Pembo, where there are many

---

[20] The ascetic practitioners who preserved Lama Atisha's tradition in Tibet.

Kadampa geshes' caves. All day long he practiced *Jorchö,* the preparatory practices for meditating on lam-rim.

During this time, he also achieved chu len, making pills and living on them. He also meditated on tranquil abiding (Skt: *shamatha*), achieving shamatha even before he escaped from Tibet.

After escaping from Tibet he lived with us at a place called Buxa Duar, which is close to Bhutan. It was the concentration camp used to imprison Prime Minister Nehru and Mahatma Gandhi when the British controlled India. Lama Yeshe and I lived in that place for eight years. Gen Jampa Wangdu was there for two or three years, then he left Buxa and lived for many years in Dalhousie with Trehor Kyörpön Rinpoche, an ascetic lama who was highly learned and highly realized, with great achievement of very high tantric paths. When Trehor Kyörpön Rinpoche passed away many years ago, he remained in meditation for twenty days. Gen Jampa Wangdu did three years of practice on the instructions of that lama.

From Dalhousie, Gen Jampa Wangdu moved to Dharamsala, where he initially stayed in a cave. One day, Lama Yeshe, another monk and I went there to have a picnic, but he wasn't there. It was a small cave with very little space inside—you couldn't actually stand up in it.

At one point Gen Jampa Wangdu got very sick, with much pain in both knees and both elbows. Even though he was in pain, however, his mind was in a blissful state. He wasn't upset about being sick, the way we would be. For many months he didn't take any medicine or try to get any treatment. He then explained the situation to His Holiness the Dalai Lama, who advised him to get some treatment. He didn't listen at first, but then his leg worsened and he listened.

No Tibetan doctor could help, so His Holiness made observations and advised Gen Jampa Wangdu to go to Ludhiana, which has one of the largest hospitals in India, with very good equipment and very good treatment. His Holiness's office took care of him. They took him to Ludhiana, which is quite far from Dharamsala, and all the expenses for his treatment were paid by His Holiness's office.

The reason Gen Jampa Wangdu had so much pain in his knees and elbows is that when he was in Sera Monastery in Tibet, he beat an old monk with a stick for no particular reason. It wasn't that the monk had cheated him or treated him badly. He just disliked that old monk. He beat the old monk on his knees and elbows, and his pain was in exactly the same places where he had beaten the old monk. While experiencing the pain, he remembered how he had beaten the old monk and felt sorry.

Very good meditators, those with realizations and thinner obscurations, experience the result of even the small karmas they have collected in this life. When Lama Drubkhangpa, a great yogi of Chenrezig, was asked by a benefactor to come to read the *Prajnaparamita* scriptures, a total of twelve volumes, at his house, Lama Drubkhangpa didn't go but instead sent another lama, one of his disciples who was also a great yogi of Chenrezig, and another four monks. The family wanted these texts read because although they had been rich before, they had then lost most of their material possessions and become poor. They had sold the *Prajnaparamita* texts that they had had before in their shrine room and used that money to offer food to the four monks and the great yogi of Chenrezig.

While eating the food bought with the money from selling the texts, this great yogi had unbelievable pain in his body, and when he checked inside he found there was a white letter AH moving around in his body. No matter what he did, this white AH would go up and down, causing much pain.

He then prayed very hard to Chenrezig. (When he prayed to Chenrezig, Chenrezig usually appeared to him and gave him advice.) When Chenrezig appeared, he asked, "What is the cause of this?" Chenrezig then explained the karma, "The reason you are now experiencing unbearable pain is that you have eaten food gained through wrong livelihood. The food was obtained with money from selling *Prajnaparamita* scriptures. You are experiencing this pain now. The four other monks are not experiencing anything now but are very comfortable and relaxed; but after death, they will definitely be reborn in the hells. They are not experiencing anything now; but because you have thinner obscurations, you have experienced the result right away." There are many such stories.

So, the white man, a transformation of Chenrezig, explained to great yogi Nyiphugpa the karma of his having pain.

Great yogi Nyiphugpa continued to do nyung näs, even when his body was very weak, and especially on the special days of the eighth, fifteenth and thirtieth. Chenrezig predicted to Nyiphugpa that right after his death he would be born in Amitabha's pure land and that he would achieve enlightenment in that pure realm. When he was seventy-seven years old,

Nyiphugpa passed away on the eighth day, on a silent day of a nyung nä, with many wonderful signs.

Trupa Dorje Gyälpo

The next lineage lama, Trupa Dorje Gyälpo,[21] was born in a place called Suyul, in Kham, and was given the holy name Tsultrim Konchog. After he turned seven, he started to experience the result of his previous good karmas. From that day he met many great yogis with great attainments, including his guru, Nyiphugpa. Afterwards, he took the vow of celibacy and became highly learned in the ways of practicing and actualizing the three vehicles. He also became expert and strict in *vinaya* practice.

Drubchog Nyiphugpa told him, "I will give you one Dharma practice that will be sufficient for you, one person." His guru then gave him the initiation and teachings of Chenrezig. Trupa Dorje Gyälpo then promised this guru that he would do nyung nä practice until he died. For five years he continuously did nyung näs in one place.

When he was thirty-six, on the eighth day of the third Tibetan month, he saw Chenrezig and Chenrezig blessed him, with no separation of his holy body, speech and mind from the three doors of great yogi Trupa Dorje Gyälpo. At that time, Trupa Dorje Gyälpo achieved infinite knowledge and clear perception. He also achieved many psychic powers. He then did amazing work for sentient beings.

Trupa Dorje Gyälpo lived by begging. He never had the experience of putting a drop of alcohol or a piece of meat on his tongue. Throughout his life he did nyung nä practice continually.

When he passed away, his holy body produced relics, tiny white pills, which were preserved in a stupa, though later the Chinese probably destroyed it. The text says that when people prayed in front of that stupa, relics were born and fell down from it. This also happens at Swayambhunath Stupa, which Western people call the Monkey Temple. If you go there very early in the morning, when it's just light, on special days such as the eighth, fifteenth or thirtieth, you can find relics born from the stupa. The Nepali man who looks after the stupa picks them all up and takes care of them.

---

[21] Both Wangchen Rinpoche and Bardor Tulku Rinpoche refer to this lama as Supa Dorje Gyälpo. In the *Blue Annals* he is called Sru-pa Do-rje Gyal-po.

Sometimes he gives them to people when they ask. The relics arise because those famous stupas have been blessed by many buddhas and bodhisattvas and by many highly realized yogis. Actually, the transcendental wisdom of many buddhas and bodhisattvas abides with those stupas.

Zhangtön Drajig

The next lineage lama is Zhangtön Drajig, who was born in a place called Trophur.[22] He wasn't born in New York or London or Hawaii—maybe next time. On the day he was born, as he was coming out of his mother's womb there were many earthquakes and frightening sounds of thunder, which terrified an enemy of the family. The name Drajig (*dra* means enemy and *jig* means frightening) was then given to the child.

Zhangtön Drajig took vows of celibacy and lived purely in the lifestyle of the Kadampa geshes. He went around to different monasteries of the four traditions to give answers in debate. All the learned monks in each monastery would debate with him, and he alone could give the correct answers. In this way he became famous as being very learned.

Zhangtön Drajig established a monastery with five hundred monks. In order to develop the monastery, Tara made the prediction to him, "You must take teachings on Eleven-Face Chenrezig from bodhisattva Trupa. After you have practiced for three years and four months, on the full moon night, in the third part of the night, you will see Chenrezig surrounded by all the Action Tantra deities.[23] In this way you will be initiated and blessed."

Tara also predicted to him, "You, my son, without eating food offered with devotion or offered on behalf of dead people, should live in solitude. And if you are able to, you should do chu len practice. If you can't live on pills, you should live by begging and work for sentient beings."

In accordance with the orders of his guru, Trupa Dorje Gyälpo, Zhangtön Drajig built a monastery within three years. Right after he had finished it, he gave away all his material possessions, including his robes and his bed and bedding.

---

[22] The *Blue Annals* says he was a native of Srug-gan-pa.
[23] This means the deities mentioned in *Limb of Prostrations*: Tara, Medicine Buddha and the various other Action Tantra deities.

Zhangtön Drajig then went to live on a high rocky mountain, where he did three months of nyung näs without anybody knowing. During this time he had such a high fever and incredible pain for seven days that he thought he was going to die. One day, around dawn, when he was in a light sleep, Chenrezig explained to him, "Before, many lifetimes ago, you were born as an Indian fisherman and cooked fish alive in boiling water and ate them. Because of that you experienced suffering in the boiling hot water hell for a hundred million years. During that time, because you were touched by beams of light from my body, you passed away from that realm and were born in the human realm. You made contact with me for sixteen human lives, and in this life you are being directly guided by me. Experiencing this disease has now purified the obscurations left over from that karma." Chenrezig then put his palm on Zhangtön Drajig's head and in that moment, he was relieved from his disease.

For three years Zhangtön Drajig then practiced austerities and meditated on the graduated path of attaining Chenrezig. Because his practice of austerities was extreme, lung arose so strongly that for seven days he was barely conscious and was unable to remember anything. To reduce the lung, he put wood ash in water, boiled the water and drank it. Sometimes he ate nettles to try to reduce the lung, and at other times he ate the dried snot of shepherds. At one stage he lived for seven months without taking even a drop of water. He practiced severe austerities.

At the end of three years he had very high attainment and was able to show the signs of various psychic powers; for example, flying in the sky and reversing the flow of a river.

When Zhangtön Drajig passed away, a large amount of relics came from his holy body and an image of Chenrezig appeared on his tongue. The relics were placed in a stupa.

There are relics of Guru Shakyamuni Buddha in Sarnath. If you pay a small amount of money, the head person at the Mahabodhi Society will bring them up from underneath the temple. There are two fine, white relics kept under glass.

There are also relics of Guru Shakyamuni Buddha in Sri Lanka and other places. Because in the future degenerate time people would be unable to see Guru Shakyamuni Buddha himself, he left relics as objects of devotion, enabling people to accumulate good karma. This is besides his statues. Guru Shakyamuni Buddha explained this in the sutra teachings.

Jangchub Päl

The next lineage lama is Jangchub Päl, who is also known as Khenpo Tsidulwa. One prostration prayer to the lineage lamas says,

> I prostrate at the feet of Tsidulwa,
> Whose holy mind was pervaded by immeasurable energy of compassion.
> When meditating on bodhicitta,
> He saw his guru as inseparable from the yidam.

Tsidulwa was born in a place called Chöden. From when he was a child, Tsidulwa had incredible compassion for sentient beings, even lice. When he found lice on his body, he would call them his parents. (It's easy to get lice in Tibet, because it's so cold that people don't wash much.) When he was very young, the words would automatically come, "My parents—how pitiful!"

From when he was ten, Tsidulwa read and studied various sutra teachings. He then realized the many shortcomings of the dissatisfied mind of attachment to the point that tears would come, generated aversion to the attachment in his own mind and developed great fear of samsara. He prayed to be able to take the ordination of renunciation.

Whenever he saw or listened to a geshe explaining teachings, he would be extremely happy and would pray, "May I also be able to reveal Dharma to many sentient beings."

He developed more and more aversion to ordinary, worldly life. Of course, whether or not family life is worldly depends on the attitude with which it is lived; you can't say that family life is worldly based on external appearances. For example, from outside, Marpa and his secret mother looked as if they were living an ordinary family life.

Even though Tsidulwa prayed all the time to be able to receive ordination, he wasn't able to do so for many years because of his parents and other reasons. However, when he reached the age of twenty-one, he left alone and went to receive ordination. He then read and listened to many teachings, and reflected precisely on their meaning. He became expert in the teachings of the three baskets. He also practiced extremely pure moral conduct[24]

---

[24] Wangchen Rinpoche explains that his discipline was so pure that the perfume of morality emanated from his body.

and his bodhicitta was fully developed. He quickly became famous for his learning, his strictness in moral conduct and his good heart. He mainly practiced vinaya, which means he mainly practiced subduing his mind, and then his body and his speech. If the mind is kept in peace, without allowing anger, attachment and other disturbing thoughts to arise, the body and speech also automatically become peaceful, or subdued.

After receiving a prediction from dakinis in a dream, Tsidulwa built a monastery called Palden Dok Tho and established a community of more than a thousand monks.

His heart practices were Medicine Buddha and Tara. One night, in a dream, a blue-colored girl approached him and said, "Son of the essence, tomorrow you should go to see Zhangtön Drajig and take him as your friend and helper. You should receive the oral transmission of the teaching *Generating the Holy Mind* from him. You will then be able to generate bodhicitta and your work for sentient beings will flourish." After saying this, Tara disappeared.

The following dawn, Tsidulwa left to see Zhangtön Drajig, from whom he received the oral transmission of *Generating the Holy Mind*, as well as initiation of Eleven-Face Chenrezig and advice on meditation practice, especially on how to do the approach retreat of Chenrezig. Zhangtön Drajig gave Tsidulwa all these teachings.

Zhangtön Drajig then advised Tsidulwa, "The Dharma of the Noble Compassionate-Eyed One is a Dharma that can give enlightenment in one lifetime on one body. Do great, extensive works for other sentient beings." He gave Tsidulwa all the teachings needed to attain Chenrezig and Tsidulwa's holy mind was then completely satisfied by Dharma.

Having promised to do one thousand nyung näs, Tsidulwa left that place with great happiness. When he had finished three hundred nyung näs, on the fifteenth day of the fourth month, Saka Dawa, he saw Chenrezig, the Great Compassionate One, with a holy body of light, and Chenrezig spoke to him.

In short, Tsidulwa accomplished Chenrezig and then ripened many sentient beings and liberated them from samsara. He accomplished extensively the holy actions of Chenrezig. After having done much work for the teachings and for sentient beings, when he was eighty-two, Tsidulwa said, "For a while I will go into the presence of Maitreya Buddha. From there I will go to Sukhavati, Amitabha Buddha's pure realm." Having said this, he then passed away.

Dewa Chän

Tsidulwa handed down the nyung nä practice to a disciple called Gangchen Dewa Chän, who was born in a place called Dok Me, in the lower part of Tibet. He took the ordination of renunciation when he was seven and, until he was fifteen, studied the *Prajnaparamita* scriptures. He also became expert in the vinaya teachings. The main meditation deities he practiced were Medicine Buddha and Tara.

One day Tara appeared to Gangchen Dewa Chän and predicted, "You should work for sentient beings. You should take the oral transmission of the Chenrezig with eleven faces and a thousand arms and eyes from the abbot Thugje Jangchub."[25] As advised by Tara, Dewa Chän went to see Khenpo Tsidulwa, the lineage lama mentioned by Tara, and received from him the initiation and teachings of the Great Compassionate One.

Khenpo Tsidulwa then advised Dewa Chän, "You should stay with me and do an approach retreat, completing the number of mantras." Dewa Chän then did one approach retreat. After the retreat, he gave an explanation of all the *Prajnaparamita* teachings twenty times.

Dewa Chän himself promised to do five thousand nyung näs. When he had finished six hundred, on the night of the Tibetan eighth, on the day of complete silence, a white light appeared in front of him and took him away to Potala, Chenrezig's pure realm. In that place everything was very calm and clear. The ground was white and there were white flowers and jewels everywhere. There were also various precious trees, with birds, transformations of bodhisattvas, singing songs of Mahayana teachings. When the wind blew peacefully through the beautiful mansion of the Potala, golden bells around the mansion made sounds of the four immeasurables,[26] satisfying to the ears.

Animals with incredibly beautiful colors (again, transformations of bodhisattvas) played with great happiness in a park, satisfying the eye sense. From the sky, a continuous rain of nectar flowed, eliminating sufferings of hunger and thirst. At certain times, divine cloth would come from the wish-granting trees, eliminating the sufferings of the body.

Three of the four doors of the mansion were open, with the other one

---

[25] An epithet of Khenpo Tsidulwa.
[26] Rinpoche says that here the four immeasurables might also have another meaning.

closed. Dewa Chän circumambulated the mansion and did prostrations at each of the doors. He then saw Chenrezig, who spoke to him. White light absorbed into his heart, and his body, speech and mind were completely filled with bliss. Chenrezig advised him, "When you die, you will benefit sentient beings. When you die, I will call you. I will invite many dakinis, and I will guide you." Surrounded by white beams, Dewa Chän woke up from the dream.

Because of this experience, Dewa Chän actualized countless concentrations, such as the concentration called *looking at all existence in the aspect of equanimity*.

He then established monasteries and wrote down the teachings that he had taught. After some time, Dewa Chän said to his disciples, "I'll be leaving soon, so if you have any questions you should ask them now." He then gave his disciples advice on what they asked him. Then, in a place called Blissful Place of Abandonment, his mind abided in one-pointed meditation. With wonderful signs, he then passed away and went to Potala, Chenrezig's pure land.

When Dewa Chän's disciples then offered fire to his holy body, many relics and even images were born from his holy body. They were kept inside a Tara statue that speaks, which had been brought to Tibet from Nepal.

Jangchub Bar

Bodhisattva Dewa Chän handed down the nyung nä teachings to his main disciple, his heart son, bodhisattva Chu Zangpo, or Jangchub Bar.[27]

Bodhisattva Chu Zangpo was born in a place called Mun. When he was eleven he took the upasika ordination at a place called Dubche, then later took the ordination of renunciation. He studied well the great teachings, such as *A Guide to the Bodhisattva's Way of Life* and *Madhyamaka*, and did extensive works for the teachings. He listened to advice on the profound path, comprehending all the words and also generating the realizations. He then lived in one place and one-pointedly did retreat. He ripened and liberated many sentient beings who were objects to be subdued. He was particularly expert in the vinaya teachings. When he was twenty, he received full ordination.

---

[27] Also known as Khenchen Chuzangwa.

One night a white man appeared to him in a dream and told him, "Jangchub Bar, there is a karmic connection between you and the lama called Dewa Chän, and there is no difference between Dewa Chän and me. You must have the method to achieve Chenrezig, so you should take the oral transmission of that teaching from him and then practice it." After saying this, the white man disappeared.

At dawn the next day, bodhisattva Chu Zangpo went to see Dewa Chän and told him the story. Lama Dewa Chän then said, "Kyab su chhi![28] The man who gave you this advice is Chenrezig. Even I myself had a good dream." Lama Dewa Chän then told bodhisattva Chu Zangpo, "I will give you the oral transmissions of all the teachings on the method of achieving Chenrezig."

Chu Zangpo then told Lama Dewa Chän that he wanted to do one hundred nyung näs. Lama Dewa Chän advised him, "Don't go away yet. Stay here until Chenrezig sees you." After a long time Chu Zangpo again requested Lama Dewa Chän to be allowed to go away to do retreat. Lama Dewa Chän advised him, "You are a pure person, different from others. Since you have perseverance, you should accomplish Chenrezig."

Chu Zangpo then did nyung näs, one straight after the other. When he'd finished three hundred, after midnight on the Tibetan fifteenth, the night of the full moon, the whole sky filled with light. He wondered whether he was hallucinating or whether it was light from his light offering. While he was looking at the sky and wondering in this way, in the sky in front of him appeared Thousand-Arm Chenrezig surrounded by all the Kadampa geshes. Many other deities were making offerings to Chenrezig. The whole sky was filled with deities. Chu Zangpo cried with joy.

Chu Zangpo said to Chenrezig, "One of your transformations told me to practice in this way, so I did. Why haven't you guided me with your compassion until now? What mistake did I, the evil-doer, make that I wasn't guided by you until now?" Chenrezig replied, "I have never been separated from you for even a second. But when I gave the prediction to you, you had superstition in your mind, thinking that something else might be better. It's because of that mistake that it took so long for you to be guided. There is now no separation between you and me. You should reveal my teachings, which come from the compassion of all the buddhas of the three times, to

---

[28] This means "I take refuge!"

fortunate sentient beings. Your body, speech and mind will then become meaningful." After Chenrezig said this to him, white light covered the whole Mun valley.

Chu Zangpo was extremely pleased that he had seen Chenrezig and been given permission to practice and to give teachings to others. The next day he went to see his guru; he prostrated and asked after his guru's health. The guru then asked, "Were you happy yesterday?" Bodhisattva Chu Zangpo told his guru, "Now my mind has been liberated from superstition, from wrong conceptions." His guru said, "That is good. Now work for sentient beings."

Chu Zangpo then went to a place called Nu, where he did great practice of nyung nä in each month. At that place, he also led others in reading the elaborate, intermediate and short *Prajnaparamita* sutras. He was also able to gather three hundred Sangha.

From that time, bodhisattva Chu Zangpo was inseparable from Chenrezig, like a body and its shadow. Many wonderful signs happened and he performed incredible, unimaginable actions. His everyday life was pure Kadampa lifestyle. After he had taken full ordination, and until he reached sixty, he did nyung näs again and again.

One night, when he was doing retreat on an aspect of Chenrezig called Amoghapasha, rainfalls of flowers dropped on the mandala. There were wonderful sounds and lights, and the Sixteen Arhats made offerings. On the eighth day he saw Medicine Buddha, and the wealth-granting protectors in Medicine Buddha's entourage offered him nectar, which stopped the suffering of thirst. On the ninth day bodhisattva Chu Zangpo saw Chenrezig, Vajrapani and Manjushri, and many wonderful things happened.

Bodhisattva Chu Zangpo then did much work for sentient beings. He left instructions in his will that whatever tsampa and other food was left when he died was to be given to people doing nyung nä practice. He said, "Invite a whole group of people who are doing nyung nä and give them *thugpa*, or at least tsampa. If you can't give them even tsampa, give them water or firewood. Chenrezig has actually told me that there will be unimaginable merit from doing this. Don't listen to anything anyone else says. Chenrezig never tells lies. I don't need merits from other offerings—just dedicate as much as possible for nyung näs."

Chu Zangpo continued, "One old woman called Chökyi did much nyung nä practice. When she died, crows took her bones from the cemetery, so no one saw that her bones had become relics. Because I know what is virtue and what is nonvirtue, until now I have practiced and lived my life in accordance with the biography of Lama Atisha. You should also do that."

Bodhisattva Chu Zangpo then went into his garden. When his servant went to offer him tea, he drank the tea and then, with many wonderful signs, passed away.[29]

Modern nyung nä yogis

Geshe Lama Konchog

Geshe Lama Konchog did a total of 2,000 nyung näs, though not one straight after the other. He kept very quiet about all his practice and attainments; he never told us about them. It was only after he died that we found out.

He did his nyung näs in Tsum, where there's a nunnery and a monastery that we're now taking care of. Geshe Tenzin Zopa, Geshe Lama Konchog's attendant, has been given the responsibility to develop them, and he has already done a lot for the nunnery. I visited Tsum one time when I was in Nepal. I was meant to go there after all the building was finished to do the blessing, but Mama Pek, a woman from Malaysia, hired a Russian helicopter to go there at a cost of 100,000 rupees. Since she was going to help with the projects up there and wanted me to go, I also went.

Tsum is an incredible place. It is similar in style to Solu Khumbu, but Solu Khumbu has now degenerated with all the many tourists going there. The people and the country of Solu Khumbu have totally changed with the introduction of modern things; and now everything is devoted to business. All the villages have roads full of shops, which weren't there before. Tsum is like Solu Khumbu was before. So far in its history, only two Western people have been there.[30] It's still the same primitive place it was originally, in the past. It's a place to do only Dharma, nothing else.

I had heard a little bit of Geshe Lama Konchog's story but I didn't know or think about his hardships and sacrifice to practice Dharma until I went

---

[29] For other versions of the nyung nä lineage lamas' stories, see *The Blue Annals*, pp. 1006–61, *Buddhist Fasting Practice*, pp. 21–38, and *Rest for the Fortunate*, pp. 108–28.
[30] This has now changed, with tour groups going to Tsum.

to Tsum. Geshe Lama Konchog's cave is up above Milarepa's. There's no actual road to it—just a track on the very edge of the mountain. If you slip you're in danger of falling down the mountain. I had to scramble up on my hands and knees. Geshe Lama Konchog lived in that cave reached only by this dangerous track and cut off all relationships with people. I think he chose to live in this isolated cave because he wanted to be alone to practice without any disturbance. He lived there in that cave with nothing for many years. Like Buddha, he lived a life of austerities for six years.

Geshe-la was totally renounced. He walked around in rags, almost naked. From the outside, he looked like the poorest beggar in that area. People had no idea that he was a great practitioner. I heard that one couple took the dirt from under their bed and threw it on Geshe Lama Konchog when he was walking along the road. It was the father or brother of a monk who was the caretaker of the main gompa at Kopan Monastery. Later, each time Geshe Lama Konchog saw the man who had thrown the dirt he would remind him of what he had done.

It's just amazing when you go to see the cave where Geshe Lama Konchog lived. He was totally renounced. There is no doubt that devotion *has* to arise when you see how much he sacrificed his life to practice Dharma. He had total renunciation; he practiced the ten innermost jewels.[31] The surprising thing is that even though we lived together at Kopan for many years, he never told us stories of how he practiced. Even Lama Lhundrup had no idea how Geshe Lama Konchog had practiced Dharma. Geshe-la told us some stories but not about how he sacrificed himself and lived exactly like Milarepa. He never told us. With that much renunciation, of course you would have realizations; you would achieve the path. There's no doubt about that.

When Geshe Lama Konchog was at Kopan (I think this was during Lama Yeshe's time), one time when I was alone with him, he told me that he had completed *Lama Chöpa* and Vajrayogini. He told me that twice. I was confused about what he meant. Did he mean that he'd finished the recitation? Or did he mean he'd completed the realizations of the path? I didn't question him. He talked about it only that one time; after that he didn't

---

[31] For an explanation of the ten innermost jewels, see chapter 9 of *How to Practice Dharma* and appendix 3 of *Lama Chöpa Jorchö* in the *FPMT Retreat Prayer Book*.

mention it to me. He underwent so much hardship, exactly like Milarepa, so of course he should have completed the path.

When Geshe Lama Konchog was living in the cave in Tsum, because he had long hair and no one knew who he was, people were frightened of him; they came up and threw rocks at him. He then left that cave and went way up the mountain, where he spent two years doing retreat under a tree. Without a roof or any other shelter, he practiced under that tree. When I was flying into Tsum, Tenzin Zopa tried to show me the tree through a window of the helicopter, but I was on the other side and the window was low, so I couldn't see it. Tenzin Zopa knew which tree it was because the last time Geshe Lama Konchog went back to Tsum, he took Tenzin Zopa to that tree and showed him.

When we lived together, I knew that Geshe Lama Konchog was definitely somebody who had experience of emptiness and of bodhicitta. I could see from the way he behaved that he had power to benefit others, but I didn't know that he was a highly attained yogi who had completed the tantric path. I had no idea.

Drupa Rinpoche

Drupa Rinpoche, the lama who built the monastery and nunnery in Tsum, an unbelievable practitioner, also did 2,000 nyung näs. He had a few disciples who did 3,000 nyung näs and many others who did 2,000 or 1,000. This lama's life story is also amazing. He was of unbelievable benefit to sentient beings. In the early times I saw a picture of him in the prayer wheel house at Boudhanath Stupa. For many years, it was there. He's the guru of Tsechu Rinpoche, who was the leader of the Buddhists in Nepal.

At first, I thought Drupa Rinpoche was a Kagyü or Nyingma lama, but later Tenzin Zopa sent me his life story. Drupa Rinpoche founded those monasteries in his past life. I read that he was actually a *lharampa* geshe from Drepung Monastery and very expert in the Dharma. He took initiations from lamas of all four traditions. He was a great practitioner of Vajrayogini, but his main practice was Chenrezig. He organized many people in Tsum and also in other places to recite together one hundred million OM MANI PADME HUMS. By organizing the recitation of one hundred million manis he helped so many sentient beings, enabling them to purify much negative karma and collect extensive merit. He gave people the chance to become so much closer to enlightenment. And mani retreats are still happening up there in Tsum.

Drupa Rinpoche went to many different places in the Himalayan region of Nepal and made laws that animals were not to be harmed, that people were not to hunt or kill animals. These laws still exist. He helped the people in Tsum and many other areas to live in vows to not hunt and kill animals. So many sentient beings received unbelievable benefit from him.

There was a similar law in Solu Khumbu in the past—I'm not sure whether it was because Drupa Rinpoche or another lama came there. Tsum still has this law, but now it has degenerated in Solu Khumbu. The Sherpas call the type of Tibetan who kills animals and sells the meat in markets by a special name, *yapas*. It was not like that in the past. In the past, animals were killed only by wolves or other animals, not by people, but now it has degenerated.

5. The Benefits of the Eight Mahayana Precepts[32]

THE TAKING OF the Eight Mahayana Precepts is known in Tibetan as *theg chen so jong*. *Theg chen* means Mahayana; *so* means to restore, or revive; and *jong* means to purify. So, the literal translation is "Mahayana restoring and purifying," and it involves restoring, or reviving, the virtue that has been degenerated and purifying negative karma.

The method of the Eight Mahayana Precepts comes from the tantric text *Dön yö shag pai kyi gyü*. Since *Dön yö shag pa* is Amoghapasha and *gyü* means tantra, the name of the text is *Tantra of Amoghapasha*. That is the reference for this practice.

WHEN TO TAKE THE EIGHT MAHAYANA PRECEPTS

It's good to take the Eight Mahayana Precepts on the Tibetan eighth, fifteenth and thirtieth days and especially on the special days of Buddha, such as the fifteen special days that celebrate Guru Shakyamuni Buddha performing miracles, when many kings and benefactors made offerings to Buddha and requested him to subdue the six Hindu founders. Any merit we accumulate during these fifteen days is increased 100 million times. Even though we mightn't normally do much practice to accumulate merit because we are busy with other things, it is skillful to practice hard at this time. Since each merit is increased by so much, we can make our life highly meaningful in such a short time.

As I have already mentioned, Saka Dawa, the fourth Tibetan month, has three special Buddha days. Some teachings say that the eighth was the day that Guru Shakyamuni Buddha showed the action of coming out of his mother's womb. The fifteenth, the full moon day, is the day that he

---

[32] See *The Direct and Unmistaken Method* for more on the Eight Mahayana Precepts.

achieved enlightenment under the bodhi tree in Bodhgaya, and the day that later he passed away in Kushinagar. There is another Buddha day that celebrates when Guru Shakyamuni Buddha first turned the Dharma wheel in Sarnath, and one that celebrates Buddha's descent from the Thirty-three Realm, where he had gone to teach his mother.

It's extremely good to take the Eight Mahayana Precepts as often as you can, especially when you do retreat and particularly if you haven't taken the lifetime ordination of thirty-six, 253 or 364 precepts.

Since the Eight Mahayana Precepts are taken for only one day, I think it's a particularly good practice for laypeople. Because a layperson's life is extremely busy with working for their family, it's very difficult for them to take vows. Therefore, Guru Shakyamuni Buddha's method is for them to take the Eight Mahayana Precepts on those special days when much more merit is accumulated. Laypeople should take the Eight Mahayana Precepts on whichever days they think they can take and keep them. Even though life is normally very busy, on certain days or once a month they should take and keep the eight precepts. Their life will then not be completely empty. When the person dies, even though they didn't become a monk or nun and live in a monastery, their life is not completely empty because they've accumulated so much merit and performed so much purification. In this way they have made preparation to be reborn with the body of a happy transmigratory being, with a human or deva body; to find a perfect human rebirth again.

When one tiny bodhi seed is planted, a huge tree with so many branches that it can cover five hundred horse carriages can grow. And each year, so many seeds come from that tree. Even with external examples, incredible results can come from a small cause. With internal examples, such as the evolution of karma, the results are much greater. From a small good karma, there can be amazing results, much greater than with external examples that you can see with your eyes. Similarly, even if a negative karma is small, the negative results can be enormous, much greater than with external examples.

Take the example of one of the past lives of Shariputra. (In thangkas, Shariputra is one of the two arhats with begging bowls next to Guru Shakyamuni Buddha.) In a past life, while traveling, he stopped in a place that had paintings on the wall. That night Shariputra was fixing his shoes, and by the light in front of him, he saw a painting of Buddha on the wall. He was very attracted to that painting and kept on looking at the Buddha.

He then generated a strong wish, "How wonderful it would be if I could be like this!"

That was the karma that enabled him in his next life to be born in India, to become a disciple of Guru Shakyamuni Buddha; to become an arhat, completely liberated from true suffering and true cause of suffering; and to always be with Buddha, hearing teachings and serving him. In fact, he was able to meet many buddhas. Just by generating the wish to become a buddha, one becomes able to meet many buddhas. That's an incredible result.

Therefore, you can enjoy the result of keeping each of the eight precepts for many lifetimes even while you are in samsara, besides enjoying the ultimate result of enlightenment, the infinite qualities of a buddha's holy body, holy speech and holy mind. Taking the Eight Mahayana Precepts for one day even once in your life has unbelievable results. If you could actually see all the results, they wouldn't fit your mind. It's like somebody who hasn't seen that a huge bodhi tree with so many seeds can come from one small seed—they wouldn't believe it. But those who have seen it can understand.

The benefits of taking vows are emphasized in lam-rim teachings. For example, if a *gelong*, a fully ordained monk living in 253 precepts, makes a light offering with butter the size of a fingernail and a wick the size of a hair, he collects more merit than someone who doesn't live in any precepts at all making a light offering with butter the size of this earth (or maybe hundreds of times the size of the earth) and a wick the size of Mount Meru. Even though the gelong's offering is so tiny, because he has a body that is living in the ordination of a gelong, the merit is much greater than that of somebody without precepts who makes a huge offering. There is an incredibly big difference in the profit, in the merit.

There are differences when someone who doesn't live in precepts and someone who lives in vows, such as the thirty-six vows, do the same thing. When they both offer one stick of incense, one butter lamp or candle, recite OM MANI PADME HUM or do one prostration, there's a big difference in the merit, like the difference between an atom and a mountain. Therefore, even though at other times it might be difficult, it's extremely important to take the Eight Mahayana Precepts and live in those vows on the days when you are making a special effort to accumulate merit and practice purification by doing retreat or by making many offerings. You then accumulate so much merit. There is much greater profit in terms of merit.

A person who lives in vows is a skillful Dharma practitioner. It's like a businessman investing his money wherever it's most profitable. But that kind of business investment is nothing. This is much more important. If you have the opportunity to make merit and don't take it, that loss of merit is a much greater loss than losing money. Ordinary people regard losing the opportunity to gain a million dollars as a great loss; but for Dharma practitioners, the greatest loss is not accumulating merit when they have the opportunity to do so. The greatest loss is the loss of good karma—money is nothing. Even for business people, all their success in business—all the money they can make and all the things they can get—depends on having created good karma. Without the good karma, that success wouldn't happen. Dharma practitioners, those who understand and practice Dharma, regard not creating good karma while they have the opportunity as a great loss.

During a retreat you make many offerings. At other times you might be busy working for your family and doing many other activities. When you live with other people, and even when you live alone, it's difficult for your activities to become Dharma. So at particular times, such as when you're doing retreat, where you're actually making offerings and doing other practices to accumulate merit, it's very important to take precepts. The more precepts you take, the more merit you accumulate. There is much greater profit in regard to good karma.

Receiving the lineage

To take the Eight Mahayana Precepts, first you need to receive the lineage of the ordination. If you haven't received the ordination of one-day precepts before, you first have to receive the lineage from somebody you wish to recognize as a guru, a virtuous friend. The person from whom you receive the lineage of the ordination becomes your guru. It's better to regard the person from whom you first received the ordination, whether Sangha or lay, male or female, as a virtuous friend.

If you don't regard the person from whom you receive the ordination lineage as a guru, it means you could take a tantric initiation from someone without recognizing that person as a guru either. However, just being there doesn't mean that you receive an initiation. It's a mental thing, not a physical thing. And if you don't have the lineage of an initiation, you can't pass the lineage to others.

Afterwards you can take the ordination from the altar. However, whether you have an altar or not, first visualize Guru Shakyamuni Buddha or Chenrezig surrounded by numberless buddhas and bodhisattvas, then take the ordination.

The benefits of taking the Eight Mahayana Precepts

Taking the Eight Mahayana Precepts has great benefits. *The King of Concentration Sutra* mentions,

> The merit from taking and keeping one precept for a day and night in this time when the Dharma is degenerating and the teaching of the Buddha is about to stop is much more than that from making offerings of food and drink, umbrellas, banners and lights to one hundred billion buddhas for eons equal in number to the sand grains of the ocean.

Taking the Eight Mahayana Precepts also has great benefit from the side of the place. You can practice virtue for eons in a pure realm, but the merit from practicing one virtue in an impure realm such as ours for the duration of a finger snap is much greater. Therefore, taking the Eight Mahayana Precepts, which involves not just one virtue but eight, for the duration of even a finger snap collects infinite merit. If the benefit of keeping the precepts for the duration of a finger snap were materialized, it wouldn't fit in space. It wouldn't fit in the great three thousand galaxies.

There are also benefits from the nature of morality. Even the great black nagas, poisonous snakes and other harmful vicious beings cannot harm someone who is living in morality, in vows.

Those who live in morality also create the cause to be able to meet a buddha.

Living in morality is like having legs: it allows you to go to whichever place you wish to go, even to liberation. Living without morality is like not having legs.

Broken morality is like a broken pot, which cannot be used to hold water. Living in morality is like an unbroken pot in which you can keep nectar.

Taking the Eight Mahayana Precepts also has the benefit of enabling you to meet Maitreya Buddha's teachings. Maitreya Buddha said,

> During the time of Shakyamuni Buddha's teachings, whoever listens to the teachings with devotion and protects the eight precepts will be born as a disciple in my retinue.

Maitreya Buddha promised that you will become his disciple when he descends on this earth, that you will meet his teachings.

By living in morality by taking the Eight Mahayana Precepts, you are protected by the devas who are beyond samsara and even worldly devas. The white-side guardians naturally protect you day and night, even though you don't ask them to do so. Wherever you are, they protect you from interferences, from obstacles, day and night, all the time.

Also, as I've just mentioned, taking the Eight Mahayana Precepts has great benefit in terms of the merit you accumulate. Take the example of someone who doesn't live in any vows making an offering to the Three Rare Sublime Ones of an ocean of butter with a wick the size of Mount Meru, and someone else who lives in just one precept making a tiny light offering using one drop of oil with a wick like the tip of a needle. This second person collects much greater merit than the first person without vows, who made such an incredible light offering. There's no comparison at all. The first person's merit becomes insignificant when compared to that of the person living in even one vow who makes one tiny offering. And with the Eight Mahayana Precepts you're taking not just one vow but eight.

Another benefit is that your prayers will succeed. Any prayers you make during times you are living purely in your vows are very powerful. By taking the Eight Mahayana Precepts and keeping them without degeneration, you will definitely be able to accomplish whatever you pray for during the time of keeping the vows purely. That is the power of pure morality.

Even the ability to heal depends on how pure your morality is. With the power of pure morality you can benefit others by using mantras and other methods to stop disease and spirit harms, which make people crazy. You can also stop the problems of drought by doing naga pujas and so forth. Pujas have much more power if the person doing them lives purely in their vows. Your work for other sentient beings through teaching and other activities is also much more effective. Your blessings also have great power. Human beings and even spirits, devas and protectors listen to a person who lives in pure vows and do what that person asks them to.

Taking the Eight Mahayana Precepts also has the incredible benefit of bringing a human or deva body in future lives. By keeping the Eight Mahayana Precepts even once you receive a special human or deva body.

Another benefit is that the Eight Mahayana Precepts are very easy to take. You can bear hardships for a long time, for months or years, doing retreat and mantra recitation, but even if you do the recitation for many eons, if your mind is distracted it won't bring any result. With other virtues, it's necessary that your mind not be distracted at the beginning, in the middle and at the end. Otherwise, it's difficult to receive the benefits as explained. But with the Eight Mahayana Precepts, you just need to be able to pay attention during the few minutes it takes to do the ceremony. During the rest of the day, even if your mind is distracted, it doesn't become an obstacle; there's still continuous great benefit. In accumulating merit by practicing the Eight Mahayana Precepts, you have to keep fewer precepts compared to other vows and for only a short time, and the ceremony is easy to recite. There is nothing more meaningful and nothing easier than taking the Eight Mahayana Precepts.

The final benefit from taking the Eight Mahayana Precepts is that you achieve liberation and enlightenment. It is mentioned in the sutra *Requested by Indra* that a person who keeps the Eight Mahayana Precepts on the Tibetan eighth and fifteenth days and on the special days when Buddha showed his psychic powers will become enlightened.

Taking the Eight Mahayana Precepts has unbelievable benefits. You're not taking them only for yourself or only for the happiness of this life, for the happiness of future lives or for even liberation. You're taking them purely to free all sentient beings from all their suffering and lead them to enlightenment.

SHORTENING THE TIME

If somebody has such an uncontrolled mind that they can't keep the precepts for one whole day, they can take them for just half a day—for the nighttime or the daytime, for example—for one hour or for even half an hour. Taking the vows for even such a short period has unbelievable benefits.

In the past, in India, Arya Katiyana gave precepts to a butcher and to a prostitute. Since butchers mostly work in the daytime and don't kill at night, it was easy for the butcher to keep the precepts at night and not during the daytime. Arya Katiyana gave the butcher the vow not to kill at night. The butcher could not keep the vow in the daytime, but it was much better for him to keep the vow at night than not to take the vow at all. There was much benefit from this.

Since it was difficult for the prostitute to keep the vow to abstain from sexual intercourse during the nighttime and easy for her to keep it in the daytime, Arya Katiyana gave her the vow to abandon sexual intercourse in the daytime.

There are such scriptural references. There are ways of doing the practice so that even those with difficult minds are able to take the vows.

Even if you have degenerated one of the vows you have taken, it's not skillful to think, "What's the point of keeping vows?" and give up the rest. That is foolish. Even if one precept is broken, the rest aren't broken, and there's much merit in keeping the rest of the precepts. It's a great loss if you give up all your vows because you have broken one.

Differences between the Mahayana and pratimoksha precepts

It might be helpful to know the differences between the Eight Mahayana Precepts and the eight general *pratimoksha* precepts. There are several differences between taking these eight precepts in the Mahayana way and taking the eight precepts to achieve self-liberation, the sorrowless state of the Lesser Vehicle path.

In regard to lay pratimoksha vows, there are the refuge-only lay vow, the five lay vows and the eight lay vows, which are called *nyer nä*. *Nyer* means near and *nä* means abiding, so near abiding. It means that taking and living in these eight precepts makes you near to liberation. The term *near abiding* has great meaning, showing the result of the practice of living in the vows. These eight precepts bring a person near to liberation. The longer they keep the vows the nearer they become to achieving liberation.

Difference of motivation

One difference between the Eight Mahayana Precepts and the eight lay pratimoksha vows is the motivation. The Eight Mahayana Precepts should be taken with a motivation of bodhicitta. One takes the eight lay pratimoksha precepts to achieve liberation from samsara for oneself. In the Mahayana ordination, we take the eight precepts with a motivation of bodhicitta, so what do we get from this? It makes us near to great liberation, full enlightenment, for sentient beings.

Difference of visualization

Another difference is in the visualization. When you take the eight pratimoksha precepts, you don't visualize all the buddhas and bodhisattvas. With the Eight Mahayana Precepts, you have to visualize all the buddhas and bodhisattvas, and you take the precepts in front of them.

One particular point is that we visualize the lama who gives the Eight Mahayana Precepts as a buddha. Why do we do this? Because the Eight Mahayana Precepts come from tantra, not from sutra. From the four types of tantra, this practice comes from Action Tantra. When you take the Eight Mahayana Precepts from a lama in relation to nyung nä, an Action Tantra practice, you visualize according to tantric guru yoga practice. Tantric practice involves training the mind in purity, in stopping impure ordinary appearances and conceptions.

To succeed in achieving realizations of the path, according to the Hinayana path, disciples devote themselves to the abbot or Dharma teacher as if he were Shakyamuni Buddha. They don't visualize the abbot as Shakyamuni Buddha, but they respect and obey him as if he were Shakyamuni Buddha.

According to the sutra path of Paramitayana, to succeed in realizing the path, the disciple devotes to the virtuous friend, or Dharma teacher, by meditating that, in essence, they are a buddha. They try to generate the devotion that sees the virtuous friend as a buddha.

In tantra, to succeed in actualizing the path, the disciple devotes to the virtuous friend not only by looking at them as in essence a buddha but by even visualizing them in the aspect of a buddha. You think of the virtuous friend with that pure appearance. In this way, with the Hinayana, Paramitayana and Vajrayana, the method of devoting oneself to the virtuous friend becomes progressively more profound. It is because of these methods that one is able to achieve enlightenment by practicing Paramitayana and to achieve enlightenment quickly by practicing Vajrayana. It is Buddha's skillful means to guide different levels of sentient beings to enlightenment.

The Eight Mahayana Precepts involve visualizing the virtuous friend as a buddha not only in essence, but even in aspect. Because this nyung nä practice is related to Chenrezig, we have to visualize the virtuous friend as Thousand-Arm Chenrezig.

Difference of ordination

A third difference is that those who are ordained, who have renounced the householder's life, can't take the eight lay pratimoksha vows. Why can't those who have taken higher vows take the eight lay precepts? Because taking lower vows while living in higher vows causes you to lose the higher vows. The Eight Mahayana Precepts can be taken by anyone, however, even by a fully ordained monk or nun. This is a third difference from the eight lay pratimoksha vows.

If you have a higher ordination, and especially if you don't keep your vows strictly, taking the Eight Mahayana Precepts helps you to be able to keep even your higher vows purely that day, since the four branches of fasting and so forth are kept that day. The higher vows are all based on these eight precepts. There is this benefit.

In regard to precepts, those who are living in higher vows have taken many more precepts than these eight, but I think the additional thing is the practice of Action Tantra. If someone has taken an Action Tantra initiation, it makes sense for that person to practice the extra Action Tantra precepts, such as the outer yoga of keeping the body clean. Otherwise, if a person were a bodhisattva, I don't think there would be much benefit for that person to just live in the vows with the motivation of bodhicitta, without the limbs of the precepts, because they have much higher vows. For someone who has taken more and higher precepts and is living in them purely, there wouldn't be much benefit in taking fewer and lower precepts. However, if someone has taken an Action Tantra initiation, it makes some difference to take the branch vows, which have to do with outer yoga.

Also, in regard to the actual precepts, the eight precepts of the Hinayana path have only the eight precepts and no branches, such as avoiding black food and so forth. Why are the branches mentioned here? Because these Eight Mahayana Precepts are part of Action Tantra practice, and Action Tantra involves avoiding black food. In Action Tantra, the main emphasis is on outer yoga, such as keeping the body clean, rather than inner yoga. The purpose of not polluting your body is so that you don't pollute your mind. You are then able to have clear concentration.

6. The Benefits of Reciting
OM MANI PADME HUM

WHY EVERYONE SHOULD RECITE OM MANI PADME HUM

Meditation on Chenrezig and recitation of OM MANI PADME HUM are most important practices in your life. They are the most important practices for the happiness and benefit of other sentient beings, so there can be no doubt that they are the most important practices for your own happiness and benefit as well. The meditation-recitation of Compassion Buddha is the most important thing.

As I often say, because they want happiness and do not want suffering, even turtles, mosquitoes, ants and wood lice all need to recite OM MANI PADME HUM. Goats and pigs need to recite OM MANI PADME HUM, in loud voices. It's the same for snakes—they also need to recite OM MANI PADME HUM. They should, but they can't. Why not? Because they don't have a human body.

Peter Wildoats, a student from Australia, says he has a dog that recites OM MANI PADME HUM. That's what he says, anyway. He taught his dog OM MANI PADME HUM and says that the dog chants it, but I don't think it could come out very precisely. It's probably mixed with the sound of barking.

Animals should recite OM MANI PADME HUM, but they can't. They should recite it because they want happiness and don't want suffering. That's why everyone should recite this mantra. It's the easiest way to achieve happiness for yourself. By reciting OM MANI PADME HUM, you can achieve all your wishes for happiness, not only for the happiness of this life but for the happiness of all your coming future lives, and also for the ultimate happiness that comes with cessation of the oceans of samsaric sufferings and their causes, karma and delusion, and even their negative imprints. Cessation of all negative imprints makes it impossible for delusions to arise again, which makes it impossible for negative karma to be accumulated, which makes it impossible for suffering to happen. There is then great liberation, or full enlightenment.

On top of that, you, the one person, want to bring all other sentient beings the happiness of this life and of all coming future lives and the ultimate happiness of total cessation of the oceans of samsaric sufferings: the oceans of sufferings of the hell beings, the hungry ghosts, the animals, the human beings, the asuras, the suras and the intermediate state beings. You want to cause the cessation of the general sufferings of samsara and the particular sufferings of each realm; you want to cause everlasting happiness to the numberless sentient beings in each realm. You also want to bring them to full enlightenment, with cessation of not only the gross defilements but even the subtle ones. You want to bring them the complete qualities of cessation and realization, which is full enlightenment. By chanting OM MANI PADME HUM, Compassion Buddha's mantra, you can easily bring these four levels of happiness to the numberless sentient beings.

In essence, OM MANI PADME HUM includes the entire Dharma, all the 84,000 teachings of Buddha, which come in three levels: Hinayana, Paramitayana (Mahayana sutra) and Secret Mantra Vajrayana (Mahayana tantra). It's a great mistake to say "Hinayana, Mahayana and Vajrayana," as it makes it sound as if Vajrayana is not Mahayana teaching. This gives people who don't understand the completely wrong idea, and in front of people who do understand, you're making a big mistake because you show that you don't know that Secret Mantra Vajrayana *is* Mahayana.

Vajrayana is practiced with bodhicitta. This is what makes Vajrayana teachings and practice Mahayana. Bodhicitta is fundamental. Without bodhicitta, Secret Mantra Vajrayana doesn't become a cause of enlightenment. What makes an action or a teaching Mahayana is that it is done with bodhicitta. Without bodhicitta, Secret Mantra Vajrayana—even *dzog rim* (completion stage) or *dzog chen* (great perfection)—does not become Mahayana, does not become a cause of enlightenment.

And without renunciation of samsara, Vajrayana doesn't become even a cause to achieve liberation from samsara for the self. Renunciation has two divisions: renunciation of this life and renunciation of future life samsara. Without renunciation of this life, even if you practice dzog rim or dzog chen, Secret Mantra Vajrayana does not even become Dharma. Your practice of dzog rim or dzog chen without renunciation of this life, without letting go of the attachment clinging to this life, doesn't even become

Dharma, doesn't even become virtue. It doesn't even become a cause of the happiness beyond this life, the happiness of future lives. Besides not becoming a cause to be born in a pure land of buddha where you can become enlightened, it doesn't even become a cause to achieve a good rebirth in your next life. Without renunciation of this life, the Secret Mantra Vajrayana you're practicing, the dzog rim or dzog chen you're practicing, doesn't become Dharma. It becomes solely nonvirtue, leading to rebirth in the lower realms.

This is very much emphasized by Lama Atisha and the Kadampa geshes in the lam-rim, and in the other traditions in texts such as *The Words of My Perfect Teacher,* the Sakyas' *Parting from the Four Clingings* and *Transformation of the Four Thoughts.* It is explained in those preliminary, fundamental teachings.

The benefits of reciting OM MANI PADME HUM

It is said that you collect greater merit from just reciting OM MANI PADME HUM than from actually offering service to countless buddhas.

Songtsen Gampo, an embodiment of Chenrezig, wrote a text called *Mani Kabum (One Hundred Thousand Teachings of the Mani).* This is one hundred thousand manis, m-a-n-i-s, not one hundred thousands of money, m-o-n-e-y. Recently in the United States, His Holiness the Dalai Lama was telling the Tibetan people that first people chant, OM MANI PADME HUM, OM MANI PADME HUM . . . , then later, OM MONEY PAY ME HUM, OM MONEY PAY ME HUM . . .

It says in *Mani Kabum* that compassion has no discriminating thought; compassion is for everyone. There's no discriminating some sentient beings as close and others as distant. There's no discrimination because of high or low, rich or poor, belief in Chenrezig or no belief in Chenrezig. Because of that compassion for all sentient beings, it's definite that Chenrezig will help you if you rely on Chenrezig.

Mani Kabum also says that all the buddhas have blessed these six syllables again and again. Praying to Chenrezig is the same as praying to all the buddhas and bodhisattvas of the ten directions and chanting the Chenrezig mantra, OM MANI PADME HUM, is the same as chanting the mantras of all the buddhas. By reciting OM MANI PADME HUM, we get the benefit of having chanted all the rest of the buddhas' mantras.

It is said that these six syllables are the heart of Arya Compassion Buddha.

In *The Mirror Clarifying History,* it says that this six-syllable mantra is the heart of the 84,000 teachings taught by Buddha. OM MANI PADME HUM contains the thought, or view, of all the buddhas embodied in one.

OM MANI PADME HUM contains the Hinayana path, the Mahayana Paramitayana path and the paths of the four classes of tantra; it contains the whole path to enlightenment. That means that all the extensive sutra teachings—*Pramanavarttika, Abhisamayalamkara, Abhidharmakosha, Madhyamaka* and *Vinaya*—are rooted in OM MANI PADME HUM, as are the extensive tantric teachings, such as *The Great Graduated Tantric Path to Enlightenment* (*Ngag Rim Chenmo*), which covers the five stages of the completion stage, including clear light. The entire extensive teachings are rooted, or embodied, in OM MANI PADME HUM. It also contains all the qualities of a buddha.

OM MANI PADME HUM is also the heart of the five types of buddha and of the deities who are the owners of the secret.

And OM MANI PADME HUM is the source of all the collections of virtue, of all the collections of happiness, and it is the root from where you and all other sentient beings receive all benefit, all happiness, all attainment.

This mantra, OM MANI PADME HUM, is a great path to achieve higher rebirth and liberation, which includes enlightenment.

If you chant Chenrezig mantras every day, whether the long dharani or the six-syllable mantra, OM MANI PADME HUM, all your wishes come true. Before, Chenrezig made the promise, "If that doesn't happen, may I not achieve enlightenment." There is no doubt that we actually receive all the benefits of the mantra as mentioned by Chenrezig. Then, at the time of death, Chenrezig will stretch out his hand to guide us to the pure land.

THE LONGEST CHENREZIG MANTRA

Tony Wong asked me about the longest Chenrezig dharani the second time I met him, and I said I would check. I think he had asked many lamas about it but didn't get an answer. When his group recited it, it didn't sound like Sanskrit.

It took me one or two years to find it. When I was at Jamyang Centre in London, Venerable Sarah [Thresher], the nun helping in the center at that time, gave me the text *Mani Kabum*. I had seen this text before in Solu Khumbu, at Lawudo Monastery, and I had read some parts of it. I saw the long dharani there in *Mani Kabum*.

I then gave a copy of the mantra to Geshe Jampa Tegchok, the abbot of Nalanda Monastery in France at that time, and he sent it to Sarnath University, where there are some monks who are excellent Sanskrit scholars. One of these monks translated the meaning into Tibetan, but he didn't translate all of it as he said some of it is very secret. I have made the dharani and the translation of its meaning into a text, but without a translation of the few secret syllables.

The longest dharani has unimaginable benefits. You can use it not only for healing, but for many other things. Reciting this dharani just once has the power to purify 800 million eons of negative karma. It seems that it's best to recite it at night, probably to benefit spirits.

The benefits of reciting ten malas of OM MANI PADME HUM

It's mentioned that if you have done even one nyung nä well or if you recite ten malas of OM MANI PADME HUM every day, there is unbelievable benefit, especially if you want to heal people. When you are in a public place, the negative karma of anybody who sees you is purified, and those people won't be reborn in the lower realms. If you are on top of a hill with many people down below, all their negative karma is purified when they look at you. That means you become meaningful to behold. This happens because of the power of mantra and also because you visualize yourself as Chenrezig. This blesses you, so that your body becomes a relic. In that way, the negative karma of anybody who sees you is purified. Even if you don't have any particular reason to go to a market, you can go there and walk around just to purify other sentient beings. Doing nyung näs and reciting ten malas of OM MANI PADME HUM every day are great practices.

Some years ago in Spain, when I mentioned that reciting ten malas of OM MANI PADME HUM every day has this benefit of purifying the negative karma of anybody who sees you, the daughter of the director of the Valencia center thought that Richard Gere should recite ten malas a day because he's seen by so many people. So many people in the world would then get a lot of benefit. This thought came in her mind. She told me that she wrote to Richard Gere about this. I didn't hear about it from Richard Gere, but I heard about it from her.

When you recite ten malas a day, if your breath touches other people when you're talking, it purifies their negative karma. When you're walking along a street, the wind that blows over your body becomes blessed, and when that wind then goes on to touch any being, fat or skinny, human or animal, ant or elephant, it purifies all their negative karma, and they won't be reborn in the lower realms. It also means that the negative karma of anybody who touches you is purified. It's the same when you touch anybody. If you touch somebody by shaking their hand or by massaging them, it purifies all their negative karma. There are these unimaginable benefits.

Some years ago I gave the oral transmission of a mantra that has the power to purify the negative karma of anybody who hears your voice.[33] This applies to even the five uninterrupted negative karmas. Your speech becomes of unbelievable benefit to other sentient beings, protecting them from the heaviest suffering of the lower realms and causing them to receive a higher rebirth or to be born in a pure land. At that time, I didn't mention that reciting OM MANI PADME HUM also has all these benefits.

If you do nyung näs or recite OM MANI PADME HUM one thousand times every day, when you then go to swim in a river or an ocean, since your body is already blessed by visualizing yourself as Chenrezig and by reciting the mantra, the whole river or ocean is blessed. All the people who then come to play in or on the water, swimming or surfing, are purified; the negative karma of anybody who is touched by the water is purified, and the same thing happens to all the numberless other beings in the river or ocean, from the large sharks and fish down to the tiny microscopic beings. All their negative karma to be born in the lower realms is purified.

If you recite one thousand manis every day and also visualize yourself as Chenrezig, it's said that if your body is cremated when you die, the smoke from the cremation fire purifies the negative karma of any being it touches, whether human or animal, and they won't be reborn in the lower realms. There's also this unbelievable benefit.

If you do this practice then go for a walk, the negative karma of all the

---

[33] See *Teachings from the Mani Retreat*, pp. 40–44. See also "Exalted Stainless Beam Totally Pure Light Mantra," *FPMT Retreat Prayer Book*, p. 24.

people who see you is purified, and it's the same with even mosquitoes, flies and other insects that land on your body.

One time at Land of Calm Abiding (previously known as Shiné Land), an FPMT retreat place in California, there were two old horses, and I wanted to read the *Arya Sanghata Sutra* for them. A couple was taking care of the land, and the woman had to give the horses food again and again to keep them there while I read the *Arya Sanghata Sutra* and chanted mantras to liberate them. She had to give them a lot of food to keep them there.

At that time many flies landed on my arms. I try to chant one thousand mani mantras every day but, of course, I miss out sometimes. I don't recite that many every day but I try to do it as often as possible. And sometimes I recite more; sometimes I recite ten thousand.

There are also other mantras you can use to bless your body so that it becomes like a stupa. If any insect lands on a stupa, its negative karma is purified. Also, when rain runs off a stupa onto the ground, that water purifies all the insects it touches on the ground. The wind that touches a stupa is blessed as well, and when it then touches any being, their negative karma is purified. Seeing a stupa, even from afar, touching it, talking about it, thinking about it or remembering it plants the seed of enlightenment in a being's mind; it brings them to enlightenment. There is unbelievable benefit. When you chant those other mantras, your body becomes like a stupa, and whenever you speak to people, no matter what you say, their negative karma is purified, and not just general negative karma but even the five heavy negative karmas. The negative karma of anyone who hears your voice is purified.

When the flies came that day, although I hadn't remembered before, I thought that because I had done those mantras in the morning, it might be meaningful for the flies to land on my arms. I don't know—maybe if a lot of mosquitoes had come I might have freaked out. I'm joking.

A long time ago, before Kopan Monastery was built, we were staying with Zina [Rachevsky]. In the evenings some Western students would come and we would meditate on lam-rim in grass huts. So many mosquitoes came! At those times, we tried to practice a little bit of Buddhadharma, a little bit of charity. The mosquitoes would land and drink our blood, and then after they went away we would feel good, as if something had been purified. I think in those times there was a little bit of Dharma practice . . .

Easy to become Dharma

It's easy for the chanting of OM MANI PADME HUM to become Dharma. Because many other mantras are recited for long life, wealth or good health, there's more danger that reciting them doesn't become Dharma because of attachment clinging to this life, to this life's comfort and happiness. Of course, if you have the thought of seeking the happiness of future lives, even though it's still attachment, your action of chanting mantra for that becomes Dharma. That's the very least Dharma motivation, and the result is happiness in future lives.

Why does chanting OM MANI PADME HUM become Dharma? Because it protects you from suffering. The action is pure because the motivation is uncontaminated by the attachment clinging to this life. By that, it becomes Dharma, and that action results in happiness, the happiness of future lives.

It's very easy for the reciting of OM MANI PADME HUM to become Dharma, and very easy for it to purify your negative karma. The motivation of people who chant OM MANI PADME HUM many times is usually to benefit others, to pacify others' sufferings and bring them happiness. That's a very special motivation. And when a person recites OM MANI PADME HUM so much, it's also a prayer, and the prayer is mostly for others.

In Solu Khumbu, it's extremely rare for the old mothers and fathers to receive teachings. A lama from a monastery sometimes gives a public long-life initiation, but there's not really any teaching about what Dharma really is, about karma, compassion and all these things. So, there are not so many people who really understand Dharma. There are many people, monks and laypeople, who can do prayers and pujas very nicely, but real understanding of the meaning is rare because there's no study of basic teachings and philosophy in the monasteries. Since these have not been established in the monasteries, it's difficult to spread the teachings to laypeople. Of course, the monks do go to different places to take teachings from high lamas, but generally it's not like that with the laypeople.

If we compare ourselves to them, we have unbelievable opportunities to learn Dharma. If you have a resident teacher at your Dharma center, you always have a teacher from whom you can learn not only lam-rim, but other profound teachings on Buddhist philosophy. There are so many different subjects you can learn. There are these most rare, most meaningful, most awakening opportunities bringing light into your life, bringing the light of Dharma into your heart, dispelling the darkness of ignorance. This is amazing! It's extremely rare in this world, but it's happening to us.

Solu Khumbu is a Buddhist place, and people generally have faith in karma, but their understanding of Dharma is limited. Most of them can't read Dharma texts. Those who can read are very few in number, and even being able to read doesn't mean that they're able to understand what they read. Simply being able to read a text doesn't mean you can understand its meaning. To be able to understand, you have to study. In the past, there were no schools, so most people didn't learn to read or write Tibetan.

The greatest thing the people in Solu Khumbu have is their faith, their devotion. There's little intellectual understanding, but there's great faith in Buddha, Dharma and Sangha. Even though they don't have intellectual understanding of the qualities of the objects of refuge, they have faith in them due to their parents, grandparents and lamas. And because they have faith, they are able to collect merit. Each day of their life they're able to collect merit many times. Before they eat or even drink chang, they first make offering to Buddha, Dharma and Sangha, so they collect inconceivable merit. Because of their faith, they collect merit through many small things they do in daily life. They do prostrations, and while they're walking, they chant mantras and prayers. They leave a lot of positive imprints and do a lot of purification and collect a lot of merit, even though they don't have the intellectual understanding that we have from receiving teachings, studying and reading books.

Compared to even a Buddhist place like that, here in the West you are unbelievably fortunate. You have to recognize this; you have to realize this. You will then understand that your life with all the opportunities you have is most amazing and most precious. You then take care of your life and don't become lazy. This life doesn't last long, and it can end any day. Even among the people we know, our fellow Dharma students and family members, some people have already left; they don't exist now.

Anyway, as I was saying, in Solu Khumbu, the old mothers chant OM MANI PADME HUM a lot. They don't have much intellectual understanding, and there's no opportunity for them to receive teachings from a lama. Even when a lama comes to give them teachings, they can't understand the language. They have no opportunity at all to learn because they can't receive teachings from a lama and can't read Dharma texts because most of them can't read. However, the effect of their reciting OM MANI PADME HUM so much is that their hearts become very compassionate. They don't do much intellectual reasoning about how sentient beings are suffering and why one should help them, they can't explain compassion according to the texts, but they have a natural feeling of compassion for others and the thought to help others, even if all they can do is pray for them. I see that the people in Solu Khumbu who do nyung näs and much chanting of OM MANI PADME HUM develop much compassion for others. Those people are very good-hearted. So, that's something to rejoice in.

One part of my advertising Chenrezig and nyung näs is finished...

Rinpoche's mother

My mother used to recite OM MANI PADME HUM 50,000 times every day. She was a nun for many years, ordained in Bodhgaya in 1974 by His Holiness Ling Rinpoche, His Holiness the Dalai Lama's senior tutor, along with ten Western Sangha, including Dr. Nick Ribush, who started Wisdom Publications.

One time when we were on the roof of the old Kopan Monastery gompa, she told me that she used to recite 50,000 OM MANI PADME HUMs every day, but she could no longer do that many. At that time a hawk landed on her head. I later saw a text where Nagarjuna explains that a hawk landing on a person's head is a sign that the person is going to die.

That year she had some sickness. It was 1991, the same year there was a Kalachakra initiation in Sarnath that we had requested from His Holiness the Dalai Lama. My mother came for the Kalachakra initiation. I brought her outside to meet His Holiness when His Holiness was going for the teachings, but I'm not sure whether she saw His Holiness as her eyes were closed. The next day, in the early morning, between one and two o'clock, she passed away.

At Lawudo, when the sun was shining, my mother couldn't really see it—she saw just a little bit of white. But she saw Buddha and many monks, as if she were actually seeing them. This is what happens when you're dying if you're going to be reborn in Amitabha pure land: you see many monks or Amitabha Buddha at the time of death. I think that even though the eyes are physically blind, when the mind is purified, when your negative karma is purified, you can then actually see such things. When I checked with somebody, it seems she was there in Chenrezig's pure land.

I talk about compassion, I say the words, but everybody knew that my mother was an unbelievably compassionate person. Anybody who saw her could feel that. When the family would go on pilgrimage with other Sherpa families, they would stop along the road, and each family would make food. My mother would make food, then give it all away to other people. Later there would be no food left for the family. At home, she would make a big pot of *shagpa*, rice soup, in the morning, then serve it to everybody who came to the house.

My mother didn't develop compassion by studying Buddhist texts or philosophy. She received many teachings and initiations from great lamas such as His Holiness the Dalai Lama, Kyabje Trulshik Rinpoche, one of the top Nyingma lamas, and Trulshik Rinpoche's root guru, Rongphuk Sangye, who had a monastery in Dza Rongphuk in Tibet, behind Mount Everest. In the past, when my father was alive, it seems they would go together to Tibet to receive teachings from Rongphuk Sangye. However, it doesn't mean that my mother actually understood the teachings. But with much devotion, she went just to listen. Even though she didn't understand the teachings, she did understand the simple pieces of advice given by the lamas and would always follow them. For example, she mentioned to me that Kyabje Trulshik Rinpoche had said, "When you chant mantras, don't chant one OM MANI PADME HUM, but then pass two beads together on your mala. Don't do that." She also understood that you shouldn't let your mind wander while you are reciting mantras and that when you go to see a lama, you sit in front of the lama with your hands folded. She told me what she understood of those small pieces of advice. However, I don't think that she could understand when a lama went over a text or talked about the path to enlightenment—she would then just recite "OM MANI PADME HUM, OM MANI PADME HUM . . . ."

My mother had so much compassion for the people who looked after her. And if she saw Nepalese people walking along the road without shoes, she would feel so much compassion for them because they didn't have shoes. One time, many years ago, my mother came to Dharamsala and stayed with us at Tushita Retreat Centre. In the morning there were pancakes for breakfast, so she would eat half a pancake, then put the other half in her pocket. When she then went down to circumambulate His Holiness's temple and palace, she would give the half pancake she had put in her pocket to some of the beggars. Since there were many beggars there, of course, it wasn't enough for all of them. She had unbearable compassion.

Rinpoche's mother's incarnation

My mother reincarnated, not at Lawudo, but at the next hermitage, from where we used to get water. She was born to the son of a *ngagpa*, a lay tantric practitioner, and his wife, who is from another part of Solu Khumbu, Rolwaling, from where Thubten Jinpa[34] and some of the Kopan tantric monks come. Rolwaling is where I lived for seven years as a child. It's a hidden place, a Padmasambhava holy place. There are many caves where in the past many great yogis lived and practiced, and there are many natural footprints left there, some small. Padmasambhava's footprint, a long-life vase and many other things are there in the caves.

My mother had been very close to the son's wife, giving her advice about not taking food from the houses of other families. It seems the baby was already there in her womb.

One monk in the monastery of Thangme village, the village where I was born, is very good at divination. That monk did a divination and said this child was my mother's incarnation. At the request of my sister, after there was some talk about this child being my mother's incarnation, Kyabje Trulshik Rinpoche also did divination and confirmed this child as my mother's incarnation.

My sister then went to see the incarnation and offered him a scarf. He took the scarf and wore it round his neck for seven days; he wouldn't let it be taken away. He always talked about Lawudo to his parents, and he could tell them about the animals and many other things there. One day, my younger brother, Sangye, who lives in Kathmandu, and one of my mother's best friends, a Sherpa called Ang Puwa, went up to see the incarnation because they wanted to invite him to Lawudo and hold a celebration there. The incarnation waited for a long time for them to arrive.

When Ang Puwa first came inside the house, the moment he sat down, the incarnation's mother served him tea or *chang,* and the incarnation immediately called him by his name, saying, "Ang Puwa, please have,

---

[34] Geshe Thubten Jinpa is currently *gekyö* of Kopan Monastery.

please have." Ang Puwa hadn't met the incarnation before. Ang Puwa then grabbed the child and burst into tears. He cried and cried. He was so surprised that the child could remember his name.

The incarnation told them that he would put the Lawudo animals (there are quite a few *dri*, or cows) in a helicopter with him and then come down to Kathmandu to see my brother and Ang Puwa. This is how he expressed his wishes.

The incarnation later came over to Lawudo for an enthronement and celebration. Even though this was the first time he had come to Lawudo, he did *exactly* the same as my mother used to do. He circumambulated the temple seven times, then went inside and prostrated to His Holiness's carved throne, then bent his head down to take a blessing from the low throne where I usually sit. This is just what my mother used to do. He then went to the altar, which is what my mother used to do every day. He behaved exactly the way my mother used to behave.

He then offered a *khatag*, a scarf, to everybody there, apart from two people. One was his father and the other was a Kopan monk called Tsultrim Norbu, who's from that area. Otherwise, he offered a khatag to everybody.

I think the reason he didn't offer a scarf to his father was that during my mother's time, we put pipes from that hermitage to bring water closer to Lawudo so that the Western students doing retreat didn't have to go so far for water to wash themselves and their clothes. One time the son, who became the incarnation's father, put earth in the pipe so that it blocked the water, and my mother got very upset. You can see how the imprint from the past life affected the mind in the next life. You can understand that what you think in this life, whether positive or negative, affects your next life. It has effects from life to life. It's a great teaching.

The incarnation didn't give a scarf to his father or to this monk at Lawudo. My mother used to whisper to me, "This monk always gets angry."

The interesting thing is that even though the child was around three years old, you could see the effects of the thoughts from the previous life. We have to understand that. That's why it's so important to practice the good heart toward everybody.

The incarnation could also remember all the Lawudo animals.

Six or seven years before my mother passed away, with Lama Pasang's help we had a handheld prayer wheel made for her, which she always turned. Every time the incarnation came to Lawudo, he would embrace the prayer wheel and offer a khatag to it. He loved the prayer wheel very much. Because of mental imprints he had the same conduct as in his past life. He would also look for things that my mother had had until he found them. He remembered many things. This is just proof of the incarnation.

My mother also collected plastic buttons: she would take the plastic buttons off her old shirts and collect them in a bottle. She behaved like in the old times when plastic buttons and spoons were regarded as very precious. People would sometimes wear a spoon around their neck because spoons couldn't be bought in Solu Khumbu and had to be brought from Kathmandu, which is far away. At the time I was born and lived in Solu Khumbu there was no sugar, no coffee, no sweet tea, nothing. In one way, it was pure—not because of not having tea or coffee, but in another sense.

After I had lived in Tibet for three years I escaped from Tibet through Bhutan to India, where I lived for eight years before returning to Nepal. When I then went back to my birthplace in Solu Khumbu, things had completely changed. At that time there were sweet tea, coffee and so many other things there.

My sister, who had become a nun, used some of the plastic buttons to make a shirt for my mother's incarnation. When she put the shirt on him, he said, "Oh, these are my buttons." My mother had taken the buttons from her own shirts and collected them in a bottle, and the incarnation remembered the buttons.

There was no debate, no discussion, about this incarnation. Sometimes there's so much debate about an incarnation, with two incarnations being recognized. One group wants this incarnation and another group wants that incarnation. Here, there was no such discussion because it was very clear. The incarnation could remember so many things about Lawudo, and he immediately recognized all the family members.

At one point my mother had spent two or three months at Kopan. Every day she would go down to circumambulate the Boudhanath Stupa, helped by two nuns, Ani Jangsem, the manager of the Kopan nuns, and another nun. When the incarnation came to the nunnery, though he was shy with the rest of the people, he recognized those two nuns and immediately talked to them.

He had such a clear memory because of chanting OM MANI PADME HUM in his previous life. Chanting OM MANI PADME HUM has benefits like the atoms of this earth. Having a clear memory is one small benefit, like one atom, among the many benefits, like the atoms of this earth, of chanting OM MANI PADME HUM.

My mother's incarnation was enthroned at Kopan Monastery when he was four years old. There was something enchanting about the way he talked. It didn't matter what he was saying—you just wanted to hear the next word, and then the next. After he mentioned something, you wanted to hear what he had to say next.

Unfortunately, because of disagreement between what I thought and what the parents thought, the incarnation was sent to Penor Rinpoche's monastery in south India. My idea was for him to be educated in philosophy at Kopan Monastery, and then later he himself could practice whichever tradition he wanted to benefit others. But somebody else did a divination and the parents followed that advice to send him to Penor Rinpoche's monastery.

About fifteen days after he went there, he was playing outside when there was a heavy storm. When he tried to run inside, he fell down and knocked his head on the corner of the cement steps and broke his skull. He was taken to small local hospitals, and we didn't hear about what had happened until much later. They tried to send a message to Solu Khumbu, where the parents couldn't do anything to help. Later he was brought to a Bangalore hospital, but he didn't improve. He then came to Nepal, but the doctors wouldn't accept to operate because his condition was already bad.

A doctor friend of my brother's wife very kindly operated on him, and the incarnation seemed to improve, but there were still pieces of shattered bone left inside. He passed away soon after that. He was about eight years old. Unfortunately, he didn't live long. After that, when I checked, the divination said that he was in Potala, Chenrezig's pure land.

7. The Benefits of Prostrations

THE GENERAL BENEFITS OF PROSTRATIONS

FOR EACH ATOM your body covers when you do a prostration, you create the karma to be reborn as a wheel-turning king one thousand times. Buddha uses the example of a wheel-turning king to give you an idea of the merit, because to be born even one time as a wheel-turning king you need to accumulate infinite merit. A wheel-turning king has much power and wealth and many supporters; many wheel-turning kings are also bodhisattvas, bringing extensive benefit to sentient beings. By being born as a wheel-turning king, you have unbelievable opportunities to create merit by bringing so much benefit to others and to the teachings.

By covering two atoms when doing one prostration, you create the karma to be born as a wheel-turning king two thousand times.

Now, from the floor where you are prostrating down to the other side of the earth, your body covers numberless atoms. Therefore, when you do one prostration, you create the karma to be born a wheel-turning king a thousand times that number of atoms. But it's not that you are doing the prostrations to become a wheel-turning king—Buddha just used this example to give us an idea of how much merit we accumulate. Of course, since you do the prostration to a buddha, it becomes a cause of enlightenment.

Therefore, when you do prostrations, it is important to stretch out your body as much as possible, even your feet. If you keep your feet supported on the tips of your toes, the upper surface of your foot doesn't touch the ground. Stretch out even your feet, so that the upper surface covers the ground. Since covering one atom has unbelievable merit, if you stretch out your feet, so many times numberless atoms will be covered by them, and there will be unbelievable merit. Stretch out as much as the space allows. If you have long hair, when you prostrate, even your long hair becomes beneficial because it covers more ground. The more area your hair covers, the more merit you accumulate. Also, the longer your nails, the more merit you accumulate. Since people who are tall and fat cover more ground, as do those with long hair and long nails, they should do as many prostrations as possible!

THE TEN SPECIFIC BENEFITS OF PROSTRATIONS

There are ten specific benefits of doing prostrations to a buddha. (This is prostrating to a holy object, not to a cow or a house.)

The first of the ten benefits is that you will receive a pure golden-colored body.

Second, you will be extremely attractive to others. This is like a buddha's holy body, which is so beautiful that you never get bored no matter how much you see it. No matter how many times you look at a buddha's holy body, you are never satiated but want to see it more.

Third, you will have an extremely sweet voice. Everything you say will sound so sweet that other people will want to listen to you, and it will be beneficial for their minds.

Fourth, you will be able to go anywhere without any fear. You will never feel shy or uncomfortable in any group of people. Like a being who has lived a holy life, like Buddha, there will be no fear no matter whom you go to see.

Fifth, you will be born in a higher realm, as a deva or a human being.

Sixth, you will make everyone who sees you happy. This is like His Holiness the Dalai Lama and many other holy beings. Everybody wants to see them, and anybody who does see them experiences much bliss or peace in their mind.

Seventh, your body will be magnificent, or glorious.

Eighth, you will always be in the company of buddhas, bodhisattvas and arhats.

Ninth, you will have great enjoyments.

The tenth benefit is that you will quickly become enlightened.

The many benefits from doing one prostration can be integrated into these ten benefits.

These benefits are in relation to prostrating to one buddha or even one statue of a buddha. It is mentioned in the teachings that the benefits of prostrating or making offerings to the actual Buddha or to a statue of Buddha are exactly the same. Since making prostration to one buddha has these unbelievable benefits, doing one prostration by thinking of all the buddhas creates infinite merit.

How to do prostrations physically

No matter which tradition you use to do prostrations, the main point is to do them respectfully. Your manner should not be disrespectful.

If there's enough space, it's good to do full-length prostrations, which are according to the tradition of Naropa, the great Indian yogi. The normal five-limb prostration is according to the sutra, or Hinayana, tradition. The time to do everything in the best way we can is now, while we have this precious human body. We should do the best we can with our life, for ourselves and for other sentient beings. If we don't do this when we have a precious human rebirth, when will we again have the opportunity to do these things and to achieve enlightenment? Therefore, do full-length prostrations.

Keep your two thumbs tucked inside your hands. This signifies offering a jewel and means that you are not offering empty hands.

Putting your hands on your crown creates the karma to receive the pinnacle, or *ushnisha*, a special sign of a buddha's holy body. Since we need these different aspects of a buddha's holy body to benefit sentient beings, we need to create their causes.

You then put your hands at your forehead, which creates the karma to receive the curled white hair between the eyebrows, the *dzö pu*, another special quality of a buddha's holy body. To have this aspect to benefit sentient beings, we need to accumulate merit.

Putting your hands at your throat enables you to achieve the infinite qualities of a buddha's holy speech and putting them at your heart, the infinite qualities of a buddha's holy mind. You are also purifying all the negative karmas and obscurations of your body, speech and mind. You are purifying the two obscurations and achieving the infinite qualities of a buddha's holy body, holy speech and holy mind.

Keep your feet together. When you put your hands on the floor, to be respectful, don't stretch out your fingers so that there is a gap between them. If you do prostrations in the wrong way, if you do them disrespectfully, you create negative karma. Even if you do them wrongly out of ignorance rather than disrespect, it still becomes negative karma.

When you lie down on the floor, don't stay there a long time. Get up as soon as you touch your head to the floor, as that signifies quickly getting out of samsara. It is disrespectful if you lie down for a long time, and that creates the cause to be reborn as a worm, a snake or other animal that pulls its body along the ground.

Do a prostration, stand up, then do another prostration. The teachings mention that if you don't stand up straight but start to do the next prostration while you are still bent over, it is a mistake and disrespectful and creates the cause to be reborn as a worm that moves in a similar way.

How to do prostrations mentally

There are two most important points to remember when you do the practice of prostrations. To make the prostrations most profitable, to collect the most extensive merit, you should think that each holy object—whether a statue or a painting of a buddha—is your guru.

The other important point is to visualize numberless large replicas of your body doing prostrations. The bigger you visualize your body, the more merit you collect. So, when you prostrate, think that each holy object you are prostrating to is your guru, and visualize numberless of your bodies, as tall as mountains, covering the whole earth.

We should especially practice guru yoga when we do prostrations to Chenrezig. Who is Chenrezig? The guru. Besides that, Chenrezig is all the beings in the merit field. Higher bodhisattvas manifest many billions of bodies with many heads, mouths and arms and then make offerings and do prostrations to the buddhas. Like that, think that on each atom there are buddhas equaling the number of the atoms, and around each buddha there are numberless replicas of you doing prostrations. If you can think that, it's excellent. Besides thinking that Chenrezig is all the holy beings in the merit field and all the holy objects, you can think that all the pictures, statues and other holy objects on all the altars where you are prostrating are the guru.

If there is one statue of a buddha, prostrate by thinking, "This is my guru." By thinking of the guru in this way, you accumulate the most merit, more merit than by prostrating to all the buddhas, because the virtuous friend is the most powerful among all the powerful objects.

You can then think that one statue is, in essence, all the holy objects of the ten directions: all the statues, stupas and scriptures. Then prostrate to every single holy object that exists in this world and in other worlds. Remember all the benefits of making prostration to one buddha or one statue of buddha. Again, when you think of prostrating to all the buddhas and bodhisattvas of the ten directions, be aware that they are also your own virtuous friend. In this way, you create unbelievable merit.

However, there are usually many holy objects in the meditation room in our own house or in a gompa. When we prostrate we should prostrate to all the holy objects, by thinking that they are our own virtuous friend. In this way we collect unbelievable merit. It is explained in the Paramitayana and also in the tantric teachings, that any time we make prostrations or offerings to a buddha statue, if we can remember our own virtuous friend and make the prostrations or offerings to the virtuous friend, we collect much more merit than from having done the prostrations or offerings to all the buddhas. Therefore, to think of the virtuous friend whenever we do a prostration or make an offering to buddha is the most skillful way of accumulating merit. In this way we quickly become enlightened, like Lama Tsongkhapa and the many other lineage lamas who achieved enlightenment by practicing lam-rim. In his hermitage, Lama Tsongkhapa did many hundreds of thousands of prostrations with the Thirty-five Buddhas' prayer and achieved many realizations.

Also, besides the material holy objects, there are actual living holy beings, your gurus and numberless buddhas and bodhisattvas (who are manifestations of your guru), in the direction toward which you are making prostrations. By doing one prostration to so many holy objects in this way, regarding every one as the highest object, the guru, you collect unbelievable merit. Your ordinary mind can't comprehend how much merit you accumulate.

Dealing with difficulties

If you experience difficulties while doing prostrations, during some prostrations just think of the benefits of prostrations, of all the merit you collect. Remember that for each atom that's under your body when you do one prostration, you create the cause to be born as a wheel-turning king one thousand times, and that to be born even once as a wheel-turning king, you have to create infinite merit. You accumulate this much merit with each atom, and there are numberless atoms from the floor where you are prostrating down to the bottom of the earth. By doing one prostration, you create countless causes to be born a wheel-turning king. Think how each prostration you are doing is creating this inconceivable merit.

With other prostrations, you can dedicate all the prostrations for enlightenment, so that each prostration becomes a cause of enlightenment, and you can dedicate all the merit for the enlightenment of all sentient beings. You can think that you are giving the incredible merit from each prostration to other sentient beings. As you're prostrating to Chenrezig, think, "I give to all sentient beings all the merit that I create each time I prostrate." As you again lie down to do another prostration, think, "I give all this merit to all sentient beings." It would be extremely good to do some prostrations in this way.

Also, with some prostrations, you can think, "This nyung nä practice of prostrations is Guru Chenrezig's way of guiding me and saving me from the lower realms. Guru Chenrezig is protecting me from falling down into the lower realms, into samsara and into the lower nirvana. By giving me the instructions of this nyung nä practice of prostrations, Guru Chenrezig is guiding me to enlightenment." Each time you do a prostration, think, "This is Guru Chenrezig's way of guiding me to enlightenment by enabling me to purify all my obstacles." Do some prostrations with just this awareness. This is very good, as it then gives you much energy to continue the prostrations.

8. The Benefits of Offerings

The power of Buddha

It is said in *Sutra of the Mudra of Developing the Power of Devotion* that if every day for a hundred eons you offered hundreds of divine food, which means nectar, and hundreds of divine dresses to Solitary Realizer arhats equaling the number of atoms of the many universes, all the merit you would collect is small compared to the merit from merely seeing a statue or a painting of Buddha. By just seeing a statue or a painting of Buddha, you immediately collect numberless merits. Even though the merit from the first offering itself is great, it's small when compared to the merit from merely seeing a statue or a painting of Buddha. Then, if you prostrate, make offerings, offer incense and so forth to a statue or a painting of Buddha, you collect far greater merit than from simply seeing the statue or painting.

Therefore, that in this life, in this perfect human rebirth, we have met Dharma and have faith in it is unbelievably precious. It's wish-fulfilling, for this life and for future lives. What you can do every day is amazing!

In the lam-rim teachings, there's the story of somebody who, having nothing else to offer, offered a medicinal drink to four ordinary, fully ordained monks. Just from that, in his next life, that person was born as King Kaushika, the most powerful, wealthy king in India. It doesn't say that those monks were highly attained monks; they were just four ordinary monks.

Now, in the example I just mentioned, you're making offerings to arhats, who are liberated from samsara, from delusion and karma, equal in number to the number of atoms of the universes every day for one hundred eons. Now, all that merit becomes small when compared to the merit you collect from simply seeing a statue or a painting of a buddha.

Therefore, it's good to have many holy objects in your house and, of course, to respect them. Don't put them on the floor without anything under them. That advice comes in refuge practice. After we have taken refuge, there are three things to abandon and three things to practice, including respecting holy objects. Since we want realizations, since we want liberation and enlightenment, in order to benefit others, we must do these things. We must respect holy objects to create extensive merits, and we must not pollute our mind through disrespecting them.

Quite a number of years ago I was returning from Australia with Thubten Yeshe, an American nun, who was acting as my attendant. (She's not a nun now, but she still helps to lead meditation retreats and courses at Chenrezig Institute.) At that time she helped me to travel from Nepal to Australia, and then return. She knew that it was less expensive to return to India and Nepal via Sri Lanka, which meant we could visit Kandy, where there's a temple with Buddha's tooth.

We flew from Australia and landed in the capital of Sri Lanka, Colombo, then went to Kandy. You can't actually see Buddha's tooth, which is inside a stupa, unless you're a member of the government and there's a big function. But there is still the power of the blessing. Even though you don't actually see the tooth, you feel an amazing vibration, or power, there.

Some Theravadin-style stupas were lined up, with the tooth in one of the stupas. There was a long table all the way along with all the offerings lined up. In the early morning people would bring food to be blessed by Buddha, then take it back home to share the blessing. If they first think of offering to Buddha as the motivation for offering, in that moment they collect causes of enlightenment equal in number to the number of rice grains in the container. Since there must be many thousands of grains in a pot of rice, they create many thousands of causes of enlightenment and, by the way, causes of liberation from samsara and the happiness of all future lives. The family collects unbelievable merit.

Offering just one grain of rice to Buddha's tooth immediately creates the cause of enlightenment, even if the motivation is related only to this life, nothing more than to be wealthy or have a good reputation. This happens even if the motivation is totally black, only attachment or some other nonvirtuous thought. Usually, for an action to become the cause of happiness, the initial motivation for the action has to be Dharma; the motivation has to be pure, such as non-ignorance, non-anger, non-attachment to this life.

If it's attachment to this life, it's nonvirtue. The best, purest motivation is non-self-cherishing. First you have to make your mind Dharma; then your action becomes Dharma and results in happiness.

So, you can't imagine how much merit each family who brings a whole pot of rice, with thousands and thousands of grains of rice, and offers it there to the Buddha's tooth collects.

There's no doubt that offering a single grain of rice to Buddha, Dharma and Sangha immediately becomes a cause of enlightenment, a cause of the highest success, as well as a cause of liberation from samsara and all the happiness of future lives, but it's the same even with statues, stupas and scriptures. This happens not by the power of your mind but by the power of the object. Your mind, your motivation, can be totally black, totally nonvirtuous. It comes from the power of the holy object.

When you offer one grain of rice to statues, stupas or scriptures of Buddha, no matter how small they are, even a tiny one in a photo, the moment you offer this single rice grain, whether with a virtuous or nonvirtuous motivation, it immediately becomes a cause of full enlightenment, great liberation, and by the way, it becomes a cause of liberation from samsara and of all the happiness of future lives—not future life but future *lives*; there are more than one. It can result in happiness, in good rebirth, in hundreds or thousands of lives.

It is explained in the sutra *Heaps of Flowers* (*Metog Tsek pai Do*) that from having offered one flower (but it's the same as my example of one rice grain) to a stupa (but it's the same with a statue or scripture), no matter how big or small, the benefit you obtain is happiness equal to all the happiness you have experienced numberless times during beginningless rebirths up to now and the happiness you will experience in the future.

And the benefit from offering one single grain to a statue, stupa or scripture doesn't stop there. You obtain all that temporary happiness, but the benefit doesn't stop there. On top of that, you obtain the ultimate happiness of liberation from samsara. That means you create the causes of all the realizations involved in generating the path of merit, the path of preparation, the path of seeing, the path of meditation and the path of no more learning. The nature of that mind is free from all suffering and its cause, karma and delusion, and from the cause of delusion, the negative imprint. There is the cessation of all that. So, that is nirvana, the truth of cessation from the four noble truths. So, it causes true cessation of suffering and true path.

And the benefits of offering one grain of rice to a holy object don't stop there. You then achieve great liberation, full enlightenment. That means you create the cause of achieving all the realizations of the five Mahayana paths and the ten bhumis.

The benefit still doesn't stop there. After having achieved all that, you then liberate the numberless hell beings from the oceans of samsaric suffering; you liberate the numberless hungry ghosts from the oceans of samsaric suffering; you liberate the numberless animals from the oceans of samsaric suffering; you liberate the numberless human beings from the oceans of samsaric suffering; you liberate the numberless asuras and suras from the oceans of samsaric suffering; and you liberate the numberless intermediate state beings from the oceans of samsaric suffering. Not only that but you bring them all to full enlightenment. Everybody! So, when you have brought every single sentient being to enlightenment, it is only at *that* time that the benefit of your offering one grain of rice to a statue, stupa or scripture will be completed.

Therefore, in our daily life it's extremely important to make as many offerings as possible to guru, Buddha, Dharma and Sangha, statues, stupas and scriptures.

Power of the object

It is very important to respect and serve your parents of this life and not show any disrespect to them with your speech or your body. Besides not getting angry with them, you shouldn't treat them in a disrespectful manner. Because your parents are powerful objects, you can start to experience the resultant problems from disrespect to them in this life. And if you offer even a small sign of respect or a small service to your parents, because of the power of the object, you can start to experience the good results in this life.

More powerful objects than your parents are ordinary Sangha, those who are living in ordination. Criticizing Sangha, your parents and other people can create heavy negative karma. The heaviness of the karma depends on how powerful the object is. Since both Sangha and parents are powerful objects, criticizing them or even giving them a negative nickname creates heavy negative karma. If you call somebody a pig, you will be born as a pig for five hundred lifetimes. The number of lifetimes you have to be born as a pig depends on how powerful the object is that you insult. If, out of anger, you tell somebody they are blind, you can be born blind for many lifetimes, and even in this lifetime you can become blind. Particularly with negative karma created in relation to parents, Sangha and any other powerful object, you can start to experience the karma in this life. Experience of all the karma is not finished in this life, however. If it's a powerful object, for five hundred lifetimes or thousands of lifetimes, you will have to be born again and again like that.

More powerful than ordinary Sangha are arhats, absolute Sangha. More powerful than arhats are bodhisattvas. If you glare at one bodhisattva, the negative karma is much worse than that from having gouged out the eyes of all the beings in the three realms. Looking disrespectfully at one bodhisattva is such heavy negative karma because the object is very powerful. Why? Because of the power of the bodhicitta realization.

More powerful than a bodhisattva is a buddha. It is said in the sutra teachings that even if you look with an angry mind at a painting of a buddha on a wall, you create the karma to eventually see ten million buddhas. This is by the power of the object. Even a painting or a statue of a buddha has this power because an actual living buddha has omniscient mind, infinite compassion and perfect power. In relation to Chenrezig, even a statue or thangka of Chenrezig has power, so just looking at it brings purification. It enables you to eventually see ten million buddhas.

The most powerful object so far is a buddha, but even more powerful than that is the guru. The guru is the most powerful object of all.

From our parents up to our guru, if we make a small mistake or do a small negative thing, it has great shortcomings, and we can start to experience them in this life. On the other hand, if we offer a small good thing, some service or even respect, it has great benefit, becoming the cause of great success.

Always remember the guru

Since the greatest, most extensive merit, comes from offering to the guru, when you make offerings to the merit field, you *must* remember the guru.

Whether you're offering to one buddha, Chenrezig, or to numberless buddhas, you must always remember the guru, who is Chenrezig. With one buddha or with all the buddhas, remember the guru. In this way you collect the most extensive merit with each offering, so it then becomes a quick path to enlightenment.

Every time you do a sadhana, in which there are always extensive offerings, make sure that you always remember that the deities to whom you are making requests and offerings are the guru. You will then always collect the most extensive merit. And when you do any practice with the guru always think of buddha. That's the essential point of guru yoga practice. It makes whatever good karma you accumulate the most profitable; in this way you very quickly achieve enlightenment. If you are wise in practicing guru yoga, you accumulate the most extensive merit every time you make offerings, and that's what makes it possible for you to achieve enlightenment quickly.

Even offering a piece of fruit, a glass of water or a candy to a disciple of your guru by thinking of that guru accumulates much more merit than making offerings to all the buddhas of the three times. Therefore, we should remember guru yoga practice every time we do a sadhana and every time we make offerings to buddhas.

If you leave out thinking of the guru, it's not a complete practice. The very basic practice is missing if you leave out this when you do a sadhana. When you make offerings, such as when you do a self-initiation where there are many offerings, if you think only of the deity, thinking that the deity is higher or more precious than the guru, you can't receive the blessings of the guru, and you then can't attain the realizations of the path to enlightenment; you can't attain the three principal aspects of the path to enlightenment.

The power of the guru

One time when Milarepa was about to pass by, Padampa Sangye, the great Indian yogi who lived during that time, manifested as a flower to check whether Milarepa could recognize him or not. Milarepa recognized that the flower beside the road was actually Padampa Sangye. If you have read Milarepa's biography you know this story.

Padampa Sangye said,

> In your heart, you must cherish the guru more than the Buddha;
> if you do that, realization will come in this life, people of Tingri.

Padampa Sangye was giving this advice to the people of Tingri in Tibet. Tingri has two parts now, Old Tingri and New Tingri. The last time we went on pilgrimage to Tibet we spent one night camping outside Old Tingri.

I'm not going to talk about the pilgrimage, but the mountain of Tsipri, which is near Tingri, was very interesting. Tsipri is a special mountain that combines the three holy places of Heruka's holy body, holy speech and holy mind: Mount Kailash, Tsari and Lapchi. People circumambulate Tsipri mountain, which takes about seven days. They load food and other things onto a donkey and then go round the mountain.

The road goes around one side of the mountain, and every stone on that side has a conch shell or some other special auspicious sign. Somebody gave me some stones that have grains as part of the stone. But on the side that's not part of the mountain, there's nothing like that.

The next morning after camping near Tingri, we did prostrations toward the Tsipri mountain from the road, because we didn't have time to go there. In the near future I'd like to be able to circumambulate the mountain. There are one hundred small monasteries there. Lama Atisha lived there, and many great holy beings came there to meditate and achieved enlightenment, achieved the rainbow body.

One monk studied the place for two years. He checked all the monasteries, all of which had been completely destroyed and hadn't been rebuilt. He asked me if it would be possible to build a small temple with a few rooms so that monks who have completed their studies at Sera, Ganden or Drepung monasteries in south India and would like to meditate and actualize the path can go there. It's an excellent idea. Before that, however, we need to build a two-story Maitreya Buddha statue there. They had one there before. There was a huge rock, and any person or animal who touched that rock would die. Lama Atisha (or somebody else) then advised that a two-story Maitreya statue be built on top of that rock, and that negative effect was then stopped. The idea is to build a two-story Maitreya Buddha statue first and then a temple. I said I will build the statue and he should organize the building of the temple.

Anyway, finding out the cost took a long time. The Chinese officials then heard that the leader of that area was receiving money from outside Tibet and put him in prison. I don't know whether he actually got any money or not. I think it hadn't yet happened, but the news went out and the Chinese officials heard about it.

As Padampa Sangye said, if you cherish the guru more than Buddha, you will have attainment in this life. This means you can achieve enlightenment in this life if you have that kind of guru devotion. You shouldn't think that the guru and Buddha are separate, that the guru is some ordinary person and the Buddha is something special. If you think that, you can't achieve enlightenment in this life. You have to totally change your thinking, and it doesn't mean that you think that Buddha is an ordinary being. You must cherish the guru more than Buddha.

"Guru" and "Buddha" are just different names, like Tara and Guru Shakyamuni Buddha and Manjushri are given different names. It is one being, but because of the different aspects they are called different names. So, "guru" and "buddha" are just different names for one being. You need to accomplish stable realization of that. Why? Because you want happiness and you don't want suffering, and especially you want to achieve the peerless happiness of enlightenment; you want this profit. Why do you need to achieve enlightenment? Because the purpose of life is to benefit others, so you need to liberate the numberless sentient beings from the oceans of samsaric suffering. Not only that, but you need to bring them to full enlightenment. So, if this is what you want to do, then you need to be enlightened. To accomplish that you need a pure mind, a devotional mind, seeing the guru as buddha by looking at the guru as buddha. Through analytical meditation, using reasoning, and through fixed meditation, you achieve the realization of seeing the guru as buddha. You need that, and if you have that, you are then able to protect your life. This protects you from all the heaviest negative karmas, the heaviest negative thoughts. You're able to protect yourself from anger and heresy, or non-devotional thoughts, toward the guru.

If you have this stable realization, no matter what ordinary, or mistaken, aspect appears to you, it doesn't destroy your devotion because of your realization that the guru is buddha. No matter what ordinary aspect appears, you see it all as an act on the part of the guru due to your mistaken thoughts, your hallucinated mind, your negative karma. You don't believe in it; you see everything as an act. It's like a play in a theater, where one person can play many different roles: a king, a minister, a beggar. Nothing causes distraction; nothing harms your devotion.

From your devotion, you then receive the blessings of the guru. Through that blessing you then receive the realizations of the path to enlightenment, the three principles of the path and the two stages. You then achieve your goal, the two kayas, and then liberate and enlighten all sentient beings.

Dangers with the guru

There are great shortcomings if you get angry or generate heresy toward the guru for the shortest duration of time (in the Mahayana, it's said that one finger snap has 365 of these instants). This is not talking about just any guru in the world or somebody else's guru. It's talking about your own guru, the person with whom you have a Dharma connection, through taking teachings, even if it's only one verse of teaching, or receiving an oral transmission, even it's of only a few syllables of mantra, with the determination that you are the disciple and that person is your guru. If you receive a teaching or an oral transmission with that recognition, that establishes the Dharma connection. This also applies to taking initiation, if you did the visualizations that the lama explained, and to taking vows, whether refuge, pratimoksha, bodhisattva or tantric vows, and to receiving commentaries with that determination.

If you commit the heavy negative karma of having killed your father, mother or an arhat, harmed Buddha or caused disunity among the Sangha, you can still purify it and achieve enlightenment in one life. If you commit one of these five heavy negative karmas, usually, without the break of another life, you immediately get reborn in the lowest hot hell, Inexhaustible Suffering, which has the heaviest suffering in samsara and lasts the longest time. However, it's not that once you're born in hell you have to remain there forever, like in Christianity. It might sometimes sound like that when it's presented, but in Buddhism you can be liberated from defilements and from suffering; there's nothing that you have to experience forever.

Even if you have collected such a negative karma, you can still achieve enlightenment in that life. But if you have made mistakes in correctly following the virtuous friend, you cannot achieve enlightenment in that life.

If, for an instant, you generate anger or heresy toward the guru, criticize or give up the guru, as mentioned in the *Kalachakra Tantra*, you will be born in Inexhaustible Hell for eons equal in number to the instants of your anger or heresy. However, being born in hell and suffering there for that many eons is not the only result: you have to understand that that many eons of your merits also get destroyed. That's the second point. Third, your realizations will also be delayed for that many eons. There are these three points. Therefore, this is the heaviest negative karma in regard to interfering with the development of your mind in the path to enlightenment.

Therefore, the way Lama Tsongkhapa guides beings to enlightenment is by first introducing the practice of guru devotion. Since success in all the realizations from the beginning of the path, perfect human rebirth, up to enlightenment depends on guru devotion, Lama Tsongkhapa presents it first. In other traditions, guru devotion comes later, usually after the introduction to samsaric suffering. But Lama Tsongkhapa taught the most important thing first. He first introduced the guru, all the advantages and disadvantages of guru devotion, so that we are aware where we should pay all our attention, where we should be most careful and protect ourselves for the benefit of sentient beings.

In conclusion, if you want to benefit others, to liberate the numberless other sentient beings from the sufferings of samsara and bring them to enlightenment, which is what they really need, then you need to achieve enlightenment. You need to achieve the whole path, which means you need to practice guru devotion. If you're not interested in that, then you don't need to practice guru devotion. This is the whole point of why you need to practice guru devotion. I think that even if you're not looking for enlightenment or liberation or the happiness of future lives, but are looking only for the happiness and success of this life, you could say that if you have guru devotion, everything in this life just comes without your looking for it. So, you could still relate achieving happiness in this life to guru devotion.

Without the guru there's no Buddha, Dharma, Sangha; there's no statues, stupas, scriptures. Without the guru, there's nothing. Without the guru, there's no opportunity at all to collect merit.

The ultimate reason is related to the unified primordial savior. The transcendental wisdom of nondual bliss and voidness, the *dharmakaya*, pervades all phenomena; it covers all existence. It's everywhere. The moment a sentient being's karma is ripened, it's just there. It manifests there in ordinary or other forms to help. It's mentioned that bodhisattvas manifest even in material forms, as mountains, bridges and so forth, if that is what sentient beings need, so there's no doubt that buddhas do this. Whether in the aspect of a buddha or of an ordinary sentient being, without even a moment's delay, it immediately manifests just there. The moment the karma has ripened to receive help, because it's bound by infinite compassion for us sentient beings, it immediately manifests. It is eternal, with no beginning and no end, and is bound by infinite compassion to sentient beings, to you. That is what the guru really is. There is the ultimate guru (*dön den pai lama*) and the conventional guru (*kün tsob kyi lama*). "Conventional guru" is a simpler translation—more literally it is "guru of the all-obscuring truth."

Practicing with holy objects

When we see a statue or another holy object, we should first think of the guru and then make offerings and prostrations. It's important to have as many holy objects—statues, stupas, scriptures—as possible in every suitable, respectful place in the house (but not in the toilet because of the bad smells). Every day, the moment you open your eyes you will then see holy objects in your room, outside, everywhere. That's mind-blowing, as you collect inconceivable merits each time you just see a holy object.

Arranging holy objects when practices are done is not something just made up by Tibetan lamas. It's a practice that came from India, from Buddha. Buddha first explained it, and when Lama Atisha came from India to Tibet, he explained the six preparatory practices before meditation on the lam-rim path, which start with cleaning (see appendix 1) and setting up an altar. Of course, in Zen or other traditions, some people might say, "You don't need a statue and all these things to meditate. You don't need an altar. You don't need anything." Maybe this comes from not having analyzed all the different teachings of Buddha and those of Lama Atisha and many other great scholars and enlightened beings.

Before you meditate, you do the six preparatory practices to purify your mind, collect extensive merits and increase the merits. So, you need to set up an altar. Of course, it's different if you're living with a husband, wife or other family member who doesn't like the idea of your setting up an altar in the house, perhaps because they belong to a different religion. In that case you would need to hide your holy objects or visualize them and then do the practice.

As mentioned in the Paramitayana and especially in the Vajrayana teachings, when you make offerings to statues or paintings of Buddha in your room or in a temple, think that you are offering to your own virtuous friend, the one with whom you have Dharma contact. The merit from any offering is then much greater than from having made offerings to all the past, present and future buddhas.

With any statues or stupas in our own house or any statues, stupas and scriptures we see in a temple when we go on pilgrimage, we should train our mind to always see them as our own guru.

We do these practices to develop our mind in the path, to achieve enlightenment. Our ultimate aim is to benefit sentient beings, to free them from suffering and bring them to enlightenment. It is for this reason that we are doing these various offering practices. The whole answer as to how long it will take us to actualize the path and achieve enlightenment depends on how quickly we're able to finish the work of accumulating merit. Therefore, we think that every holy object, whether one or many, in a temple or in our meditation room, is our own virtuous friend and then make offerings. There is no comparison between doing this and making offerings to all the buddhas of the three times, to all the holy objects: statues, stupas and scriptures. This is the most skillful way to accumulate extensive merit.

You can then elaborate by making offerings to all the buddhas and bodhisattvas of the ten directions, thinking that they are all your guru. You can also offer to all the statues, stupas, and scriptures of the ten directions, thinking that they are all the embodiment of your own virtuous friend.

The specific benefits of offering flowers

Offering flowers has ten benefits. One of the results of offering a beautiful flower to Buddha is that you become like a flower in the world. In other words, you make many sentient beings happy. Everybody likes to see and to have beautiful flowers. When there are beautiful flowers in a park or a garden, everybody wants to come to enjoy them. By becoming like a flower in the world, you are then able to benefit many sentient beings. Holy beings taking a perfect, beautiful, holy body is the result of these offering practices.

Also, your sense of smell never degenerates. Some people, because of a disease or some other condition, cannot smell. Such people need to make more flower offerings.

Another benefit is that your body doesn't have a bad smell; instead, a scented smell comes from it. Also, there is the fragrance of morality in the directions and corners.[35] Wherever you go you spread the scented smell of morality. There are many holy beings—high lamas and meditators—like that. I have even seen small incarnate lamas with the scent of morality. Even when very young, they have a natural scented smell coming from their holy body.

Another benefit of offering flowers is that one becomes higher than others, and one goes before others. This could be related to the physical body, but it's possible for it to be related to the mind as well. *One goes before others* could mean that physically one is a leader or a holy being, and it could also refer to development of the mind.

Other benefits are that you receive beautiful objects; you have great wealth; you are born in the deva or human realm; and you quickly become enlightened. (As long as an offering is made to a buddha, it always becomes a cause of enlightenment.)

THE SPECIFIC BENEFITS OF OFFERING LIGHT

Offering light to a buddha also has ten benefits.

You become like a light in the world, which means you are bright, or radiant.

You achieve clairvoyance of the eye, which means you can see very distant things.

You achieve the clairvoyance of a deva's eye. (There are six types of clairvoyance. The sixth one is that you are able to read the minds of other sentient beings.)

You receive Dharma wisdom, understanding what is virtue and what is nonvirtue.

You are able to eliminate the darkness of ignorance.

You are able to achieve the illumination of wisdom.

---

[35] The corners are the four sub-directions.

While you are in samsara, you are never in a place where there's no light.
You have great enjoyments.
You take birth in a deva or human realm.
And the last benefit is that you quickly achieve enlightenment.

How to make offerings

Before making an offering, first generate bodhicitta by thinking, "I must free all sentient beings from all their sufferings and lead them to enlightenment. Therefore, I must achieve enlightenment, and therefore, I'm going to make this offering." Generate bodhicitta and then make the offering.

When you make an offering, it's also very good to recite the *Offering Cloud Mantra*, the mantra for blessing and multiplying offerings, three times:

> OM NAMO BHAGAVATE VAJRA SARA PRAMARDANE /
> TATHAGATAYA / ARHATE SAMYAKSAM BUDDHAYA /
> TADYATHA / OM VAJRE VAJRE / MAHA VAJRE / MAHA TEJA
> VAJRE / MAHA VIDYA VAJRE / MAHA BODHICITTA VAJRE
> / MAHA BODHI MANDO PASAM KRAMANA VAJRE / SARVA
> KARMA AVARANA VISHO DHANA VAJRE SVAHA.

If you are making light offerings in front of an altar, think in a similar way to when doing prostrations. The additional thing to think when you're offering light is, "This light is the light of Dharma wisdom." Relate to *Dharma wisdom* according to your understanding of the path to enlightenment. For example, if you understand tantra, you can relate it to the wisdom of clear light of the Highest Yoga Tantra path.

This wisdom light completely eliminates the ignorance of all sentient beings of the six realms. It eliminates all their suffering and its causes, karma and delusion, especially the ignorance not understanding emptiness and the ignorance not knowing Dharma. You can then think that all sentient beings generate the path. For example, you can think that all sentient beings achieve a buddha's five transcendental wisdoms and become enlightened.

A food offering is done in a similar way. Think of the food as nectar and offer it to a buddha such as Chenrezig visualized in front of you or in your heart. (See also *The Yoga of Eating*, chapter 19.)

When you eat and drink, at that time don't visualize yourself as an ordinary being. Purify yourself in emptiness, then generate into the guru-deity: you, the guru and the deity, all three are one. Then take every spoonful of food and every mouthful of tea by thinking that you are offering it to the guru; you then collect the most extensive merit with each spoonful. By offering to yourself as the guru-deity, you collect more merit than from having made offerings to the numberless buddhas, numberless Dharma, numberless Sangha, numberless statues, numberless stupas and numberless scriptures. As I mentioned before, the merit from offering one grain of rice to a statue, stupa or scripture is unbelievable. But it cannot be compared to the merit you collect by meditating on offering to yourself as the guru when you do the yoga of eating and drinking. With just the first sip of drink or spoonful of food, you collect the most extensive merit, so much more merit than from having made offerings to numberless holy objects. All those merits are small compared to the amount of merit you collect when you make offerings to the guru. And, depending on how big the mug is, there are so many sips in one mug of tea. If you practice the tantric yoga of eating and drinking every time you eat and drink, you collect merit far greater than from having made offerings to numberless buddhas, numberless Dharma, numberless Sangha and numberless statues, stupas and scriptures. All those merits are small compared to this.

Dedicating the offering

After making an offering, you should immediately dedicate the merit collected by you and by others to achieving enlightenment for the sake of all sentient beings. Especially, you should seal the dedication with emptiness so that if you later give rise to anger or heresy, the merit you have collected by putting so much effort into making offerings and doing other practices won't be destroyed.

If you don't dedicate the merit immediately, especially by sealing it with emptiness, and don't dedicate the merit to achieving enlightenment, since the merit you have accumulated doesn't become unceasing, it is quickly exhausted. Even though it's not destroyed, it doesn't last long. Like rejoicing, dedicating merit is a means of increasing, or multiplying, merit. If you put a drop of water into an ocean, that drop is always there until the ocean dries up; it never finishes. Like that, if you collect even a small amount of merit and dedicate it for enlightenment, it then becomes unceasing. Even after you have achieved enlightenment, your leading every sentient being to enlightenment is a result of having dedicated that merit for enlightenment.

The other dedication you should make is to generate bodhicitta. You dedicate in the same way for all sentient beings. You also dedicate for those who have bodhicitta to increase it. This is a very important practice to do every day.

There are five or six other dedications that are good to practice every day, especially when you are dedicating merits at the end of the day.[36]

---

[36] See "Standard Dedication Prayers," pp. 321–24, in *FPMT Retreat Prayer Book*.

Part Two

The Preparatory Ritual

Initially perform ablution, take the restoring and purifying ordination,
Invoke the merit field, do prostrations and so forth,
Confess negative actions and recite the (dharani of)
immaculate morality:
These are the five preparatory practices.

9. Brief Motivations

1. Take the responsibility

Think, "I'm going to do this nyung nä session to free every hell being from all their suffering and its causes and to free every hungry ghost from all their suffering and its causes. I must also free every animal from all their suffering and its causes; I must free every human being from all their suffering and its causes; and I must free every deva from all their suffering and its causes. I must free all sentient beings from all their suffering and its causes."

Take the responsibility to free all sentient beings from suffering and to lead them to enlightenment solely upon yourself. Make this strong determination now, and remember that your only opportunity to do this is at this time, in this life.

2. Bodhicitta is of the utmost need

When we meet a sentient being who has problems, who is suffering in samsara, that itself is the reason to generate bodhicitta. When we see a country, a society or a person suffering, it is the reason that we need to generate bodhicitta and to become enlightened.

Think, "It is not just one sentient being who is suffering—numberless sentient beings are suffering. If I had generated bodhicitta and already become enlightened, not only this one sentient being but the numberless other sentient beings, who are dependent on me, would have already been enlightened. But because I have followed only the self-cherishing thought, this one sentient being has suffered again and again, so many times, from beginningless rebirths, and there are numberless sentient beings who are suffering. Since this is due to my self-cherishing thought, the self-cherishing thought is unbelievably harmful to all the numberless sentient beings. I must eliminate it right now.

"If I had already generated bodhicitta, I would already have become enlightened, and those sentient beings would already have been enlightened. Bodhicitta is of the utmost need. Therefore, I must generate bodhicitta right now, without a second's delay.

"In order to generate bodhicitta and achieve enlightenment, I have to rely upon a special deity of compassion, Chenrezig, embodiment of the compassion of all the buddhas. Relying upon such a special deity will enable me to develop compassion. I must generate the path and develop bodhicitta, but to do so I need to accumulate a lot of merit. To achieve enlightenment, Buddha accumulated merit for three countless great eons and did so much purification in life after life. Therefore, I'm going to do this Chenrezig practice, this nyung nä, to achieve enlightenment for the sake of all sentient beings."

3. Every sentient being is your dearest one

You have received numberless past happinesses during beginningless rebirths from the numberless hell beings, hungry ghosts, animals, human beings, asuras, suras and intermediate state beings. Since you have received all this past happiness from them, think how unbelievably kind and precious they are. On top of that, you receive all your present happiness from them, so they are even more precious, unbelievably precious. And you will receive all your future happiness from them, so now they are much more precious, much more kind.

You also receive the ultimate happiness of liberation from samsara from all these sentient beings, so now they are even kinder and more precious. And you also receive full enlightenment from them, so now they are the dearest, kindest, most precious ones. Every sentient being is your dearest one. Every hell being is your dearest, kindest, most precious one. Every hungry ghost is your dearest, kindest, most precious one. Every animal is your dearest, kindest, most precious one. (Every insect or animal that you hate—rat, cockroach, spider, snake—is your dearest, kindest, most precious one.) Every human being is your dearest, kindest, most precious one. Every asura is your dearest, kindest, most precious one. Every sura is your dearest, kindest, most precious one. Every intermediate state being is your dearest, kindest, most precious one.

Think, "I must free every sentient being from all their suffering and its causes and bring them to enlightenment by myself alone (*alone* is very important). Therefore, I must achieve full enlightenment. Therefore, I'm going to do this nyung nä session."

4. Repaying the kindness

Doing this Chenrezig practice is how you enjoy life. This is the best way to enjoy life, to make life happy. Here we're talking about being happy because what we're doing is most meaningful, most beneficial, for sentient beings. Normally, in the world, being happy is related to your self-cherishing thought, your selfish mind. You're happy when you get what you want, what your attachment wants. Being happy is mostly related to delusions. But here happiness is not connected to the delusions, to samsaric pleasure, but to your doing the best you can for sentient beings.

Think, "Doing this nyung nä is my contribution to world peace. I'm doing this to bring peace and happiness to all sentient beings, but it's also my best contribution to world peace."

And this is the best way to repay the kindness of others, including your parents. Think of the kindness of your parents in giving birth to you, in taking care of you, in educating you and so forth. Even if somebody else took care of you after you were born, that person was also kind. First of all your parents were kind, because they gave birth to you, then all the others who took care of you were also kind.

Doing this nyung nä is the best way to repay their kindness, because by this you are able to bring all happiness to sentient beings. You are able to complete the path and achieve full enlightenment yourself, and then do perfect work for sentient beings.

5. Numberless, kind and precious

Think, "There are numberless kind and precious hell beings, and this nyung nä is for every single hell being, for their temporary and ultimate happiness.

"There are numberless kind and precious hungry ghosts, and this nyung nä is for every single one of them, for their temporary and ultimate happiness.

"There are numberless kind and precious animals, and this nyung nä is for every single one of them, for their temporary and ultimate happiness.

"There are numberless kind and precious human beings, and this nyung nä is for every single one of them, for their temporary and ultimate happiness.

"There are numberless kind and precious asura beings, and this nyung nä is for every single one of them, for their temporary and ultimate happiness.

"There are numberless kind and precious sura beings, and this nyung nä is for every single one of them, for their temporary and ultimate happiness.

"There are numberless kind and precious intermediate state beings, and this nyung nä is for every single one of them, for their temporary and ultimate happiness."

6. Developing great compassion is of utmost importance

It is through generating the root of enlightenment, great compassion, that the realization of bodhicitta, the door to the Mahayana path to enlightenment, comes. From bodhicitta then come all the Mahayana realizations— the six paramitas, the five paths, the ten bhumis and the realizations of the Highest Yoga Tantra path. Then the state of omniscient mind comes, with the infinite qualities of a buddha's holy body, holy speech and holy mind. We are then able to do perfect work for all sentient beings, bringing them from happiness to happiness to enlightenment.

Think, "Therefore, the most important thing in my life is to develop compassion, great compassion. This is of utmost importance. Just understanding the teachings on how to develop compassion is not sufficient. Even if I have all the information on how to develop compassion, I must still have the realization. For that, I must receive the blessing of the special deity of compassion by doing the practice that persuades the holy mind of the Buddha of Compassion. It is for this reason that I am going to do the meditation-recitation of Compassion Buddha."[37]

---

[37] All these brief motivations are also suitable to use to renew the bodhicitta motivation before doing the mantra recitation. The final two motivations come from *Teachings from the Mani Retreat*, pp. 45–47.

10. Intermediate Motivation

1. This practice is for every sentient being

Think, "I'm going to do this nyung nä session to free every hell being, who has so much suffering, from all their suffering and its causes. I can't stand one hell being to suffer for even one second. I *must* free them *right now* from all their suffering and its causes and lead them to enlightenment."

It is the same with the preta beings, the hungry ghosts. Think, "I'm going to do this session to free every hungry ghost from all their suffering and its causes. It is unbearable to me that one preta being is suffering for even one second. I can't stand it. Therefore, I must free them from all their suffering and its causes and lead them to enlightenment right now.

"I must also free every animal being from all their suffering and its causes. I can't bear one animal being to suffer for even one second. It is unbearable!"

When our body starts to degenerate and becomes bent over, we find it unbearable. We are still human, we still have a human body, but when such changes happen we find them unbearable. Even when we see a few more wrinkles on our face we are unhappy. We can't bear to see them; it disturbs our mind. So if we were a pig, a turtle or a conch animal it would be unbearable for us.

Until an animal has finished experiencing that karma, there's nothing it can do. When you experience various mental and physical problems as a human, you can be helped in so many ways. You can ask for help from your parents, from your friends and other people you know, from doctors or the government. You can ask for help from so many different sources. Even if there's no way for you to be helped, you can still tell other people about your problems and get some kind of support. Even if they can't completely solve your problems, they can still give you some kind of help.

Think, "Therefore, I must free each animal being from all their suffering and its causes and lead them to enlightenment by myself right now.

"I must also free every human being from all their suffering and its causes and lead them to enlightenment right now. Besides already being under the control of karma and delusion and experiencing so much suffering as the result of their past karma and delusion, they're constantly, day and night, creating more negative karma. All the time they're creating causes to again reincarnate in samsara, particularly in the three lower realms. Therefore, I must free them from all their suffering and its causes and lead them to enlightenment right now."

For example, when fighting in a war, people might think they are winning but they are actually creating the cause for another problem, for another war, in the future. The result is an even bigger war. There are many instances of people thinking they have defeated somebody but they themselves have actually lost because they have created the cause to lose and to experience more problems in the future.

Think, "I must free all the human beings from all their suffering and its causes and lead them to enlightenment by myself alone.

"I must also free all the devas, who are under the control of karma and delusion, from all their suffering and its causes and lead them to enlightenment by myself alone."

Each deva being has so much suffering, not only near the time of death with the five major and the five close signs of death, but from fighting and being killed and from being controlled by others. Not only do they experience these sufferings, but they also live their lives in a great hallucination. Even though their wealth and enjoyments are a million times greater than those of the richest human being, their life is lived completely in distraction. Because they are distracted by sense pleasures, they have no opportunity to practice Dharma. The result of living their whole life with attachment to such great sense pleasures is that they are then reborn in the lower realms. When death comes, all those pleasures mean nothing; they all have to be left behind.

The result of living their life with attachment and distraction is to be reborn in the lower realms, in the hells, where they see nothing but fire. As Nagarjuna explains in *Letter to a Friend*, the result is the complete opposite to their previous existence. Instead of drinking nectar, in their next life they drink molten iron, like lava, which burns their insides. Nagarjuna mentions many other things they experience that are the complete opposite to what they used to enjoy with attachment.[38] In reality, there's no real happiness in that deva life, and there's no doubt that there's no happiness in their next life.

Think, "I must free all sentient beings from all their suffering and its causes and lead them to enlightenment by myself alone. Therefore, I must achieve enlightenment quickly and more quickly. Therefore, I'm going to do this practice of Compassion Buddha. This nyung nä retreat is not for me but for everybody else: for every hell being, every preta being, every animal being, every human being, every asura and every sura. Any merit I accumulate from this practice is for every sentient being."

2. My mothers are suffering

Think, "The numberless sentient beings have been my mother and have been kind to me numberless times. They have been kind in giving me a body; they have been kind in protecting my life from danger hundreds of times even in one day; they have been kind in guiding me in the path of the world, giving me a general education for my short-term happiness; and they have been kind in bearing much hardship in taking care of me.

"These mother sentient beings, who have been kind to me in these ways numberless times, are now suffering in the hells, experiencing the heaviest sufferings of heat and cold."

It's exactly as if our present kind mother or father or our most beloved friend had fallen into the hells and were experiencing all this. We couldn't stand it. We couldn't relax. We couldn't stand by and ignore what was happening—we would have to do something to help them. Day and night we would be thinking of them and working to find some way to help them.

The hell beings who are now suffering are no different from the kindest person in our life, our mother or father or our best friend. They are the same, and they are the same in having been our kind mother, father and friend numberless times. They have been kind to us, and they are kind to us now. As beings with suffering, they give us bodhicitta; they give us enlightenment. They give us reasons to develop our mind and achieve ultimate happiness.

Think, "Therefore, I'm completely responsible for all these hell beings. No matter how much I suffer it's nothing to be shocked about. And even if

---

[38] See *Nagarjuna's Letter*, vv. 98–101.

I were to achieve liberation from samsara, it would be nothing to be excited about. So many of my mothers, who have been most kind to me in all three times, are now suffering there in the hells.

"Also, my kind mother sentient beings, the pretas, are passing their time in the greatest hunger and thirst. My kind mother sentient beings, the animals, are extremely foolish and are being eaten by each other. And my kind mother sentient beings, the human beings, have various problems. Besides the sufferings of birth, old age, sickness and death, they have many other problems. They have problems of being unable to make a living. If that is not the problem, they have relationship problems. If lack of wealth is not a problem, loneliness is a problem. If loneliness is not the problem, they have some other problem.

"The devas, because their minds are distracted by their great pleasures, find it difficult to think of practicing Dharma and developing their minds. They don't have the opportunities that we have here in the human world. They also suffer when they fight and kill each other and when they experience the signs of death.

"The beings in the form and formless realms are still under the control of karma and delusion, and they don't have the opportunities we have to meet and practice the whole Buddhadharma, including Mahayana teachings and especially tantra. Even though they have the realization of stable concentration, for them it doesn't become the cause of liberation.

"I'm completely responsible for freeing all these mother sentient beings from all their sufferings and for leading them to enlightenment. Therefore, I'm going to do the nyung nä practice. Everything—all the meditation, recitation of mantras, offerings and prostrations—is for them. It's not for me—it's for my mother sentient beings."

3. Giving up self, cherishing others

I often quote the following verse from great bodhisattva Shantideva:

> If you don't drop the fire,
> The burning cannot be stopped.
> Like that, if you don't give up the I,
> Suffering cannot be abandoned.[39]

---

[39] *Guide*, ch. 8, v. 135.

This means that if you don't give up the I, let go of the I, you can't abandon suffering; you can't be free from suffering.

> Therefore, in order to pacify the sufferings of yourself
> And the sufferings of other sentient beings,
> Give up yourself for others
> And cherish others as yourself.[40]

This is the very heart practice of Buddhism, especially Mahayana Buddhism. It is not sufficient for just you yourself to not be reborn in the lower realms and achieve the happiness of future lives. And even achieving liberation from samsara for yourself is not sufficient. As mentioned here, you must make your life meaningful for sentient beings. By letting go of the I and cherishing other sentient beings, you can free all sentient beings from the oceans of samsaric suffering and bring them to full enlightenment. You can bring the numberless hell beings, the numberless hungry ghosts, the numberless animals, the numberless human beings, the numberless asuras, the numberless suras and the numberless intermediate state beings to full enlightenment. That's the real meaning of your life, the real purpose of your life. That's why you have been born a human being at this time—to benefit others. To succeed in doing that, you must achieve full enlightenment.

Think, "From my side, even if it takes eons equal in number to the drops of water in the ocean to achieve enlightenment, I will do it. Even if I have to suffer in the hell realms for eons equal in number to the drops of water in the ocean or the atoms of this earth, I will suffer in hell to achieve enlightenment for the benefit of sentient beings. From my side I can do that, but I can't stand the thought that from the side of the sentient beings, they will have to suffer for such a long time. That thought is unbearable. Therefore, I must free them from the oceans of samsaric suffering. They need to achieve full enlightenment quickly, so I need to achieve enlightenment more quickly than I can through the Paramitayana path. Therefore, I need to practice the tantric path to achieve enlightenment the most quickly, within one life.

"Especially, I need to develop compassion for sentient beings. Even though Maitreya Buddha generated bodhicitta long before Guru Shakyamuni Buddha, Guru Shakyamuni Buddha became enlightened before

---

[40] Ibid, ch. 8, v. 136.

Maitreya Buddha. Why? Because, when they were still bodhisattvas, the compassion Guru Shakyamuni Buddha generated was much stronger than that generated by Maitreya Buddha."

When they were both bodhisattvas, Maitreya Buddha and Guru Shakyamuni Buddha saw a family of five tigers dying of starvation. Both of them then returned home. Later, Guru Shakyamuni Buddha went back alone to give his holy body to the tiger family. When he first offered his body to the five tigers, they were too weak to eat it, so he used a stick to make himself bleed. They were then able to lick the blood, and then later they ate his body.

Through that connection, in their next life those five tigers became Guru Shakyamuni Buddha's disciples. They were born as human beings and Guru Shakyamuni Buddha revealed Dharma to them.

You may not be able to make a connection with a bodhisattva through positive actions such as serving or making offering to them, but even if you make a connection with a bodhisattva by harming them, because of their bodhicitta, you will receive only benefit in return. Even if you harm a bodhisattva, in return you will receive only help from that bodhisattva. The bodhisattva will make prayers to benefit you, as in this story and in the story of those five *yakshas* who drank blood from the holy body of Guru Shakyamuni Buddha when he was a bodhisattva. In their next life, the five yakshas were the five disciples when Buddha turned the first Wheel of Dharma in Sarnath.

This is the last benefit of bodhicitta Shantideva mentions in the first chapter of *A Guide to the Bodhisattva's Way of Life*. The whole chapter is on the benefits of bodhicitta, and the last verse is,

> A bodhisattva brings happiness even to those who harm him:
> To this source of happiness, I go for refuge.[41]

Even if you harm a bodhisattva, you don't receive harm in return, only happiness and benefit. Even harming them makes a connection that enables you to receive happiness.

The stronger the compassion you are able to generate, the quicker you are able to achieve enlightenment, like with the story of Guru Shakyamuni

---

[41] Ch. 1, v. 36.

Buddha. Think, "Therefore, I need to receive the blessings of the Buddha of Compassion, Chenrezig; for that, I need to do the meditation-recitation of Chenrezig. Therefore, I'm going to do this nyung nä session."

4. Beginningless kindness

At this time we have been born as human beings but we're not free from suffering, from true suffering and the true cause of suffering. We don't experience one moment of pure happiness. Even what we call "pleasure" is only labeled on suffering. Suffering appears to us as pleasure.

We must free ourselves from all suffering, but that alone is not sufficient. We can't be satisfied with just that because all sentient beings have been our mother and as kind as our present mother numberless times, giving us our body, protecting us from hundreds of dangers to our life even in each day, leading us in the path of the world by giving us education and bearing much mental and physical hardship, including worry, fear and exhaustion for us. They have also created much negative karma to obtain happiness for us. We should feel very strongly that all sentient beings have been our mother and kind in these four ways numberless times—even a buddha's omniscient mind cannot see the beginning of their kindness.

First feel the kindness of the mother in giving you a body numberless times. It is because your present mother gave you your body that you have the opportunity to practice Dharma, and all sentient beings have done this numberless times.

They have also protected your life from hundreds of dangers each day. Unless someone is watching a baby, within a minute its life is in danger. There are so many dangers. If your present mother hadn't protected your life from danger, you wouldn't now be a human being with the opportunity to practice Dharma. All sentient beings have been kind to you in protecting your life from danger numberless times.

They have also led you in the path of the world: teaching you how to walk and speak and sending you to school to be educated. If your present mother hadn't educated you you wouldn't now have all these opportunities to read Dharma books, write, study, work at a job and do many other things.

If your present-life mother hadn't borne hardships for you, starting from the time you were conceived in her womb, you wouldn't now be a human being and you wouldn't have the opportunity to practice Dharma and obtain the happiness of future lives, liberation and enlightenment. Therefore, your present mother has been unbelievably kind. But this is not the first time; she has been kind to you in these four ways numberless times, and so have all other sentient beings.

Since all sentient beings have been your mother and kind in these four ways numberless times, you should repay their kindness. Think, "I must repay the kindness of all sentient beings. The best way to do this is by freeing them from suffering and leading them to enlightenment. To do that I must achieve enlightenment, and to do that I must practice Dharma. Practicing Dharma is the best way to repay the kindness of my mother sentient beings.

"My mother sentient beings lack temporary happiness, and even when they have temporary happiness, they lack ultimate happiness. How wonderful it would be if all mother sentient beings had happiness. I will cause them to have happiness." This is the way to generate loving kindness.

You then take the responsibility upon yourself: "I will cause them to have happiness, both temporary and ultimate, especially the ultimate happiness of enlightenment."

It's very important to feel this in your heart. It's very important to generate not just loving kindness but great loving kindness. Simply wishing them to have happiness is loving kindness, but here you need to generate *great* loving kindness, which means taking the responsibility upon yourself to cause them to have happiness.

Then think, "Even though the mother sentient beings don't want to suffer, they are constantly suffering and creating the causes of suffering. Even though they want happiness, they are devoid of happiness and always destroying the causes of happiness. Therefore, how wonderful it would be if all sentient being could be free from all suffering and the causes of suffering. I will cause them to be free from suffering and its causes."

Next generate the special attitude, in which you take the responsibility for other sentient beings completely upon yourself. This attitude is much stronger than before. "I will take responsibility for doing this work of bringing sentient beings happiness and freeing them from all suffering by myself alone.

"At the moment, however, I can't guide even one sentient being to enlightenment. In order to perfectly guide sentient beings, I need to understand the mind of every single sentient being and every single method that fits the different minds of sentient beings. Since the only mind that knows all this is the omniscient mind, I must achieve the omniscient mind in order to lead all sentient beings to enlightenment."

It is very important to generate this thought.

"Since the omniscient mind cannot be achieved without causes and conditions, I must generate the path. The fundamental ways to achieve the omniscient mind are to protect karma, live in morality and generate compassion. Therefore, I'm going to do this nyung nä session."

It's very important to generate the thought to do the nyung nä session purely for all sentient beings.

5. By myself alone

Think, "The numberless hell beings, from whom I receive all my past, present and future happiness, all realizations and enlightenment, are the most precious and most kind ones in my life—I must free them from all their suffering and its causes and bring them to Compassion Buddha's enlightenment by myself alone.

"The numberless hungry ghosts, from whom I receive all my past, present and future happiness, all realizations and enlightenment, are the most precious and most kind ones in my life—I must free them from all their suffering and its causes and bring them to Compassion Buddha's enlightenment by myself alone.

"The numberless animals, from whom I receive all my past, present and future happiness, all realizations and enlightenment, are the most precious and most kind ones in my life—I must free them from all their suffering and its causes and bring them to Compassion Buddha's enlightenment by myself alone.

"The numberless human beings, from whom I receive all my past, present and future happiness, all realizations and enlightenment, are the most precious and most kind ones in my life—I must free them from all their suffering and its causes and bring them to Compassion Buddha's enlightenment by myself alone.

"The numberless asuras, from whom I receive all my past, present and future happiness, all realizations and enlightenment, are the most precious and most kind ones in my life—I must free them from all their suffering and its causes and bring them to Compassion Buddha's enlightenment by myself alone.

"The numberless suras, from whom I receive all my past, present and future happiness, all realizations and enlightenment, are the most precious and most kind ones in my life—I must free them from all their suffering and its causes and bring them to Compassion Buddha's enlightenment by myself alone.

"The numberless intermediate state beings, from whom I receive all my past, present and future happiness, all realizations and enlightenment, are the most precious and most kind ones in my life—I must free them from all their suffering and its causes and bring them to Compassion Buddha's enlightenment by myself alone.

"To do this, I must achieve Compassion Buddha's enlightenment; therefore, I'm going to do the meditation-recitation of Compassion Buddha."

Also, you can then specifically think, "Every single OM MANI PADME HUM that I recite is for every hell being, every hungry ghost, every animal, every human being, every asura being, every sura being, every intermediate state being. Each OM MANI PADME HUM that I recite is for the benefit of every single one of my most precious, kind mother sentient beings."

6. IF I HAD GREAT COMPASSION

Think, "If I had the realization of great compassion, Mahayana compassion, the numberless hell beings, who are the most kind and most precious ones in my life and who are experiencing unbearable suffering, would be liberated from all that suffering and its causes and achieve enlightenment.

"If I had great compassion, the numberless hungry ghosts, who are the most kind and most precious ones in my life and who are experiencing unbearable suffering, would be liberated from all that suffering and its causes and achieve enlightenment.

"If I had great compassion, the numberless animals, who are the most kind and most precious ones in my life and who are experiencing unbearable suffering, would be liberated from all that suffering and its causes and achieve enlightenment.

"If I had great compassion, the numberless human beings, who are the most kind and most precious ones in my life and who are experiencing the unbearable suffering of samsara and all the problems of human beings, would be liberated from all that suffering and its causes and achieve enlightenment.

"If I had great compassion, the numberless asura beings, who are the most kind and most precious ones in my life and who are experiencing unbearable suffering, would be liberated from all that suffering and its causes and achieve enlightenment.

"If I had great compassion, the numberless sura beings, who are the most kind and most precious ones in my life and who are experiencing unbearable suffering, would be liberated from all that suffering and its causes and achieve enlightenment.

"If I had great compassion, the numberless intermediate state beings, who are the most kind and most precious ones in my life and who are experiencing unbearable suffering, would be liberated from all that suffering and its causes and achieve enlightenment.

"Therefore, I need to develop great compassion; therefore, I'm going to do the meditation-recitation of Compassion Buddha."[42]

---

[42] The final two motivations are bodhicitta motivations for doing the mantra recitation taken from *Teachings from the Mani Retreat*, pp. 1–3 and 47–48 respectively.

11. Extensive Motivations

1. If I had generated bodhicitta

THIS IS ANOTHER WAY to generate a motivation of bodhicitta before the meditation-recitation of Compassion Buddha so that it becomes not only Dharma but most beneficial not only for you but for every single hell being, hungry ghost, animal, human being, asura, sura and intermediate state being. Each realm has numberless beings. In the human realm there are numberless human beings. We can easily understand that there are numberless beings in the animal realm. Even in regard to one type of insect, ants, there are numberless ants. In the same way, there are many other different types of animals that are numberless. This is without mentioning the countless sentient beings in the other realms.

All these beings, who are the source of all your own past, present and future happiness, are continuously suffering; totally overwhelmed by karma and delusion, they do not have any freedom at all.

Even though there are numberless buddhas and bodhisattvas working for sentient beings, there are many sentient beings—people, and even animals—who received help only through meeting you. They had some problem they couldn't resolve until they met you and you were able to help them. Or they didn't meet Dharma until they met you. You have had many such experiences of sentient beings being dependent upon your help.

There are numberless beings with whom you have a karmic connection and who depend upon you. Their being free from suffering, from samsara, and achieving liberation and enlightenment depends on you. You can understand from your experiences in this life of the many beings who depend on your help that there are numberless other beings who depend on your help to free them from samsara; they depend on you to meet, understand and practice Dharma and to achieve enlightenment.

Now think, "If I had generated bodhicitta much earlier, this one hell being who is dependent on me wouldn't have to experience this unimaginable, unbearable suffering, the heaviest suffering in samsara." One tiny spark of the fire of the hot hells is seven times hotter than the fire at the end of the world, which can melt rocky mountains and concrete. And the fire at the end of the world is sixty or seventy times hotter than the fire energy of our present human world.

"For one hell being to be suffering now in the hell realm for even one second is like they are suffering for eons—it is unbearable. If I had generated bodhicitta much sooner, that hell being would already have been enlightened. And there are numberless other hell beings who could have already been enlightened by me so that they now wouldn't have to suffer. They have been suffering up to now because I have been following the self-cherishing thought, ego. Even when I think of that one hell being who is experiencing unimaginable suffering, it becomes urgent that I generate bodhicitta without the delay of even a second. Now there are numberless hell beings; therefore, I need to generate bodhicitta without even a second's delay. Because there are numberless hell beings who are suffering, the need for me to generate bodhicitta is much more urgent.

"If I had generated bodhicitta much sooner, this one preta being, who is so precious and kind and from whom I receive all my past, present and future happiness, would have already been enlightened. But because I followed the self-cherishing thought, this one preta being has been suffering so much, experiencing all the unbearable sufferings of heat, cold, exhaustion, hunger and thirst, outer obscurations, food obscurations and inner obscurations. And there are numberless preta beings. If I had generated bodhicitta sooner, all these numberless preta beings would already have been enlightened. Because I didn't generate bodhicitta, they have been suffering up to now. Therefore, it is urgent: I must generate bodhicitta without the delay of even a second, not just for this one hungry ghost but for the numberless other hungry ghosts as well.

"If I had generated bodhicitta much sooner, this one animal who has been suffering so much up to now—being extremely foolish, experiencing hunger and thirst, heat and cold, being tortured, being used for food—would have already been enlightened a long time ago. There are numberless animals, and they would all have already been enlightened if I had generated bodhicitta much sooner. It is because I didn't generate bodhicitta but followed the self-cherishing thought that they have been suffering up to now. Therefore, the need for me to generate bodhicitta, to change my mind, is unbelievably urgent, not only for this one animal but for the numberless animals who have been experiencing so much suffering.

"It is the same with the human beings. If I had generated bodhicitta, if I had changed my mind, a long time ago, this one human being, who is constantly suffering, would already have been enlightened. Instead they are experiencing the suffering of pain; if not that, the suffering of change; and if not that, pervasive compounding suffering, by having these aggregates, this samsara, the nature of which is suffering. These aggregates are caused by karma and delusion and contaminated by the seed of delusion, so this person constantly, without even one second's break, experiences pervasive compounding suffering. This human being is totally overwhelmed by karma and delusion; they are living in a total hallucination, with piles of wrong concepts, and suffering. If I had generated bodhicitta earlier, this most precious and kind human being who has been suffering up to now and who is the source of all my own past, present and future happiness would already have been enlightened and not have to suffer. And there are numberless human beings. Because I did not change my mind but followed ego, not only this one human being but numberless human beings have been suffering from beginningless time up to now. Therefore, without even a second's delay, I must change my mind into bodhicitta, into cherishing others.

"It is the same with the suras. If I had generated bodhicitta much sooner, this one sura being, who has been suffering so much, would have been enlightened a long time ago. The sufferings of the suras are similar to those of human beings, but suras are also totally distracted by objects of desire. They cling to and are distracted by sense pleasures. No matter how many eons they live, their life is totally overwhelmed by desire. In this way, they are constantly creating the cause of suffering, the cause to again be reborn in the lower realms. Their having great enjoyment is just temporary. How wonderful it would have been if this one sura being could have been enlightened a long time ago. And there are numberless sura beings who could have been enlightened a long time ago. How fantastic that would have been. But because I didn't change my mind and followed only my ego instead, not only this one sura being but numberless sura beings have been suffering up to now. And it is the same with the asuras.

"My kind mother sentient beings have been suffering from time without beginning; they have never had a break for even one second from the suffering of samsara, from pervasive compounding suffering. Therefore, without delay, I *must* generate bodhicitta.

"Generating bodhicitta depends on receiving the blessing of the special deity of compassion. Trying to develop bodhicitta just by remembering the words of the teachings is not enough. Even meditation alone is not enough. I need to receive the blessings of the special deity of compassion. For that reason, I need to meditate on Compassion Buddha and to recite the mantra that persuades Compassion Buddha's holy mind. I need to recite the mantra that brings me closer to the deity of compassion, that causes me to receive the blessings of the deity of compassion. Therefore, I'm going to do the meditation-recitation of Compassion Buddha."[43]

2. Freedom to practice Dharma

We have received a human rebirth at this time through our practice of pure morality in past lives. By looking at the world, we can see that living in pure morality is extremely difficult. Most people do not understand how and do not like to live in morality. It is difficult to understand the importance of living in morality, of abstaining from negative karma, from harming ourselves and others with our body, speech and mind; and even if we do understand the importance of living in morality, and even if we take vows, it doesn't mean we can live in them purely. It's very difficult to live in even one vow purely. By looking at our own experiences, we can see how difficult it is to live purely in any vows that we have taken. Therefore, we must have practiced pure morality in many previous lifetimes and have thus received a higher rebirth, the good body of a happy transmigratory being. There are also suffering transmigratory beings, but we have achieved the body of a happy transmigratory being.

---

[43] This was a bodhicitta motivation before mantra recitation, taken from *Teachings from the Mani Retreat*, p. 95.

Not only that, but this time we have received a human body qualified by eight freedoms and ten richnesses, or endowments.⁴⁴

By not being born in hell, we have the freedom, the opportunity, to practice Dharma.

By not being born as a preta, we have the freedom to practice Dharma.

By not being born as an animal, we have the freedom to practice Dharma.

By not being born as (or by not being) a barbarian, we have the freedom to practice Dharma. (I think that if there's not enough merit, it's possible for someone to be a Buddhist and then later become a barbarian.)

By not being born as a long-life god, we have the freedom to practice Dharma. Even though such gods have very long lives, since they have only awareness of their birth at the very beginning and their death at the very end, they have no opportunity at all to practice Dharma.

By not being born as (or by not being) a heretic, we have the freedom to practice Dharma. We can relate this to our present situation, our present life. If we had been born in a place where Buddha hadn't descended, we would have no freedom to practice Dharma. But it's not like that for us. We are in a world where Buddha has descended and revealed the teachings and where the teachings still exist—we have just made it before the teaching of Buddha degenerates and stops in this world. That's unbelievable success.

If we were to be born in this world later, when the Buddhadharma had degenerated, it would be no different from being born as an animal. We might have some temporary pleasure, but we would not have the freedom to practice Dharma. There would be no way for us to use our intelligence to learn Dharma, to actualize the path, to overcome our samsaric sufferings and liberate ourselves by ceasing the cause of suffering, karma and delusion.

One time in the temple in Dharamsala, when His Holiness was giving all the rare initiations related to the Fifth Dalai Lama's pure appearances, His Holiness pointed to His Holiness Karmapa and Ling Rinpoche and said that during their lifetime the Buddhadharma would be okay, but that after the lifetime of these young lamas, it would be very difficult in this world for the Buddhadharma.

So, we have been born just before Buddhadharma degenerates and stops in this world, and not as animals but as human beings having, especially, the eight freedoms and ten richnesses.

---

⁴⁴ See Rinpoche's *The Perfect Human Rebirth* for extensive teachings on this topic.

The complete teachings of Buddha exist. There are the Hinayana teachings, with which one achieves liberation for oneself from the oceans of samsaric suffering and its cause, karma and delusion. There are the Paramitayana teachings, with which one achieves enlightenment for sentient beings. And there are the Secret Mantra Vajrayana teachings, with which one achieves enlightenment for sentient beings quickly because one cannot stand that sentient beings are suffering in samsara.

The last freedom, the eighth freedom, is having the freedom to practice Dharma by not being born a fool. This can refer to somebody who is born a fool or who becomes a fool. Sometimes a person is not born as a fool but later becomes a fool due to past negative karma ripening.

So, we have all these eight freedoms to practice Dharma. With the first freedom, the freedom to practice Dharma by not being born in a hell realm, we can achieve the first great meaning, a higher rebirth; the second great meaning, liberation from samsara; and the third, enlightenment. Since we can achieve all that with this first freedom, this one freedom is *so* meaningful, *so* precious—unbelievably meaningful and precious. But this first freedom can be stopped at any time. So, not only must we practice Dharma but we must practice Dharma right now.

How precious is this first freedom, the freedom to practice Dharma by not being born in a hell realm? It's more precious than a wish-granting jewel. I'm not talking about gold, silver or diamonds but about a wish-granting jewel. This first freedom that you have is more precious than the whole sky filled with wish-granting jewels. The value of all that is nothing compared to the value of this human rebirth that you have, especially this perfect human rebirth. The value of all that is nothing compared to even this first freedom. The value of this one freedom is just amazing, because if you don't have this freedom, you can't practice Dharma.

Nagas, who belong to the animal realm, are very wealthy and always have a wish-granting jewel on their crown. We have been born as nagas with all that wealth numberless times in the past but it didn't do anything for us. It didn't liberate us from samsara; it didn't cause us to actualize bodhicitta or realize emptiness or renunciation. None of that. Under the control of karma and delusion, we've continued to be born in samsara, experience suffering and die.

Milarepa, on the other hand, had nothing—not even one dollar, not even one rupee. He had no money and not even one tiny jewel, but he had a human body, and he used that human body to practice Dharma. He had very strong guru devotion to Marpa, an enlightened being, the actual Vajradhara. For many years Marpa never gave Milarepa teachings or initiations. Marpa only scolded and beat Milarepa and gave him hard work to do, such as building a nine-story tower by himself. After he had finished the tower, Marpa then told him to take the stones back to where he got them from and then rebuild the tower. Then again he had to demolish the tower and return the stones, then again build the tower.

One day Milarepa came with the other students to receive teachings, but when Marpa saw Milarepa, he immediately scolded him in public, beat him and kicked him out. For years he never gave him any teachings—nothing!

Marpa's wisdom mother (his wife, in ordinary language) pushed Marpa, begging him to give teachings to Milarepa. Marpa then manifested the mandala in his hermitage and initiated his disciple, Milarepa. After that he gave Milarepa all the initiations, commentaries and practices. He then advised Milarepa about places in the mountains where he should go to meditate.

Milarepa followed Marpa's advice exactly. By bearing all the hardships to do the practice, Milarepa achieved full enlightenment in that life. He completed the entire tantric path and achieved enlightenment within a number of years.

Marpa made the comment that if his wisdom mother hadn't pushed him to give Milarepa initiations and teachings, from his own side he would have given Milarepa more hardships to bear, and in that case Milarepa would have achieved enlightenment even sooner. He would have achieved enlightenment much quicker. But because Marpa's wisdom mother pushed Marpa to give the teachings earlier, Milarepa took a longer time to achieve enlightenment, even though he still achieved it in the brief lifetime of a degenerate time.

During all the hard work, Milarepa never got angry or gave rise to one single thought of heresy toward his guru Marpa. He followed Marpa's advice exactly, by looking at Marpa as a buddha. Because he did everything with that pure mind of devotion, within a few years Milarepa achieved enlightenment.

You've been born as nagas and had wish-granting jewels numberless times, but that didn't liberate you from samsara; that didn't cause you to achieve the realizations of renunciation, bodhicitta and right view or even the common attainments. However, without any of that wealth, just by having this perfect human rebirth you can achieve all these realizations and full enlightenment. With this human body you can practice Dharma in every second and not only liberate yourself from the oceans of samsaric suffering and enlighten yourself, but you, one person, can liberate the numberless hell beings from the oceans of samsaric suffering and bring them to enlightenment. In the same way, you can liberate the numberless pretas from the oceans of samsaric suffering and bring them to enlightenment. You can liberate the numberless animals from the oceans of samsaric suffering and bring them to enlightenment, and you can do the same with the numberless human beings, asuras, suras and intermediate state beings. Therefore, this perfect human body that you have received, with its eight freedoms and ten richnesses, is unbelievably precious.

As I said before, with one freedom you can achieve all the three great meanings. The first freedom is most precious, more precious than the sky filled with wish-granting jewels. Every freedom is unbelievably precious, more precious than the sky filled with wish-granting jewels. But if you don't understand this, you might think that the sky filled with billions of dollars or with diamonds or gold is more precious.

To make it short, this perfect human rebirth that you have achieved is the most precious one. Every second of this human rebirth, especially this perfect human rebirth qualified by eight freedoms and ten richnesses, is most precious.

Now, it is the same with the ten richnesses that you have received. Each richness is unbelievably precious, more precious than the sky filled with wish-granting jewels. Your precious human body is qualified by eight freedoms and ten richnesses, so with these eighteen qualities, it's much more precious, unbelievably precious.

So, in this life you must do your best. How can you dare to waste this precious human body? Only an ignorant person would be careless and waste this precious human body. And you don't have it for a long time. Death is definite and the actual time of death is indefinite; it's uncertain when it will happen. It could happen even today, in any hour, at any moment. So, you must practice Dharma right away.

If it's the case that you want happiness and you don't want suffering, then you have to practice the cause of happiness, Dharma, and abandon the cause of suffering. The very first thing is that you have to make sure not to be reborn in the lower realms and to receive a higher rebirth so that you can continue to practice Dharma and actualize the path. The method to achieve that is to take refuge and then protect karma. The very basic way to protect karma is to abandon the ten nonvirtues and practice the ten virtues as much as you can.

However, that alone is not sufficient. You must free yourself from samsara and achieve the ultimate happiness of liberation. But just achieving liberation for yourself, with cessation of all suffering and its causes, is still not sufficient. That's still not the real meaning of life. The real purpose of life, the real meaning of life, is to benefit others, to free the numberless sentient beings from all their suffering and its causes and bring them to full enlightenment. This is the thought of seeking enlightenment for others. The way to succeed in that is for you yourself to achieve enlightenment. In order to seek enlightenment for other sentient beings, you first seek enlightenment for yourself. This is what makes life the most meaningful, most productive and most beneficial for all sentient beings and yourself.

For the success of this, you must actualize bodhicitta, the door of the Mahayana path to enlightenment. For that, you must actualize the root of bodhicitta, great compassion. For that, meditation alone is not sufficient. You need to receive the blessings of the special deity of compassion, Chenrezig. It is for this reason that you are going to do the nyung nä practice.

3. YOUR HUMAN BODY IS SO PRECIOUS

It is said that Buddhism is differentiated from other religions by compassion for all living beings. *Compassion* doesn't mean feeling compassion only for the friends who love you or for those who smile at you for as long as they like you or need something from you. When they don't like you or don't need anything from you, they don't smile at you. You have compassion for them at the times they smile at you; but you need to develop compassion for them even at the times they don't smile at you or don't love you. You have to have compassion for them even at those times when they don't pay attention to you, when there's nothing they need from you. You have to have compassion for them even at the times they harm you.

You have to develop compassion not only for friends but also for strangers and even enemies. You have to develop compassion for every sentient being—not only for every human being, but even for every animal: for every single fish, every single lobster. Due to karma such animals have been born with unimaginable kinds of bodies. In this life, if your body slowly started to change into that of a lobster, thoughts of suicide would arise. You would prefer to die rather than to have a lobster's body.

As I often mention, when you look down at the ocean from an airplane, if you don't understand the reality of the world and just think in a superficial way, the blue ocean looks very peaceful. It looks as if there's no suffering there. But if you look deeper and think about what's happening inside the ocean, there are numberless sentient beings there. I'm not talking here about human beings, hell beings, hungry ghosts, asuras or suras, but just about animals. The animal beings alone are numberless.

In the ocean, animals as large as mountains, whales, are eating so many small animals, and then so many small animals are living on their body, eating them. Buddha mentioned that in the deepest ocean, where there's no light, where it's totally dark, there are large animals with many small animals around their mouths. They just eat whatever is there in front of them; they just eat each other. It's unimaginable.

If you look at the animal world inside the ocean, there are animals as large as mountains and ones so tiny that you can see them only with a microscope. Every one of them is constantly looking for food for their own happiness; and much of their finding food involves eating other sentient beings, who are scared of being eaten and always try to escape. Animals' lives are always full of fear. Animals are always scared, trying to escape being eaten by their enemies and looking for protection, and at the same time they're looking for food, which is other living beings. It goes on and on like that continuously, from those animals as large as mountains down to the tiniest ones. It's unbelievable. They are constantly trying to escape from their enemies and looking for safety; but at the same time, they are looking for food. That's the nature of their life—the result of their past negative karma. We can't even imagine their suffering.

The root of all that suffering is the ignorance not knowing ultimate nature, or emptiness. There are two types of this ignorance: ignorance not knowing the selflessness of the I, the person, and ignorance not knowing the selflessness of the aggregates. Or you can say: ignorance not knowing the ultimate reality of the I and ignorance not knowing the ultimate reality of the aggregates. This ignorance is the root of each individual being's suffering of samsara. With that as the root, ignorance, anger and attachment then motivate karma, leaving karmic imprints on the mind, which then produce the various rebirths.

So, we have experienced all this animal suffering. The ocean has been our home, our residence, numberless times. We have been born as fish, lobsters and all those other animals, including the tiniest microscopic ones. We have been born as every single animal and insect numberless times. There's no ocean where we haven't been born with bodies similar to the bodies of those animals. The main cause is attachment. Attachment to water is nothing new—it's a very old story. During beginningless rebirths we have had this attachment, and we have been born in the water and lived like those animals numberless times.

In the world animals live in under the ocean, there's unbearable suffering, worry and fear. They are totally ignorant and live in fear of being eaten by other animals and experience heat and cold and many other sufferings as well. Wherever you are, wherever you escape to, even between rocks, your enemies are always there. It's karma; it's because of the past karma of having harmed others. Due to karma, wherever you are, your enemies are close by.

Your enemies have exactly the right kinds of hands and mouth to be able to catch and eat you. It looks as if somebody designed them precisely for that. Some birds, for example, have very long beaks with a hook on the tip, as if somebody designed it exactly to catch their prey. Pelicans have long beaks with a huge pouch down below, like a handbag, to catch big fish inside. They collect all the food there.

In an animal documentary on TV, I remember seeing a big orange rock and a lizard with what looked like thorns or pimples on its body whose color was exactly the same as that of the rock. It's similar to the way insects born inside a flower are the same color as the flower. If it's an orange flower, the insect born there is orange in color.

I remember one time at Mahamudra Centre in New Zealand, an elderly Western nun was cooking and she sprinkled orange flowers on the yogurt as decoration. You can eat such flowers but you have to be careful as many insects live in the center of them. If you don't watch for them, of course, you don't see them, but you have to look. I have a lot of karma to see insects in food . . .

Anyway, this orange lizard was sitting on top of the orange rock. Then a snake, also the same color as the rock, came from down below the rock to eat that lizard. Can you imagine? If you're an animal, your enemies are just there, wherever you are. That is life as an animal.

I also saw in a TV documentary many seals on the sand at the shore of an ocean. The seals, which are full of fat, are eaten by polar bears, and the seals themselves eat penguins, and the penguins eat other beings in the water. One animal eats another animal, which eats another animal, which eats another animal.

As human beings, we can't even imagine it. We don't have that constant fear, day and night, all the time, of being attacked and eaten by an enemy. We don't experience constant danger. (Of course, a person could be in danger of being killed by somebody, but this is only sometimes; it's not that it lasts the whole life.) We have unbelievable freedom. Even in terms of food, we have so many choices. We don't have to eat just one type of food, and the food we eat doesn't have to be only other sentient beings. We can find and eat so much food that is not a living being. In our life we have so much comfort and so many choices in regard to food, clothing and shelter.

While we have this amazing opportunity, it's unimaginable for us not to practice Dharma, not to do something meaningful at least for ourselves, if not for others. Our practice of Dharma can rescue us, liberating us from all sufferings (from the general sufferings of samsara and the particular sufferings of each realm; from the suffering of pain, the suffering of change, which means all the samsaric pleasures, and pervasive compounding suffering) and from the cause of suffering, karma and delusion. We have an unbelievable opportunity: whatever Dharma we wish to practice, we can practice.

We have unbelievable freedom if we compare our lives to those of animals in the ocean. We can understand that their lives are lived totally in worry and fear. They're looking for food, and at the same time they're in danger of being eaten by other animals. They live their whole life always being attacked by others. We're free from those kinds of problems. We have the most unbelievable freedom.

Now, this is not for long—just for a very short time. We mustn't deceive ourselves. We need to think about life deeply, not just superficially. If we don't get to practice Dharma, our life will have been completely wasted; we will have completely deceived ourselves, cheated by the ignorance not knowing Dharma and particularly by attachment and sometimes by anger.

When death suddenly happens, our human life is gone. At that time, we can't go back. No matter how much we think we have made mistakes in our life, no matter how much we think, "I should have practiced Dharma seriously every day" or "I should have done many years of retreat," the time is gone—we can't go back. We can't think, "I made a mistake. I wasted my time—I must go back," and go back to this morning and really practice. We can't go back even one second. As His Holiness often says, we can't go back to the previous second. Time is always finishing; life is always finishing. Of course, we can purify negative karma, but we can't go back in time.

Therefore, there's nothing more ignorant than not practicing Dharma while we have found this unbelievable opportunity, this unbelievable freedom, and instead totally cheating ourselves by following ignorance, anger and attachment.

After our death, when we're in front of Yama, Yama will question us about or show us in a mirror all the negative karmas we have collected in the past. We won't be able to hide anything or lie about anything before having to reincarnate and experience the resultant suffering.

As I mentioned at the beginning, compassion for all living beings is what differentiates Buddhism from other religions. In Christianity, it's believed that pigs, fish and other animals were created by God and given by God to human beings for their food. It is not like that in Buddhism, where there is compassion for every living being, for every suffering, obscured being. Compassion is not only for your friends but also for strangers and even for your enemies. Compassion is for everybody.

The most important thing in your life is to develop compassion for all living beings. Having generated great compassion, you're then able to take full responsibility upon yourself for liberating sentient beings from the oceans of samsaric suffering and its causes. The numberless sentient beings, especially those who have a connection with you and who rely upon you, will then be liberated.

From great compassion, you then develop the special attitude, taking the responsibility to liberate the numberless sentient beings from the oceans of samsaric suffering and its causes and bring them to enlightenment by yourself alone. You then generate bodhicitta. With bodhicitta, the extraordinary principal consciousness with the five similarities,[45] there are two intentions: the intention seeking the works for other sentient

---

[45] A principal consciousness and its mental factors have similar basis, duration, aspect, object and substance.

beings—freeing them from suffering and bringing them to enlightenment—and the intention related to you yourself—to succeed in that, you yourself have to achieve enlightenment.

Bodhicitta is the door of the Mahayana path to enlightenment, and the root of bodhicitta is great compassion. By generating great compassion, you are able to have bodhicitta and thus enter the Mahayana path. You are then able to achieve the five paths and ten bhumis and then the tantric path, including the generation and completion stages of Highest Yoga Tantra. After achieving the gross and subtle stages of the generation stage, you then achieve the isolation of speech and the isolation of mind, then the unification of clear light and the illusory body, and then the unification of no more learning. You are able to actualize the completion stage paths and achieve full enlightenment. With practice of the Paramitayana path, it takes three countless great eons to complete the two collections of merit: the merit of wisdom and the merit of virtue. Tantra, even the lower tantras, is a quicker path to achieve enlightenment, making it possible to achieve enlightenment in one life. You don't need to take three countless great eons to complete the collection of merit—you can complete it within one life.

Why are you able to do that? Tantra has greater skillful means, with the one mind practicing method and wisdom together. In Mahayana sutra, you practice the paths of method and wisdom together but with separate minds, not with one mind. That's why it takes such a long time. In order to achieve the deity's holy mind, dharmakaya, and the deity's holy body, *rupakaya*, you need to complete the merits of wisdom and virtue, which takes three countless great eons with the Paramitayana. But tantra has greater skills. Since with one mind you practice both method and wisdom, you're able to complete all that merit within one life, which means you can achieve the dharmakaya and rupakaya within one life.

With the lower tantras—Action, Performance and Yoga tantras—*within one life* means that first you have to prolong your life so that you can live for hundreds or thousands of years. You can achieve enlightenment within one life, but by prolonging your life in that way.

The Highest Yoga Tantra path has greater skillful means than the lower tantras and is the quickest means to achieve enlightenment, allowing you to achieve the unification of the deity's holy body and holy mind in the brief lifetime of a degenerate time, even within a few years. This is the quickest way to complete the two types of merit and achieve the dharmakaya and rupakaya. The Highest Yoga Tantra path is the only one that has the advanced method to cease the gross mind and to actualize the subtle mind of clear light, which is the direct cause of the dharmakaya, and the illusory body, which is the direct cause of the rupakaya. You cannot actualize these two by practicing the lower tantras—only by practicing Highest Yoga Tantra. Once you actualize the simultaneously born great bliss of clear light in this life, you're certain to achieve enlightenment in this very lifetime.

Lama Tsongkhapa's disciple's disciple, Drubchen Chökyi Dorje, and his disciple, Gyalwa Ensapa, as well as many other great meditators, great holy beings, achieved enlightenment in the brief lifetime of a degenerate time. Milarepa wasn't the only one to do this—there were many others. When Padmasambhava was in Tibet, twenty-five of his closest disciples definitely achieved enlightenment, and I think eight of Milarepa's disciples also achieved enlightenment.

The most important thing is for our life to become most beneficial for sentient beings. For that we need to develop compassion, the wish to free sentient beings from all their sufferings and bring them to enlightenment. We need to develop great compassion for each and every single obscured, suffering sentient being. To develop great compassion, we need to meditate on the lam-rim, the stages of the path to enlightenment. The root of the path to enlightenment, what brings all the success up to enlightenment, is guru devotion. The actual path then begins with the first meditation, the perfect human rebirth, realizing how this human rebirth with the eighteen precious qualities of the eight freedoms and ten richnesses is the most precious one. However, learning the lam-rim from the beginning of the path is not sufficient. We can't have realizations just by meditating on the lam-rim. In order to achieve realization of great compassion, and from there up to enlightenment, we need to receive the blessings of the special deity of compassion, Chenrezig. And to receive permission to do the meditation-recitation with ourselves generated into Chenrezig, we need to be empowered by receiving a Chenrezig great initiation.

Because they don't have a human body, animals can't do meditation-recitation; they can't meditate on Chenrezig or recite the mantra. Not having a human body blocks their understanding the words and meanings. Since we have received a human rebirth, when somebody tells us to repeat "OM MANI PADME HUM," we can immediately imitate them. It doesn't take us even a minute to be able to recite the mantra. Cows, donkeys, snakes, lizards, tigers, elephants, mosquitoes, cockroaches, frogs and crickets can't do this. Animals can't recite words. No matter how long they lived, even if they lived for billions of eons, they have no karma to be able to chant mantras. But we human beings can learn to repeat a mantra even within a minute. Imagine the difference. Imagine the freedom we have to practice Dharma.

We have unbelievable freedom to purify negative karma and to collect extensive merit, to develop compassion and bodhicitta, to achieve enlightenment quickly and to liberate numberless sentient beings from the oceans of samsaric suffering and quickly bring them to enlightenment. While having this incredible opportunity, imagine if we then live our life in complete laziness? Or with the concept of permanence? Even though life is impermanent, we have the wrong concept that it's permanent. Every day, when we get up, we think, "I'm going to live for many years." Even the morning of the day that we're going to die, we think, "I'm going to live for many years." Even five minutes before the car accident or plane crash in which we die or before we collapse with a fatal heart attack, even one minute before, we have this concept, "I'm going to live for many years."

We are living our lives with the concept of permanence and with other wrong concepts. While samsaric pleasures are only suffering in nature, we are living our lives with the wrong concept that they are all sources of real happiness. We completely cheat ourselves in this way, and we have been doing so from beginningless rebirths up to now. That's why we have still not achieved liberation. Not only have we not achieved enlightenment; we haven't achieved even liberation from samsara for ourselves.

Also, this body is unclean, or impure, and suffering in nature. After clean food goes inside our body it becomes dirty. Food is dirty when it comes out of this body, not only from the lower door but even from the mouth. Nobody wants to eat vomited food. As Nagarjuna says, the body is the container for thirty-two impure substances. But we have the wrong concept that it's clean, that it's pure.

Also, if you look for the I from the top of your head down to your toes, there's nowhere you can find it. It's neither outside nor inside the body. You can't find it inside your chest or anywhere else inside your body. You can't find it anywhere. But at the same time, because these aggregates exist, the I, which is merely labeled by mind, exists. That's the reality.

There's no I there, from where it constantly appears and where you believe it to exist. It's like a dream, an illusion, a mirage. This wrong view, this hallucination, of a real I is projected by the negative imprint left by ignorance on the mental continuum. This real I is projected there the moment after the I is merely imputed by mind, by thought. The real I is a mental fabrication, a total hallucination, and you let your mind believe in it one hundred percent. You have no doubt that it is true.

You then live your life with this wrong concept. Every day, every hour, of your whole life is lived with the belief that this I is really true. You live every day, every hour, of your life with this wrong concept, this hallucination.

From birth to death, you live your life with this hallucination. For you, this hallucination is true; you let your mind believe it is totally true. But it is not only that. There's a continuation of this hallucination from your previous life, from before the consciousness took place on the fertilized egg in your mother's womb. This belief existed in the life before this; it did not start with this life. Ignorance didn't begin with this life; it has a continuation from the past life, whatever that past life was. There's a continuation of that hallucination and the total belief that this I is true from the life before this.

From beginningless rebirths you have had this hallucination and the total belief that it is true. You let your mind believe that it is true, instead of looking at it as a hallucination, instead of looking at it as empty, as it is empty. Instead of looking at the real I as empty, you believe that it's true. You believe that it inherently exists, that it exists from its own side, that it exists by its nature. Instead of looking at the real I as nonexistent, you believe it exists. The I appears to be truly existent, inherently existent, and you believe this to be true, instead of believing it to be nonexistent, empty. During beginningless rebirths, you have been living your life with this hallucination, this wrong concept. While there's no such I at all, you have been believing that it exists as it appears to exist, from its own side.

In reality, the I exists as a dependent arising, dependent on the aggregates, the label and the mind that labels. The I exists because the base, the aggregates, exist; the I exists in mere name, merely imputed by the mind, by thought. While the I exists as a subtle dependent arising in this way, we hold that the I is not merely labeled by mind, but exists from its own side. That is a wrong concept, and we have been suffering from beginningless rebirths up to now because of it. However, *this* is the life in which we have all the opportunities to realize the ultimate nature, the emptiness, of the I.

As Buddha said, the way Buddha liberates us sentient beings from the oceans of samsaric suffering and its causes is not by washing away negative karmas with water. Nor does Buddha liberate us from the oceans of samsaric sufferings with his hand, like taking a thorn from the body. Nor does Buddha transplant his realizations within us, like transplanting a heart. The way Buddha liberates us sentient beings is by revealing ultimate reality, the truth. Buddha doesn't transplant his realizations into us but introduces us to the truth.

We have received teachings from many great teachers, including His Holiness the Dalai Lama, Compassion Buddha in human form. If, from our side, we don't put effort in this life into developing this realization that can directly cease karma and delusion, the cause of suffering, of samsara, it's not sure when it will happen. If we don't make it possible for this to happen in this life, it will be extremely difficult, almost impossible, for it to happen at all.

If we develop compassion for sentient beings and then generate bodhicitta, we will collect limitless skies of merit all the time. With the power of that great collection of merit, we will incidentally be able to realize emptiness. We should also study teachings on emptiness to leave as much imprint as possible. Even if we don't understand what we're reading, by reading teachings on emptiness as many times as possible and meditating on them, we will leave so many positive imprints that sooner or later we will be able to realize emptiness.

The great lama, Trehor Kyörpön Rinpoche said,

> It is only difficult to realize emptiness for those people who don't have much merit. Those with much merit have no difficulty realizing emptiness.

Trehor Kyörpön Rinpoche was a great meditator, with great attainments, and the leader of many meditators in Dalhousie. He achieved the path of merit and the preparatory path, and the tantric paths of clear light and illusory body.

Rinpoche became a lharampa geshe in Tibet, where there were many thousands of learned geshes. After his geshe examination Rinpoche went to the mountains to meditate, to integrate and actualize the extensive Buddhadharma, the extensive study of *Pramanavarttika, Abhisamayalamkara,*

Madhyamaka, *Abhidharmakosha* and *Vinaya* he had done in the monastery. He went into the mountains carrying only the two types of monks' robes, the *chögu* and *namjar*, and a lam-rim text.

Trehor Kyörpön Rinpoche went looking for a cave on a very high mountain near Lhasa, the top of which is always obscured by clouds. Rinpoche saw stones coming down the mountain, one after another, so he decided to follow the stones to their source. After some time he came to a cave, and inside the cave was a skeleton sitting in meditation position. Rinpoche didn't enter the cave, but sat outside and offered a mandala. The skeleton sitting in meditation then collapsed. A stone landed on top of this cave, so Rinpoche decided, "This is the cave in which to meditate."

His disciples, other geshes, then came and meditated on the mountain under his guidance. They didn't live together but at some distance from each other on the mountain.

When Communist China invaded Tibet, Trehor Kyörpön Rinpoche escaped, and later went to Dalhousie, where he led a group of meditators in integrating the extensive Buddhadharma into lam-rim and then actualizing the realizations. Rinpoche didn't accept everybody who came, but selected some geshes who could live an ascetic life, who could really sacrifice themselves to actualize the path and who could meditate. First he gave them elaborate lam-rim teachings for a few months. Many other learned geshes, such as Geshe Sopa Rinpoche, attended those teachings.

What I'm saying is that if you practice great compassion and bodhicitta, which collect the most extensive merit, then you can actually realize emptiness by the way.

I want to mention again the unbelievable freedom that we have compared to animals and to other sentient beings, especially those in the lower realms, and compared even to the devas in the higher realms and the human beings in the other continents (the eastern, western and northern continents). The human beings in the other human worlds don't have the great freedom that we have. We are able to meet the Buddhadharma. We are able to meet the Hinayana teachings, where we can recognize true suffering and the true cause of suffering and then abandon them by actualizing the true path to achieve liberation from the oceans of samsaric suffering and its causes for ourselves. We have the freedom to make it impossible for us to experience suffering again.

Not only that, but we have met the Mahayana Paramitayana teachings, with which we can achieve enlightenment for sentient beings. We also have this unbelievable freedom.

Not only that, but we have already met the Mahayana Vajrayana teachings, which make it possible for us to achieve enlightenment in one lifetime, even in the brief lifetime of a degenerate time. Receiving Chenrezig initiation allows us to receive teachings on the Chenrezig path and attain Chenrezig's enlightenment. We also have this unbelievable freedom. Even the human beings in the other worlds don't have this most amazing freedom that we have.

I want to mention again that even if animals—turtles, pigs, horses and even cats and dogs, the animals that normally live with human beings—lived for many billions of eons and even if you explained to them that the cause of happiness is virtue day and night for billions of eons, there's no way they could understand what you were saying. There's no way they could understand even the words, let alone the meaning. The definition of virtue is "any action of body, speech or mind motivated by a pure mind, by non-ignorance, non-anger or non-attachment, which results in happiness." Even if you explained this definition to an animal continuously, without even a second's break, for billions of eons, there is no way that animal could understand. No matter how much animals suffer, due to ignorance they cannot understand Dharma. They have no way to practice Dharma, no way to attain the path, no way to achieve liberation or enlightenment.

As human beings, if somebody explained this definition to us, within a few seconds we could understand that the cause of happiness is virtue and that virtue is any action motivated by a pure mind that results only in happiness. As human beings, we can understand not only the words but even the meanings within a few seconds. That shows the value of this human body, how precious this human rebirth is. Having a human body that can understand words and meanings and can communicate makes it so easy for us to learn Dharma, compared to animals and to other sentient beings. It's unbelievably easy for us, as human beings, to learn and to understand Dharma.

You can now see how foolish it is if you don't learn Dharma, if you don't practice Dharma. There's nothing more foolish than this. As Shantideva said,

> While you have such incredible freedom to practice Dharma, if you don't practice Dharma, there's no greater ignorance than this.[46]

While you have this unbelievable freedom to practice Dharma, if you don't practice, it's most foolish.

Because animals don't have a human body, they're completely blocked from understanding words and meanings. There's no way they can understand. It's so easy for us to learn and understand the words and meanings, which makes it so easy for us to practice Dharma, which makes it so easy for us to achieve realization, to achieve liberation and enlightenment. We have to appreciate the unbelievable opportunity we have. It's unimaginable! Having this human body is the easiest way to learn, to practice and to have attainment. We must realize this and practice Dharma—this is the only life in which we can do it.

Even devas don't have virtuous friends who explain the complete path to enlightenment to them. They hear Dharma through the sounds of drums. In the Thirty-three Realm, on the fifteenth day they hear teachings through the sounds of drums, but they do not have the opportunities that we have. Even though devas have sense pleasures that are a hundred thousand or a million times greater than ours, they don't have the opportunity to practice Dharma, to be liberated from the oceans of samsaric suffering and its cause: all the defilements and all the wrong concepts related to ignorance that have made them suffer from beginningless rebirths.

Therefore, since this is the only life with this unbelievable opportunity, if you don't get to practice Dharma, there's no greater ignorance than this, and no greater loss than this. If you don't get to practice Dharma, you will have wasted this life. If you pass not only a day, an hour or a minute but even a second without practicing Dharma, without practicing bodhicitta, it's a greater loss than losing the sky filled with not only billions of euros or dollars or pounds, but diamonds or gold or even the highest, rarest, most precious one, wish-granting jewels. If even one second passes without your practicing Dharma, it's a much greater loss than losing the sky filled with wish-granting jewels. That loss is nothing compared to wasting

---

[46] A paraphrase of *Guide*, v. 23, ch. 4.

this precious human body for even one second. If you don't have a precious human body, even if you have the sky filled with wish-granting jewels, you can't achieve a good rebirth next life, you can't achieve liberation from samsara, you can't achieve enlightenment. But if you have this body, even if you don't have a single jewel or a single penny, even in every second you can create the causes of the happiness of future lives, liberation from samsara and enlightenment. This is why this human body is unbelievably precious.[47]

4. WE NEED TO PURIFY RIGHT NOW

The great bodhisattva Shantideva said,

> This precious human body, qualified by freedom and richness, will be extremely difficult to find again. If I don't get to obtain benefit on this body, how can I receive a perfect human body again in the future?[48]

At this time, we should think in the following way: "If I had already died, where would I now be? It's not sure. I might have been born as a lobster and be in a glass tank in a restaurant waiting to be put into boiling water. I might have been born in the shape of a scallop, with my body between two shells. Or I might have been born as a fish, swimming in the water or caught on a hook by a fisherman, who would then slice my body in half. Or I might have been born as a worm and be attacked by ants. Or I might now be in a hot or a cold hell or be born as a preta.

"If something like this had already happened what could I do? Nothing! No matter how much I was suffering and how much I didn't want that suffering, there would be nothing I could do. I would have to go through that experience.

"So far I haven't died, and today I'm again able to be a human being and again have the opportunity to practice Dharma—how fortunate I am!"

Many of our relatives have already died; they have already left this human world. For some of us, our father or mother has died, or both have died, or our grandfather and grandmother or other relatives have already died. It's

---

[47] This was the motivation for a Chenrezig great initiation.
[48] *Guide*, ch. 1, v. 4.

difficult to say where they now are. If they're now in the lower realms, they have no opportunity at all to practice Dharma and are experiencing only suffering.

Think, "At this time, I have received a precious human body qualified by eight freedoms and ten richnesses. I have the freedom to practice Dharma by not being born in a hell realm; I have the freedom to practice Dharma by not being born a preta; I have the freedom to practice Dharma by not being born an animal; I have the freedom to practice Dharma by not being a barbarian, with no understanding of Dharma at all and totally wrong views; I have the freedom to practice Dharma by not being born as a long-life god; I have the freedom to practice Dharma by not being a heretical being; I have the freedom to practice Dharma by not being born in a place where Buddha has not descended; and I have the freedom to practice Dharma by not being born a fool. My precious human body is qualified by these eight freedoms.

"In regard to the ten richnesses, I have the opportunity to practice Dharma by being born a human being. Second, I have the opportunity to practice Dharma by being born in the center of a religious country. I have the opportunity to practice Dharma by being born with perfect senses. I have the opportunity to practice Dharma by not having committed the extreme actions.[49] I have the opportunity to practice Dharma by having faith in the teachings that subdue the mind."

Here, *the teachings that subdue the mind* are the teachings of the lam-rim, the graduated path to enlightenment. Why is this particular title used? Because when listening to and studying the extensive sutra and tantra teachings don't subdue your mind, the lam-rim teachings are able to do so. Why? Because the lam-rim teachings are presented in a special way that focuses mainly on subduing the mind. When the extensive teachings don't affect your mind, listening to, reflecting and meditating on the lam-rim can subdue it. *Having faith in the teachings that subdue the mind* means having faith in the lam-rim teachings, especially the teachings on karma.

"I have the opportunity to practice Dharma by being born in a time when a buddha has descended. Not only that, but I have the opportunity to practice Dharma because the Buddha's teachings still exist at this time. Not only do the teachings still exist in this world, but I have the opportunity to practice Dharma because I follow the teachings. Finally, I have

---

[49] The five uninterrupted negative karmas.

the opportunity to practice Dharma because the virtuous friend has compassion. If the virtuous friend didn't have compassion, I wouldn't receive teachings, I wouldn't receive guidance. But because the teacher has compassion, I receive teachings and guidance."

Since the precious human body that we now have is qualified by these eight freedoms and ten richnesses, it is unbelievably precious. At this time, this one time, we have received a perfect human body and have met the Buddhadharma and the virtuous friend, who has revealed the path. During this time, since we have received all the necessary conditions to practice Dharma, we can achieve whatever happiness we wish. We can achieve any of the three great meanings that we wish. We can achieve the happiness of future lives because we can create the cause with this perfect human body by practicing morality and charity, dedicating the merit to achieving a perfect human body and so forth. Even if we wish to achieve the ultimate benefit of liberation from samsara, we can obtain it, because with this perfect human body we can create the cause with the three higher trainings. Even if we wish to achieve the ultimate happiness of full enlightenment for sentient beings, we can obtain it, because with this perfect human body we can generate bodhicitta and practice the bodhisattva's deeds of the six paramitas and so forth.

If we don't accomplish these benefits now, it will be difficult to do so in the future. Why? Such an opportunity as this will be difficult to find again. It will be difficult to receive a perfect human body again, because it is extremely difficult to create its causes.

Also, this life is very short. Death is definite, and the actual time of death is uncertain. Death can happen at any time. We have accumulated so many negative karmas in this life, such as the ten nonvirtuous actions. There are three nonvirtuous actions of body (killing, stealing, sexual misconduct), four negative actions of speech (telling lies, speaking harshly, slandering, gossiping) and three nonvirtuous actions of mind (covetousness, ill will, heresy). These are just the basic examples—there are many other negative karmas. We have accumulated many negative karmas during this life, and during beginningless rebirths.

Take covetousness, for example. When we go shopping, during those hours, how many times do we accumulate the negative karma of covetousness? With attachment, we are always thinking, "If only I could have that." After those many hours of looking around at all the different things, we come back home with big piles of the negative karma of covetousness. There are many other similar examples of which we are not aware.

After our death of this life, even though our body disintegrates, our consciousness doesn't cease. A candle flame stops when the wax is finished, but our consciousness is not like that. Our consciousness continues, and if we haven't done anything to purify our negative karma and our nonvirtue is stronger than our virtue, we will take rebirth in the lower realms.

When death happens, it's not like a flame going out when the wax finishes. The flame stops and has no continuation. The consciousness continues after this life, even though this gross physical body doesn't. Where our consciousness migrates accords with our karma. If we didn't get to purify all our negative karma (the actions motivated by disturbing thoughts that are the cause of the lower realms) accumulated in the past and if we didn't get to accumulate virtue, the cause of the realms of the happy transmigratory beings, and if we have been accumulating heavy negative karma (such as the karmas that become heavy because of the nature of the object itself; because of the motivation, such as strong anger; or because of the action being very harmful), we will be born in the hell realms.

If we are going to be born in a hot hell, no matter how many blankets or heaters we have at the time of our death, due to karma, we feel very cold and crave heat. That craving is the immediate cause to be born in a hot hell. If we don't apply meditation at the time of death to stop this craving and to stop the disturbing thoughts of ignorance, anger and attachment, we will die with this mind craving heat. Like having a dream, we will then be born into the intermediate state. Like waking up from sleep, from the intermediate state we will suddenly have the karmic appearance of ourselves in a hot hell.

If we are born in a hot hell, we have all the obstacles and none of the necessary conditions to practice Dharma. One tiny spark of hell-fire is millions of times hotter than all the fire energy of the human realm. To give you some idea of the heat, think of the fire of a volcano, which is much hotter than the usual kind of fire we make. The heat of lava gives you some idea of the heat in hell.

All the hot hells have red-hot burning iron ground that is one with fire. To understand the red-hot burning iron ground consider touching a hot pot when you're cooking. Even if the pot is not red hot, to touch it is extremely painful. We can't imagine doing that for even a second. There in the hells everything is completely red hot, one with fire. If you were to drop food or liquid on the burning ground, it would immediately get burnt up. But because of heavy karma you don't immediately get destroyed in that way. You have to abide on the burning iron ground or in the burning iron house, which is many thousands or even hundreds of thousands of times hotter than a red-hot pot.

Also, you are cooked in molten metal in a large pot and suffer so much. The karmic guardians put you into this liquid and then stir it. When you're deep inside the molten metal, it's so hot that your skin and flesh separate from your bones. When your body comes out of the liquid, it becomes alive again and gets flesh on the bones. You have to experience that again and again.

If the body of a hell being were tiny, like some insects, there would be less pain; but since the body is huge and tall, like a mountain, there is much suffering. The skin is also extremely thin and sensitive, like the skin over an abscess, which is painful even when touched by a hair. The sufferings of the hot hells are much greater than that. They're unbearable.

The first hot hell is called Being Alive Again and Again. When you are born there, even though there are no hell guardians, due to your own negative karma, every sentient being that you see in that realm becomes your enemy. On seeing each other, the hell beings get angry and attack each other. If 360 short spears were put through your human body in one day, you would find it unbearable. If even a tiny thorn goes into the sole of your foot, you can't stand or walk; you find it unbearable. If you were born in this hell realm, Being Alive Again and Again, the suffering would be much heavier than 360 short spears being put through your body.

Due to karma, everything you hold in your hand becomes a weapon. Your body is then cut into pieces, which all fall on the ground. Again, due to karma, a voice comes from the sky, "May you be alive!" Cool air comes and touches the scattered pieces of your body so that they come together again. Once again you revive and become alive.

Everyone again fights each other and cuts each other to pieces. The pieces of the body falling to the ground is defined as death, and that death happens many hundreds of times in one day. You are alive, die, are again alive, again die, and so on. In this hell, hundreds of times each day you are killed and again become alive.

The length of life in this first hot hell is also extremely long. Fifty human years is one day for a deva, such as one of the four guardian kings, who live for five hundred years, and the length of life of those devas is one day for the hell beings in Being Alive Again and Again. The length of life of the beings in this first hell is many trillions of human years. These hell beings have to suffer for that duration of time.

The next hell is called Black Line. This hell has karmic guardians as huge as mountains, with big, red, terrifying eyes, and they make terrifying sounds urging the hell beings to kill, hit and so forth. (The guardians, as well as the red-hot iron ground and everything else, are your own karmic appearances, the appearances of your own negative karma.) The guardians capture the hell beings and stretch out their bodies on the red-hot iron ground. They then mark many black lines on their huge hell bodies with iron rope that is one with fire.

After that, like carpenters cutting wood, the guardians cut the bodies into pieces, some with axes and others with swords. The pieces of body and even the scattered drops of blood have consciousness. When we have a wound, the blood that drops on the ground and the small piece of skin that's separated from the body don't have consciousness. But here, due to karma, the flesh that drops on the ground and even the small drops of blood have consciousness, so there's much suffering. You have to experience that for a long time.

The causes to be born in these hells are all the ten nonvirtuous actions and beating human beings or animals.

The third hot hell realm is Gathered and Destroyed. Two mountains in the shape of animal heads (it could be a goat, a sheep or another animal you have killed—the animal accords with your own past karma) come from your right and left sides and crush you between them. This hell is mainly the result of killing, and the shape of the mountains is related to the type of being you killed in your past life. There is no way to escape. You are crushed between the two mountains.

Like sugar cane being pressed to give the juice, rivers and waterfalls of your blood flow. You experience so much heavy suffering in this way. Here, at this time as a human, the blood that comes out of your body doesn't experience suffering; but there in the hells, even the blood that comes out experiences suffering. Due to karma, even the blood has consciousness, and as it spreads it experiences suffering.

When the mountains then pull apart, your body again revives. You are then again crushed. Like fruit in a juicer, your body is crushed by the mountains again and again. Due to karma, some of the hell beings here are ground between two round iron stones, like grinding barley into flour. Other hell beings get crushed, like someone beating grain inside a large container with a huge stick to separate the husks from the grain. Other hell beings suffer as when dough is put into a machine and forced out of small holes to make noodles. Hell beings suffer in many different ways.

When we are born in this hell, the things that crush our body appear in the form of the tools we used to kill animals in our past life. If you used sticks to kill animals, what tortures you appears in that form.

The next hell realm is Crying. Due to karma, you are caught inside an iron house that is one with fire. Since it has no doors or windows, you have no way to escape. You are caught inside and experience much suffering for an incredible length of time.

The next hell is called Great Crying. After experiencing karma similar to that in Crying for a long time, even when that karma finishes and you are able to get out of that burning house, there is no real freedom because there's another similar world. Even if you become free from one burning iron house, you can't get free from the next one. The suffering is much greater, and you experience that suffering for a long time.

The causes to be born in these Crying hot hells are all the ten nonvirtuous actions, and the particular nonvirtue of carelessly drinking alcohol. A person who drinks alcohol is born in these Crying hell realms, and a person who gives alcohol to others is born in the surrounding hell realm. This is mentioned in the sutras. (There are four surrounding hell realms around each major hot hell.)

In the next hell, Hot Hell, you are stretched out on the red-hot iron ground, and the karmic guardians ask you what you want. When you reply, "I want something to eat and drink," they put red-hot iron balls or molten metal from a pot into your mouth. It then burns the inside of your body. They also put a flaming skewer through your anus so that it emerges through the crown of your head. In this way it burns all the inside of your body. Flames come from all your openings—mouth, nose, ears, eyes—and everything is burned. You are also cooked in a large pot full of molten iron. Your body disintegrates into pieces, but then your bones come back together and you again become alive. This happens again and again.

The next hell is called Extremely Hot because it is twice as hot as the previous hell. Your whole body is cooked in a large pot so that all the flesh disappears, and all that is left is bones. The pieces then come together again and you are revived. You experience this suffering again and again. Due to karma, your flesh is revived, and you are again burned.

The bodies of some of the hell beings are rolled in red-hot iron sheets, with no way to escape. The bodies of other hell beings are tied so tightly with burning iron thread that the flesh oozes out, like the pulp of fruit crushed in a machine. Some hell beings have a red-hot trident put through their body from below, with the middle prong coming through the crown and the other two prongs coming through the shoulders. They are then burnt in this way. The karmic guardians stretch out the tongues of other hell beings for many miles, then use animals to plow the top of the tongue, like plowing a field. Some hell beings are tied between two red-hot flat pieces of iron, like the covers of a Tibetan text, and squashed. There is no way to escape. There are various types of sufferings in the Extremely Hot hell.

The eighth, and last, hot hell is Inexhaustible Suffering. Among all the hot hells, this one has the greatest suffering. When a blacksmith makes an iron pot or iron tools, the iron is red hot, one with fire. Like that, the body itself here in this hell is one with fire. The only way you can discriminate that a sentient being is there is by the sound of their screaming. Otherwise, you can't tell there's a sentient being. You can't discriminate a living being by the shape.

There is also the karmic appearance of fire coming from the ten directions: from the four cardinal directions, the four intermediate directions, above and below. When we're near a fire, we find it hot. Even if a fire were coming from four sides and not even touching us, we would find it unbearably hot. This is a thousand times hotter than that. Not only that, but fire also comes from inside the body. So, there are eleven fires in all. Like the wick of a candle, the hell being's body is one with fire. The suffering is unbelievable.

In *Letter to a Friend*, Nagarjuna says,

> Among all happiness,
> The cessation of craving is the best happiness.
> Among all suffering,
> The Inexhaustible Hell is the most unbearable.[50]

[50] V. 85.

Even if you put together all the other sufferings of the three realms, all the other sufferings that exist in samsara, the suffering of the Inexhaustible Hell, this last hell realm, is much greater.

Each of the major hot hells is surrounded by four branch hells, with different types of sufferings. The first is the karmic appearance of being caught in the center of a blazing fire.

The next branch hell is like being in a septic tank, like being drowned in a quagmire of filthy things. While you are drowning, tiny worms with sharp, pointed mouths, like mosquitoes or certain kinds of fish, pierce your body.

There is then the karmic appearance of your most beloved friend, the object of your attachment, calling to you from the top of a tree, "Come here! I'm up here." As you start to climb up the tree, all the branches of the tree bend down and pierce your body so that it is difficult to climb up. While this is happening, there is also the karmic appearance of iron dogs that come to eat you.

Even if you manage to reach the top of the tree, the person you are attached to then calls to you from the ground down below the tree, "I'm down here!" When you then start to climb down, the branches of the tree now turn up and again pierce your body and there is the karmic appearance of birds with sharp beaks that eat you.[51]

In the cold hells, you experience the suffering of your body being one with ice. Different names are given to the cold hells as the skin becomes more and more blistered and cracked. It is completely dark, windy and unbelievably cold. To be naked in such a cold, windy place for an hour or even a minute would be unbearable. The cold hells are hundreds of thousands times colder than winter on the human earth.

Where do all these hells come from? They're productions of our disturbing thoughts and karma. We have created so many causes to be born in these hell realms in this life and during beginningless rebirths. If we don't do anything to purify our negative karma, as soon as our death happens we might be born in these hell realms. We can't have any confidence that this won't happen as we haven't reached the level of the path that makes it impossible to be reborn in the lower realms.

There are five paths to liberation and five paths to enlightenment: the

---

[51] For a slightly different presentation of the branch hells, see *Liberation in the Palm of Your Hand*, pp. 332–33.

paths of merit, preparation, seeing, meditation and no more learning. The second path, the preparatory path, has four levels: heat, tip, patience and sublime Dharma. It is only when we achieve the path of patience that we can be confident that we will never again be reborn in the lower realms. Before that we can't be completely confident. We haven't got that confidence as we haven't achieved those paths. Before our death, we have to make sure that we won't be born in the lower realms and that we're able to create the causes to be born as a deva or a human being. But even that is not sufficient, because it's still in samsara, still suffering in nature.

Therefore, the solution is to purify the karma that has been accumulated during beginningless lives. We are extremely fortunate to have met the teaching of Buddha, which can purify these causes—especially the most powerful practice of nyung nä, which combines three powerful practices that bring great purification and accumulate merit like infinite space: the Eight Mahayana Precepts, prostrations and recitation of the Chenrezig mantra.[52]

---

[52] This was a motivation for taking the Eight Mahayana Precepts.

12. Ablution and Lam-Rim Prayers

Ablution

At the very beginning of the nyung nä practice, do the samaya mudra of the lotus race: hold both hands at your heart, with the palms facing upwards, in the mudra of a blossoming lotus.[53]

Action, or Kriya, Tantra has three divisions: tathagata, lotus and vajra race. It's important to know the mudras of the three different races.[54] Since this aspect of Chenrezig, Thousand-Arm Chenrezig, belongs to the lotus race, say OM PADMA UDBHAVAYE SVAHA as you hold your hands in that lotus mudra at your heart.

Next offer your body to all the buddhas and bodhisattvas. It is said that if you offer yourself in this way you will be guided by the buddhas and bodhisattvas and will also be protected from harm from others, whether human beings or nonhuman beings.

Visualize all the buddhas and bodhisattvas of the ten directions in front of you. Thinking that you are prostrating at their holy feet, recite the following mantra and verse:

OM SARVA TATHAGATA KAYA VAK CITTA VAJRA PRANAMENA
SARVA TATHAGATA VAJRA PADA BANDHANAM KAROMI

> I offer my body at all times to all the buddhas and bodhisattvas of the ten directions until I achieve the essence of enlightenment. Please, all you buddhas and bodhisattvas, accept me. Please grant me the peerless realization.

---

[53] In one commentary, Rinpoche also says that the mudra is like the shape of a lotus petal.
[54] See *Deity Yoga*, pp. 79–81.

Think that, having offered your body to all the buddhas and bodhisattvas, you now belong to them. Think, "I should now do what the buddhas and bodhisattvas want, what accords with their holy minds, which is to always benefit sentient beings."

Please grant me the peerless realization means that, in order to lead all sentient beings to the peerless happiness of full enlightenment, you request the buddhas and bodhisattvas of the ten directions to grant you the peerless realization. To be able to receive that, you first need to achieve the realizations of the graduated path to enlightenment.

Lam-rim Prayers

There are many different lam-rim prayers, many of which have been translated into English. We recite these short lam-rim prayers to inspire us to have a pure attitude to do the practice and to develop devotion, the root of the path to enlightenment, and compassion. It's good to read such a prayer before the nyung nä session starts.

Calling the Guru from Afar

When you recite *Calling the Guru from Afar*, whether the long or short version, visualize your root guru above your crown, with the awareness that this guru is the embodiment of all other gurus, buddhas, Dharma and Sangha. The root guru is the one among all your gurus who has most benefited your mind, who has most directed your mind into Dharma. So, you could have two or three root gurus.

Always meditate that this root guru is all your other gurus. In fact, every guru is one with all your other gurus. The basic thing you have to realize is that they are all one. All the buddhas are one, and all the buddhas are the guru; and all the gurus are buddhas. They're all just one. When you think that the guru is buddha, all the gurus have to be one. Thinking otherwise interferes with having the realization of guru devotion.

In the long version of *Calling the Guru from Afar* there is quite an elaborate description of what the guru is and of the kindness of the guru.

When the prayer describes the different manifestations of the guru, it might be helpful and effective to visualize a specific object like the *Lama*

Chöpa merit field in front of you so that you can relate to it. All those different aspects manifest in one, the guru, and the guru manifests in countless aspects. The many manifest in one, and the one in many.

> Please bless me to follow after the ocean of conquerors with the will to cross to the very end of the great waves of deeds of the conquerors' children.[55]

This verse is related to bodhicitta, renouncing the self and cherishing others, which enables you to bear the greatest hardships to work for sentient beings. No matter how hard it is to work for others, you have no worry or fear, and you don't get discouraged. You have a big mind, a strong, altruistic mind, to accomplish the extensive works for sentient beings and bring them to enlightenment. Even if you need to make charity of your body for eons equal in number to the atoms of this earth to achieve enlightenment for sentient beings, you are able to bear all those hardships. Instead of your mind getting smaller and more discouraged, it gets bigger and stronger, willing to bear whatever responsibility is involved. You're willing to bear the whole responsibility for freeing each and every sentient being from all their suffering and for gradually leading them to enlightenment. You have great will to practice the conduct of the bodhisattvas.

Calling the Guru from Afar (abbreviated version)

With the first part of the abbreviated prayer, you remember the kindness of the guru. You can relate the lines to yourself in the following way:

> Magnificently glorious guru, dispelling the darkness of my ignorance;
> Magnificently glorious guru, revealing the path of liberation to me;
> Magnificently glorious guru, liberating me from the waters of samsara;

---

[55] Rinpoche's translation is: "Please grant me blessings to have the dauntless will of the altruistic mind of the conduct of the sons of the Victorious Ones."

> Magnificently glorious guru, eliminating the diseases of my five
> poisons…

In the second part of the prayer you request for success in realizing the whole graduated path to enlightenment.

> Magnificently glorious guru, who is my wish-granting jewel,
> I beseech you, please grant me blessings.
> Magnificently glorious guru, please grant me blessings
> To remember impermanence and death from my heart.
> Magnificently glorious guru, please grant me blessings
> To generate the thought of no-need in my mind.

No-need means anything that interferes with Dharma practice, with achieving the happiness of future lives, liberation and, especially, enlightenment.

At the end of *Calling the Guru from Afar*, whether the long or short version, make the strong request that you and all sentient beings, from life to life, never give rise to heresy for even a second, do actions only pleasing to the guru and accomplish all the guru's holy wishes by yourself alone. Since this is a most important prayer, with the root of all development dependent on it, pray not only for yourself but also for all sentient beings. Every time you dedicate merit or recite a prayer, you should also dedicate for all other sentient beings.

> May I not give rise to heresy even for even a second
> In regard to the actions of the glorious guru.
> May I see whatever actions are done as pure.
> With this devotion, may I receive the guru's blessings in my heart.

After this, you can also make the request from the mahamudra teaching by Panchen Losang Chökyi Gyältsän, who also composed *Lama Chöpa*:

> Please grant me blessings to see the guru as buddha, to have renunciation of samsara and to take upon myself the whole responsibility for liberating all sentient beings from all their suffering.

You can also recite the following verse:

> O virtuous teacher, whatever your holy body,
> Retinue, life span, realm and so forth,
> Whatever your supreme and excellent name,
> May I become only like you, to benefit all sentient beings.

The guru then absorbs into you, blessing your body, speech and mind. You can do the same meditation of the guru entering the heart as at the end of *Lama Chöpa* or *Lama Tsongkhapa Guru Yoga*.

Praise and Prayer to Noble Avalokiteshvara

Because this prayer is so long, you might think, "What's the point of saying all this? It takes such a long time." But this is the admiring prayer to Chenrezig written by His Holiness the Seventh Dalai Lama. This prayer has the benefit that if one recites it every day, at the death time, when one passes away, one will be able to see Chenrezig, and one's life will always be guided by Chenrezig. It contains the lam-rim, including the sufferings of the beings in the six realms, and also the qualities of Chenrezig. It's a very interesting prayer. It causes to arise unbearable devotion and also strong renunciation of samsara, because it describes the nature of people in degenerate times. It also mentions that the pure teachings of the Buddha are about to finish.

In previous times, when the Seventh Dalai Lama was living in Lhasa, one old monk in Drepung Monastery used to say this praise to Chenrezig every day. He wasn't a monk who knew much Dharma; he wasn't a geshe or a particularly learned monk.

One day, looking surprised, His Holiness the Seventh Dalai Lama suddenly mentioned to the people around him, the monks and servants, "What has happened this morning? It has become so quiet. The old monk isn't making any noise. I think he has gone." This means that every morning His Holiness could hear the old monk saying this praise to Chenrezig that His Holiness had written, even though Drepung was many miles away from the Dalai Lama's palace. The morning that His Holiness said that the old monk must have gone, the old monk had actually died in Drepung. Somehow the Dalai Lama's holy mind could understand and see this.

Request to the Supreme Compassionate One

I received the oral transmission of this requesting prayer from Kyabje Trulshik Rinpoche, a former head of the Nyingma tradition. It was composed by Kyabje Trulshik Rinpoche's root guru, who had many visions and other good things happen while doing Chenrezig retreat when he was fifteen years old. He wrote this requesting prayer to Chenrezig during that retreat. I find this prayer very inspiring; it's very soothing and very effective.

> Behold with compassion tough-skinned beings like me
> Who maintain a religious manner but do not achieve the great meaning . . .

Here, *great meaning* refers to practicing Dharma. On the basis of guru devotion, correctly following the virtuous friend once you have found him, you then practice the graduated path of the being of lower capability, seeking the happiness of future lives, such as a good rebirth and so forth. You seek rebirth in a pure land of buddha where you can become enlightened or rebirth with a perfect human body qualified by eight freedoms and ten richnesses. Also, there is the human body with seven qualities[56] and the one with eight ripening qualities (*nam min gyi yön tän gyä*),[57] highly recommended by Lama Tsongkhapa. If we want to have quick development and great achievement of the path to enlightenment, we must achieve a human body with the eight ripening qualities. Lama Tsongkhapa emphasized that very much.

By practicing the graduated path of the being of middle capability, the three higher trainings, then with renunciation, the determination to be free from samsara by realizing how it is only of the nature of suffering, you can then achieve liberation from samsara, freedom from the oceans of samsaric suffering and its causes, karma and delusion.

Then, by practicing the graduated path of the being of higher capability, with the bodhicitta motivation that seeks enlightenment in order to bring other sentient beings to enlightenment, you achieve enlightenment.

These are the three great meanings, or purposes, of life.

---

[56] High caste, perfect body, wealth, power, wisdom, long life and healthy body and mind.
[57] Having a long life, a handsome body, a good family, wealth, honest speech, a good reputation, a male body and a strong body and mind.

> Look upon us with compassion, O Lama Chenrezig,
> Mother attached by compassion to all sentient beings,
> Who is the special sole refuge of the Snow Land.
> May I and all others quickly attain your state of enlightenment.

The compassion of all the buddhas manifests in Chenrezig, and Chenrezig manifests to us in the human form of His Holiness the Dalai Lama. You can see that this description exactly fits Chenrezig. You can also say, ". . . Mother attached by compassion to us, all sentient beings."

In the past, many years ago, during Lama Yeshe's time, I used to go to Lawudo to do nyung näs. I did this when I was building the monastery at Lawudo, of course, but even after that. The Thamo nuns from the nunnery-monastery down below Lawudo used to come up to do the nyung näs, and they would chant *Request to the Supreme Compassionate One*.

It's a very good prayer, in which you are expressing your mistakes. You are trying to practice Dharma with your body, speech and mind, but when you check, in reality, nothing has become Dharma. Nothing has become pure Dharma because your motivation has always been the eight worldly concerns. You have been looking for the happiness of this life, with attachment to the pleasures of food, clothing, a good reputation and other things. And because of your attachment to the happiness and comfort of this life, you dislike it when there's discomfort. Because of your attachment to having a good reputation, to having people say nice things about you, you dislike having a bad reputation. Because of your attachment to receiving praise from other people, you dislike it when you don't receive praise or when you receive the opposite, criticism. Because of your attachment to people giving you presents or offerings, you dislike it when you don't receive them. Both are suffering: attachment clinging to these four desirable things is suffering; and because of the attachment, your mind becomes unhappy with these four undesirable things, so this is also suffering. Your life is tormented by attachment to this life. These eight worldly dharmas torment you, keeping you suffering in the prison of samsara. And if you think about from life to life, the eight worldly dharmas make you to be born again and again in samsara.

I cried for quite a long time when the Thamo nuns chanted this prayer during a nyung nä at Lawudo.

13. Taking the Restoring and Purifying Ordination

REFUGE AND BODHICITTA

AFTER TAKING REFUGE, think, "I'm going to generate bodhicitta in order to successfully accomplish the works for myself and the works for other sentient beings."

PURIFYING THE PLACE

> Everywhere may the ground be pure,
> Free of the roughness of pebbles and so forth.
> May it be in the nature of sapphire,
> And as smooth as the palm of one's hand.

After *Refuge and Bodhicitta* comes the prayer for purifying the place, for transforming the place into a pure realm. This is a means of accumulating extensive merit. Before we invoke the holy objects of Guru, Buddha, Dharma and Sangha, we should clean the place and then also mentally visualize it as a pure realm, as beautiful as possible, with all good qualities.[58]

Doing the practice of purifying the place has a purpose. For example, if we were going to invite a king or some other important person to our house, we would first clean the house to receive them. In a similar way, we need to clean the place where we are going to invoke all the buddhas and bodhisattvas.

Buddhas do not see phenomena as clean or dirty, as we do. To a buddha's senses, everything appears as only pure, as only of the nature of great bliss. However, even though nothing is dirty to the buddhas, we need to purify and accumulate merit in order to create the causes to generate the

---

[58] For the benefits of cleaning the place, see appendix 1.

graduated path to enlightenment for sentient beings. This is why we visualize a pure place, as described in the prayer.

The place becomes like a pure realm, not an ordinary place with suffering. The ground is sapphire and smooth like the palm of a hand. The ground isn't solid, but soft and blissful in nature; stepping on it is like stepping on an innerspring mattress. There are no rocks, thorns or anything else to hurt you as you walk on it. There are no dirty or ugly things. Instead, the pure realm is filled with many beautiful things, such as pools with huge lotuses having petals the size of a drum. Like in a park, there are many huge flowers and beautiful trees. Birds are flying around making the sounds of Dharma. When the wind blows through the beautiful flowering trees, you also hear the sounds of Dharma. And the whole atmosphere is filled with a fragrant smell.

Think that the place is as beautiful as possible. The purer and more beautiful you are able to visualize it, the more merit you will accumulate.

Invocation

Next is the invocation of the merit field, where we invite all the buddhas and bodhisattvas to be present.[59]

> Savior of every single sentient being;
> Destroyer of all the multitudes of maras;
> Completely understanding all phenomena:[60]
> Qualified Destroyer, with all your entourage,[61]
> I'm requesting you to be here.

This prayer was recited by Sumaghada (Magadha Zangmo), a woman from Magadha, the area around Bodhgaya in India, when she wanted to invite Buddha and his entourage to her home to offer them a meal. Her husband, who was a Hindu, said, "Even if you invoke Buddha and his entourage, they won't come." She replied, "They will come."

So, holding incense in her hand, Sumaghada sat at the door of her house

---

[59] Previously, *Invocation* came after *Extensive Power of Truth*.
[60] Past, present and future.
[61] The bodhisattvas and the rest of the holy beings.

and recited this prayer. When she said the prayer, many of the Buddha's disciples, looking glorious, immediately appeared in space between the mountains and her house. As each one appeared, because he looked magnificent, Sumaghada's husband thought, "Maybe this is Buddha." He kept asking, "Is that Buddha?" and Sumaghada kept saying, "No." With their psychic powers, Buddha's entourage flew through space riding on lions, elephants and other animals. The very last one to come was Buddha.

Buddha one-pointedly, continually, thinks only of working for sentient beings. Therefore, as Sumaghada had the karma to receive Buddha and make offerings to him, when she recited the invocation, Buddha and all his disciples immediately came, and she was then able to make offerings to them.

In reality, it is similar for us, though we don't see it because of our karma. Whenever we do an invocation or make a request, Buddha is there all the time with us, whatever we are doing, wherever we are, and whether we are happy or suffering. It's just that because of our impure karma, our karmic obscurations, we don't see it. The only problem is from our side.

Offering Prayer

This verse is for blessing and multiplying the actually arranged and mentally transformed offerings. Visualize that the whole of space is filled with offerings. Besides all the beautiful objects on the earth, which appear according to our karma, mentally transform offerings that fill the whole of space.

Offering Cloud Mantra

> OM NAMO BHAGAVATE VAJRA SARA PRAMARDANE /
> TATHAGATAYA / ARHATE SAMYAKSAM BUDDHAYA /
> TADYATHA /OM VAJRE VAJRE / MAHA VAJRE / MAHA TEJA
> VAJRE / MAHA VIDYA VAJRE / MAHA BODHICITTA VAJRE
> / MAHA BODHI MANDO PASAM KRAMANA VAJRE / SARVA
> KARMA AVARANA VISHO DHANA VAJRE SVAHA

We then recite three times the mantra that blesses and multiplies the offerings so that they become clouds of offerings filling the whole of space.

Reciting this mantra has two functions: it blesses the offerings we have arranged and it causes each buddha in all the ten directions to receive clouds of offerings.

In addition to the offerings we have actually arranged, we visualize that each buddha and bodhisattva receives numberless offerings.

When you chant the *Offering Cloud Mantra*, you can also think of all the offerings in your own room; in the gompas of all the FPMT centers; in Khachö Dechen Ling, the house in Aptos, California; and in Amitabha Buddha Pure Land, the retreat place in Washington state. Offer all the flowers, both outside in the gardens and inside the houses. Offer also the many thousands of light offerings, outside and inside, large and small (there are many of the small Christmas lights, as well as bigger ones). Also offer the many water offerings in various rooms, but especially in the offering rooms. Offer the tea and food offerings. Even though you haven't been to the two houses and don't have an exact picture of the places, just think of offering all the many flower, light, water, tea and food offerings that are there.

Then chant the *Offering Cloud Mantra*, and by the power of the mantra each of the numberless buddhas and bodhisattvas receives skies of offerings. Each flower offering, whether big or tiny, increases to become skies of flower offerings to each buddha and bodhisattva. Each small Christmas light offering at the centers and at the Aptos and Washington houses appears as numberless light offerings to each buddha and bodhisattva. If you just think of all the offerings and then chant this mantra, each buddha and bodhisattva receives all those offerings.

Extensive Power of Truth

> By the power of truth of the Three Rare Sublime Ones,
> The blessings of all the buddhas and bodhisattvas,
> The great wealth of the completed two types of merit,
> And the pure and inconceivable sphere of phenomena;
> May these piles of clouds of offerings arising through transformation by the bodhisattvas Arya Samantabhadra, Manjushri, and so forth—unimaginable and inexhaustible, equaling the sky—arise and, in the presence of the buddhas and bodhisattvas of the ten directions, be received.

After the *Offering Cloud Mantra*, we recite a prayer called *The Power of Truth* to ensure that what we pray for actually happens, that the holy objects actually receive the many offerings we have visualized. We pray for all the offerings to happen as visualized and for all the buddhas to receive all the offerings as visualized.

When you recite *The Power of Truth* you *must* visualize that each buddha and bodhisattva has received numberless offerings, skies of offerings. The more offerings—one hundred, one hundred thousand, one million, one billion—you are able to think they have received, the more causes of enlightenment you collect. If you visualize a billion offerings, you create one billion causes of enlightenment as well as, by the way, one billion causes of liberation from samsara, of the happiness of all future lives, and also of the happiness of this life. All the happiness and success of this life comes by the way, even if you are not thinking about it or looking for it. It comes through Dharma—everything comes through Dharma practice. You might be looking only for enlightenment, but liberation, the happiness of future lives and the happiness of this life also come. Everything comes.

Seven-Limb Prayer

After this, we accumulate merit with the seven-limb practice.

> I prostrate with my three doors.
> I make all the offerings both mentally and actually transformed.
> I confess all negative karmas.
> I rejoice in all the merits accumulated by ordinary and higher beings.
> Please abide well until samsara ends.
> Please turn the Dharma wheel for transmigratory beings.
> I dedicate all the merits accumulated by me and by other sentient beings to achieve enlightenment.[62]

I will explain more about how to do the seven-limb practice when it comes later in the sadhana (see chapter 15). I will try to explain the important practices we have to do every day to purify and to generate realizations of

---

[62] One version of Rinpoche's translation of the seven-limb prayer.

the graduated path to enlightenment. Anyone who wants to actualize the path to enlightenment has to do these different practices many times a day. These explanations will be helpful for understanding not only this Chenrezig practice, but other deity practices as well.

Mandala Offering

Once you have received the lineage of the Eight Mahayana Precepts you can take them at the altar in your own house. At that time, offer a mandala to Chenrezig, Shakyamuni Buddha, Amitabha or whichever buddha you have visualized.

However, when a lama is giving the Eight Mahayana Precepts, do the seven-limb practice and mandala offering in relation to that lama and to all the rest of the buddhas and bodhisattvas, but not with the appearance of the lama as an ordinary human being. Stop that ordinary appearance and here, in this practice, visualize the lama as Thousand-Arm Chenrezig. The essence is Chenrezig and the aspect is also Chenrezig. And Guru Chenrezig is surrounded by the numberless buddhas and bodhisattvas of the ten directions. However, whether or not a lama is giving the vows, you always visualize the buddhas and bodhisattvas.

Visualization and Motivation

Before taking the actual ordination, do three prostrations then kneel down with your palms together at your heart in the mudra of prostration. As I just mentioned, if a lama is granting the vows, visualize him as Thousand-Arm Chenrezig, surrounded by all the numberless buddhas and bodhisattvas. Since you have visualized the guru as inseparable from Chenrezig, think that you're repeating the prayers of the ceremony after Guru Chenrezig.

To generate a bodhicitta motivation for taking the Eight Mahayana Precepts, you can use one of the motivations I gave earlier (see chapters 9, 10 and 11) or, feel deeply from your heart: "I and all other sentient beings have experienced the general sufferings of samsara[63] and the particular suffer-

---

[63] Here you can think of the eight, six or three types of suffering.

ings of the lower realms numberless times from beginningless rebirths. This suffering is depthless and beginningless. Even the Omniscient One cannot see the beginning of the samsaric suffering experienced by me and other sentient beings.

"We have experienced the hell sufferings numberless times, again and again, again and again, as well as the preta sufferings. We can see how animals are suffering, and we have been through all those sufferings again and again, again and again, without beginning. And it is the same with the human and deva sufferings.

"To take another rebirth, another set of deluded aggregates of desire, another samsara, is like jumping again into a fire. Taking another rebirth is like running from one fire into another. It's like eating food that you have vomited.

"From bodhicitta, from cherishing others, I can achieve the happiness of future lives; I can achieve all the three great meanings. Also, by having bodhicitta, I can bring each suffering sentient being, who is more precious than I am, all the temporary happiness of the three times, as well as liberation and enlightenment. Bodhicitta is unbelievably important and precious, more precious than a wish-granting jewel. Therefore, until I achieve enlightenment, until I die, this year, this month, this week and especially today, I won't allow myself to be under the control of the self-cherishing thought for even a second. Until enlightenment, until my death, this year, this month, this week and especially today, I won't allow myself to be separated from bodhicitta for even a second.

"What sentient beings want is happiness, including the peerless happiness of enlightenment, and what they do not want is suffering. There's no way to accomplish this except through my achieving enlightenment. Achieving enlightenment depends on the fundamental practices of protecting karma and practicing morality. Therefore, to lead all sentient beings to enlightenment, I'm going to take the Eight Mahayana Precepts and keep them until sunrise tomorrow."

Actual Ordination

The special animals, *the divine wise horse and the great elephant*, are examples related to the works that Buddha accomplished. Cessation of all mental stains is the work for self and completion of all realizations is the work for others.

The purpose of mentioning your name— *. . . I, who am called [say your name] . . .*—is to make sure that you are sincere in doing the practice for sentient beings.

. . . in order to benefit means you bring temporary happiness to all sentient beings and *in order to liberate* means you bring not only temporary but ultimate happiness to all sentient beings. Think, "I am taking the Eight Mahayana Precepts to bring temporary and ultimate happiness to all sentient beings, to free them from true suffering and true cause of suffering."

As you say "in order to eliminate famine," remember all those countries in the world that have problems of famine. Taking the Eight Mahayana Precepts is a solution to famine in the world and helps the economy, helping to bring plentiful production of food and so forth. It helps to bring prosperity.

Remember that in the past, as I explained in the benefits of the Eight Mahayana Precepts (see chapter 5), many Dharma kings had rules about taking the Eight Mahayana Precepts, and taking them completely changed the country. Since rains came at the right time and crops grew well, there was no scarcity of food. The whole environment changed when the people started taking the Eight Mahayana Precepts.

As you say "in order to eliminate sickness," think of curing and preventing mental and physical sickness. Remember all the sick people in hospitals and at home, those who aren't sure whether they will survive today or not. Think of the people who are dying now and those who are having operations and don't know whether they are going to survive or not. However, they have no choice: there is no other way for them to live. Think of all the people with cancer, AIDS and other incurable diseases who are experiencing so much suffering, so much worry and fear. There are many diseases for which there is no treatment.

Think, "I'm taking and keeping the Eight Mahayana Precepts today for all the sentient beings who have problems of famine and sickness, to free them from the suffering of famine and sickness. I'm taking them for those who have problems of birth, old age, sickness and death. I'm taking these Eight Mahayana Precepts today for all those who are under the control of karma and delusion, whose life is not free but determined by karma and delusion."

Taking the Eight Mahayana Precepts also helps to stop war. With *in*

TAKING THE RESTORING AND PURIFYING ORDINATION 171

order to eliminate war,[64] feel in your heart, "My taking and keeping the Eight Mahayana Precepts is the solution for world peace, and for the peace of all sentient beings, not only those in this world. What I'm doing is a method to stop all quarrels, fighting and war between sentient beings." Ultimately, it is a method to actualize the path and to lead all sentient beings to enlightenment.

You can also dedicate the merit that you accumulate by living in the vows to all the people with relationship problems. It is as if they are living their life in hell or in a nest of rattlesnakes. They have no happiness, day or night. They are so suffocated by their many problems that they can't breathe freely. Think, "My taking the Eight Mahayana Precepts today is also to pacify the suffering of those in difficult relationships and to bring them happiness."

Think, "My taking and keeping the Eight Mahayana Precepts is to bring all these benefits to the world. It is for the peace and prosperity of the world and of all sentient beings."

At the end of the third repetition of the actual ordination, without a wandering mind, you must generate the thought, "I have received pure Eight Mahayana Precepts, the Restoring and Purifying Ordination, from Guru Chenrezig, surrounded by all the buddhas and bodhisattvas."

If you are taking the precepts from a lama, when the lama then says, "Thab yin no," which means, "This is the method," you reply, "Leg so," which means, "Yes." Here, *This is the method* might be related to the Eight Mahayana Precepts rather than to enlightenment.

On the second day of a nyung nä, when you say "from this time until sunrise tomorrow" (*ji si sang nyi ma shar gyi bar du*), you should make the time precise in your mind so that you don't break the precepts. Think that you are going to completely fast from this moment until sunrise tomorrow: "To achieve enlightenment for sentient beings, I won't eat or drink until sunrise tomorrow."

The text says that on the final morning of a nyung nä you are liberated from silence when the dawn time starts, and after dawn, you can have soup.

---

[64] Rinpoche has added this, along with *in order to stop the harm of the four elements*, to the original ordination ceremony.

In some monasteries the vase water is passed around at that time. At this time there's already much light, and you can see the palm of your hand and everything else clearly. If there are surrounding mountains, the mountains have sun on them or are about to be hit by sunlight. At that time, when everything is clear, you can then serve soup.

Generally, the day starts when the east is whitish and the rest of the sky is dark. That's the very beginning of the day. Dawn time has three divisions: the first is when the eastern sky is whitish, the second is when it becomes red and the third is when it becomes whiter. In his teachings, Pabongka Dechen Nyingpo says that the change comes in three colors.

When the eastern sky starts to become a little white, that's the very beginning of the day, the first phase of the dawn time. However, it depends on what you intended when you said "until sunrise tomorrow" in making the vow. If you decided that it's when sunlight actually comes to the place where you are, you should wait until then.

There are many details when it comes to *until sunrise tomorrow*. Does it mean the sun rising in this world? Or in a specific place? There are many different sunrises. If somebody is in a house in a hidden corner between huge mountains, maybe the sun won't even reach there. And there are places like Iceland where there's no sun for six months, so you would have to do a very long nyung nä, a six-month nyung nä, until the sun rises.

In the vinaya and in other teachings, the beginning of the day is generally defined as when the stars have lost their brightness. So, you can have food at that time. But it is up to the individual person. You might want to sleep for many hours and eat later—even when the sun sets. The Sherpas in Solu Khumbu like to get up very early in the morning and have food early. It makes it easier for them to do nyung näs. It helps them not to lose the inspiration to do nyung näs. They don't get fed up because it's so difficult and then think, "I won't ever do a nyung nä again!"

Basically, it depends on what you decide when you make the vow. If, by knowing this, you then make a particular commitment, that's correct. That is what is explained in the vinaya teachings.

The Commitment Prayer to Keep the Precepts

After thinking, "I have received the restoring and purifying ordination in the presence of Chenrezig and all the buddhas and bodhisattvas," then recite or repeat after the lama the *Commitment Prayer to Keep the Precepts*. As you do so, think, "As the previous Tathagatas kept these eight precepts for the sake of sentient beings, today I am also going to keep these eight precepts until sunrise tomorrow in order to free each and every sentient being from all their suffering and its causes and lead them to enlightenment."

On the second day of a nyung nä, in the parts where it mentions actions of speech ("I shall not speak false words" and "I shall avoid singing . . . "), it's good to think, "I'm going to keep silence to achieve enlightenment for the sake of sentient beings." Remember that precisely at that time. When it comes to abstaining from telling lies and from singing, remember to dedicate your keeping silence for sentient beings so that it becomes virtuous.

In the eight precepts of the Lesser Vehicle path *intoxicants* generally refers only to alcohol, but here in the Eight Mahayana Precepts it also includes tobacco. Tobacco is a black food, or substance, along with meat and eggs. Taking the eight precepts of the Lesser Vehicle path involves abstaining from only alcohol; the words of the vow don't mention to abstain from cigarettes. I think that's why many Theravadin monks smoke cigarettes. Perhaps they're not emphasizing the mind so much, even though generally in Buddhism the main emphasis is the mind.

Tobacco and other drugs pollute the mind. Opium is the worst, the most polluting. Even the smell of opium is a great pollution. It destroys merit and blocks the channels and chakras. Here, *intoxicants* refers to things that don't give energy to the mind to do virtuous things. On the other hand, things like Tibetan tea give you energy to read, study or do virtuous activities instead of being lazy.

When you say "I shall not eat food at the wrong time" on the first day of a nyung nä retreat, you should also think that you will eat only one meal. When you take the Eight Mahayana Precepts regularly or at least quite often, you can have breakfast, even if you are not taking the precepts every day. But if you take them very rarely, it's better to keep them strictly. It is better to be stricter the one time you do the practice. The prayer itself says not to eat at the wrong time, which means in the afternoon—it doesn't specify one meal or anything else. So, here you should think, "I will eat one meal and I will not eat at the wrong time." You should motivate to eat one meal, and the reason is to achieve enlightenment for the sake of sentient beings. There are these two things. This renunciation becomes powerful because you're making this sacrifice to benefit all sentient beings.

If you are completing a nyung nä while the rest of the group is continuing, you can still take the Eight Mahayana Precepts again on your final day, either after breakfast or even before breakfast, even though you are not going to do the nyung nä. By taking the ordination, you are practicing some part of the nyung nä. You're not practicing exactly according to this text of Chenrezig practice; but you are making vows to abstain from committing a certain number of negative karmas for that day, so it becomes that much of a nyung nä.

According to His Holiness Serkong Rinpoche's advice, after making the vow to eat just one meal you should eat well and as much as you want, then when you've finished eating, stop completely. You shouldn't decide to stop eating, then change your mind and eat again. If you do that, it's not eating one meal, even though it might not be after 12 o'clock. First eat well and then, when you decide not to eat, stop completely so that it's one meal.

There's an interesting story about two friends who used to take the Eight Mahayana Precepts. The wife of one of them pushed her husband to eat some fruit in the afternoon. Since she insisted so much, he ate the fruit. The other person didn't break the precepts.

The person who didn't break the precepts was reborn as a king. The person who broke the precepts by eating fruit in the afternoon at the insistence of his wife was reborn as a naga in the land of that king, who was his friend before.

The king had a pond, and one time a beautiful fruit came out of the pond. The king's gardener picked the fruit and gave it to the bodyguard who stood at the palace gate. The bodyguard then gave the fruit to a minister who was going inside the palace to see the king. That minister gave the fruit to the prince, and the prince gave it to the king. The king asked, "Who gave you this fruit? The king checked back and back and back, until he came to the gardener. Since the gardener had never given him such fruit before, the king thought that the gardener must have been getting such fruit all the time and eating it all himself. (I think the fruit wasn't commonly found around there.) So when the king finally found out that the fruit had come from the gardener, he threatened to imprison or kill the gardener if he didn't give him more.

The gardener then cried and prayed hard at the pond for another fruit to be produced. I've forgotten the last part of the story. I think the naga told the king about their both taking the Eight Mahayana Precepts in their past

TAKING THE RESTORING AND PURIFYING ORDINATION 175

life and about how the king didn't degenerate them, but his eating food in the evening became the cause for him to be born as a naga.

Here in the nyung nä practice you should also avoid black food, which is not mentioned in the eight pratimoksha precepts. Black foods such as meat, onion and garlic make the body impure; they pollute the body. When the body becomes impure, it makes the mind foggy, or unclear, so that you can't meditate well. Nyung nä practice is from Action Tantra, which is why there is an emphasis on keeping the body clean, which involves avoiding black food.

If you do nyung näs rarely and do a nyung nä on your own in a place where food is easily available, it's good to eat the three whites (yogurt,[65] milk and butter) and cheese, rice, flour and those types of food. That's the best way to do a nyung nä. However, when a big group of people do a nyung nä together, as happens in Lawudo, or it's a place where food is difficult to get, you then have to use vegetables and other types of food.

There are gradations in the strictness of the practice. The main black foods are meat, alcohol, garlic, onion and radish. I think this refers especially to the round radish that has a very bad smell and makes the body have bad gas. The best is to eat just completely white food. You can have rice, flour, yogurt, cheese, milk and butter. You can arrange something like the section in a supermarket where there are seventy different types of cheese. Ice cream and similar sweet white foods are also fine. That's the purest way to do a nyung nä.

There are other Action Tantra samayas, such as not eating food from leaves, from broken pots or from the palm of your hand. Drinking from the palm is there in the nyung nä practice. You put the nectar in the palm of your hand and drink it, but it says not to eat from the palm.

In the evening of the first day, you can have honey and melted brown sugar, but not thick liquids like yogurt, fruit juice with pulp or straight milk. After noon, there should be no yogurt and no whole milk when you are fasting.

This applies not only to nyung näs but even when taking the eight precepts of the pratimoksha vow or the Eight Mahayana Precepts. The prayer of the precepts says not to eat after noon, so you shouldn't eat yogurt, whole

---

[65] Rinpoche usually says "curd."

milk or anything substantial that makes kaka. It doesn't say, and I haven't heard, that you can't have milk tea, but in the Theravadin tradition you can have only black tea. I wouldn't suggest having thick milk tea if you're fasting, but I think you can have thin milk tea made with less milk, so that drinking it doesn't break the vow. It actually says that you can't have milk, but you can have thin milk. Essentially, when you do a nyung nä, the milk used to make tea should be thinner, with much more water than milk. It is better that way.

But a candy or anything else that melts in your mouth is allowed.

On the second day, the actual fasting day, from dawn you stop talking and don't take even one grain of food or one drop of water. In the traditions of some lamas and some monasteries, you're not allowed to swallow even your saliva. At one Kagyü monastery in Darjeeling, people doing nyung näs carry a bottle into which they spit. This is the very strict tradition according to some lamas; but the Seventh Dalai Lama says, "I haven't heard that and I haven't seen any reference for doing that in the scriptures of any Indian pandit."

I would like to emphasize generally that eating vegetarian food is very important. Especially in Singapore, Hong Kong and Taiwan, people who are not vegetarian eat so many animals in one day. One person's food for one day contains so many shrimps, scallops and other animals. Therefore, you should follow vegetarian practice as much as possible and also explain to other people the negative karma of harming and killing other sentient beings. In this way, if one person you have talked to becomes vegetarian through understanding karma, you have liberated so many animals even in one day, because that person then won't harm or kill those animals. Since for the number of years that person lives they stop giving that harm, you have liberated all those animals that that would have been killed.

Be vegetarian as much as you can and also tell others about it, especially people in Singapore, Hong Kong and Taiwan. It has incredible benefit. Since the person who becomes vegetarian stops creating that negative karma, you protect them from the lower realms. Each of those negative karmas makes them to be reborn in the lower realms. You also protect them from all the suffering in the human realm that results from that negative karma. You also protect all the animals from suffering and shortage of life.

In Tibet, it is common for people to eat meat, but many people eat one big animal. In countries such as Singapore, Hong Kong and Taiwan, since one person eats many small animals in one day, there is more benefit in being vegetarian there.

The Mantra of Pure Morality

Then recite twenty-one times the mantra that purifies and revives the precepts that have been degenerated.

> OM AMOGHA SHILA SAMBHARA [SAMBHARA] / BHARA BHARA / MAHA SHUDDHA SATTVA PADMA VIBHUSHITA BHUJA / DHARA DHARA / SAMANTA / AVALOKITE HUM PHAT SVAHA

> Due to all the merits that I have accumulated now by taking the Eight Mahayana Precepts, all my past merits and all my future merits and all the merits of the three times accumulated by all other sentient beings, including the bodhisattvas, and by all the buddhas, may I and all sentient beings be able to complete the paramita of morality by keeping it purely and without pride.

In the *Mani Kabum*, Songtsen Gampo explains that reciting the mantra of pure morality has three benefits: you purify past degeneration of morality and precepts, you receive the bodhisattvas' pure morality and you're also able to practice, or preserve, pure morality.

My suggestion is that, as part of refuge practice in the morning, do prostrations by reciting the Thirty-five Buddhas' names or do at least three prostrations, and at the end kneel down and recite this mantra five, seven, ten or more times. (In the ceremony of the Eight Mahayana Precepts, you recite it twenty-one times.) There is no doubt that it's very good for Sangha, for monks and nuns, to recite this mantra even when not taking the Eight Mahayana Precepts. But it would also be good for laypeople who have taken five or any other number of lay vows to recite this mantra to be able to keep those vows purely. It's very good to be able live purely in the vows that you have taken, to not degenerate them. Even if you're not taking the Eight Mahayana Precepts, it's still good to recite this mantra to be able to live purely in the vows that you have taken.

In Tibetan, this mantra is called *tsul trim nam dag zung*, the *zung* of pure morality, where *zung* means a mental state that is mindful, or conscientious, in abandoning negative karma and living in virtue. That is its essential meaning, even though *zung* is generally translated as "mantra." In Tibetan, mantra is actually *ngag*, which means protecting the mind. Again, mantra doesn't mean something you just chant. It contains the whole path to enlightenment and all the qualities of a buddha's holy body, holy speech and holy mind. It contains the four noble truths and all the paths: the Hinayana path, the Paramitayana path and the tantric path. The meaning is similar to that of OM MANI PADME HUM. Mantra performs the function of protecting the mind, and within that comes all the tantric paths: the paths of Action Tantra, Performance Tantra, Yoga Tantra and Highest Yoga Tantra. Those paths protect the mind from the defilements, from the disturbing-thought obscurations and the subtle obscurations, and bring one to enlightenment.

Chanting this mantra of pure morality helps you to keep purely the vows you have taken and also to purify vows you have degenerated in the past. Those who have recently taken vows should recite this in the morning to be able to continue to live in pure vows. If you have pure vows, everything then happens: you're able to achieve the whole lam-rim, up to enlightenment.

At this point, if you have taken the restoring and purifying ordination from a lama, do three prostrations, as before, to the lama visualized as Thousand-Arm Chenrezig.

Dedication

You can then dedicate the merit with the following verses:

> May bodhicitta be generated within my mind
> And in the minds of all sentient beings.
> May those who have generated bodhicitta develop it.
>
> Just as the brave Manjushri and Samantabhadra, too,
> Realized things as they are,
> I, too, dedicate all these merits in the best way,
> That I may follow their perfect example.

I dedicate all these merits
With the dedication praised as the best
By all the buddhas of the three times,
To quickly enlighten all sentient beings.

Due to all the merits of the three times accumulated by me and by all buddhas, bodhisattvas and other sentient beings, which are merely labeled by the mind, may the I, which is merely labeled by the mind, achieve enlightenment, which is merely labeled by the mind, and lead all sentient beings, who are merely labeled by the mind, to that enlightenment, which is merely labeled by the mind.

Feel that taking the Eight Mahayana Precepts is your contribution to world peace—to the peace of this world and all sentient beings. You have taken eight precepts, which means you have made vows not to do eight actions that harm sentient beings directly or indirectly. Since other sentient beings don't receive those eight harms, it means they receive peace, directly or indirectly, from you. The absence of those eight harms is peace. This is a real, practical contribution to world peace. For all the hours that you are living in these vows, all sentient beings are receiving peace from you.

Therefore, rejoice. Feel happy that you have made your life beneficial for sentient beings.

14. Requests through to Invocation

REQUESTS TO THE LINEAGE GURUS

AFTER TAKING the Eight Mahayana Precepts, make requests to the lineage lamas of this nyung nä practice, which was handed down from Chenrezig to Bhikshuni Lakshmi. All these lineage lamas, who achieved Chenrezig, have incredible life stories describing how they practiced and achieved realizations (see chapters 3 and 4). Request each of them to grant you the same realizations. As you do, it's good to remember their life story and generate a strong wish to become like them. It is very inspiring.

Recite the requesting prayer with the awareness that all these lineage lamas generated bodhicitta, renouncing themselves and cherishing others. While they generated all three principles of the path, especially remember how they all generated bodhicitta and how they all achieved Chenrezig. By bearing much hardship in doing many nyung näs, they purified all their past mental stains and completed the path to enlightenment. They then brought great benefit to other sentient beings and to the teaching of Buddha. Being aware of their qualities and actions, you then make the requests.

You can visualize all the lineage lamas piled up above your crown, with each lama seated above the crown of the one below. After you have made the request to one lama, he absorbs into the one below. The lineage lamas gradually absorb in this way until they have all absorbed into your direct guru, the lama from whom you received the Chenrezig initiation. That direct guru then absorbs into your heart and you think that you have generated all the realizations of the direct and indirect nyung nä lineage lamas.

If this isn't effective for your mind you can also do the visualization in another way. Visualize all the lineage lamas in front of you, emitting white nectar beams that constantly purify you and all other sentient beings. As you finish the request to each of the lineage lamas, with mention of his name a replica of that lama absorbs into your heart and you think, "I have achieved all the realizations of the path and the result. I have completed the two paths of method and wisdom and achieved the result, the two kayas."

Once the actual requests to the lineage lamas are finished, with Kelzang Gyatso, the Seventh Dalai Lama, the rest of the verses in the requesting prayer describe the three principles of the path and the graduated path of Action Tantra, the path having sign and the path not having sign.

The verse that begins *Please bless me to renounce all the perfections of cyclic existence...*, talks about renouncing all samsaric perfections and then generating bodhicitta.

The next verse, *Please bless me to eliminate ordinary appearance and grasping...*, describes the six graduated steps in generating yourself as Chenrezig.

With the next verse, *Please bless me to accomplish each and every common attainment...*, you ask to be granted blessings to generate the realizations of Action Tantra, from the practices of the concentration with four-branched recitation, and then to complete the eminent concentration with the yogas of concentrating on fire and sound.

With *Please bless me to uproot the two obscurations...*, you then ask to be granted blessings to achieve the great concentration that gives pure liberation, and in that way, with the accumulation of skillful merit, to eliminate the two obscurations.

With the dharmakaya and the holy form bodies that fulfill the wishes of sentient beings, you then liberate all sentient beings: *Please bless me to attain soon the complete direct exalted wisdom regarding all phenomena...*

INSTANTANEOUS GENERATION

After all the lineage lamas have absorbed into you, you become empty. Out of emptiness then generate yourself as Chenrezig.[66]

> I instantaneously arise as the holy body of the Great Compassionate One.

---

[66] This is only if you have received a Chenrezig great initiation or a Highest Yoga Tantra initiation. Otherwise visualize Chenrezig in space in front of you, on the crown of your head or in your heart.

Generate yourself as one-face, two-arm Chenrezig, who is like White Tara but male and without the eyes on the hands, feet and forehead. Like White Tara, Chenrezig holds a lotus in his left hand, and his right hand is in the mudra of granting sublime realization.

You have to generate yourself as the deity because you can't do the blessing of the offerings to the merit field with the appearance and conception of yourself as an ordinary being. The purpose of generating yourself as the deity at this point is to be able to bless the offerings. This is besides the general tantric purpose of meditating on the path that is similar to the four result-time purities. The general purpose of visualizing yourself as the deity, the place as the mandala and so forth is to transform everything into pure appearance.

The person who is most qualified to do nyung nä practice is someone who has received a Chenrezig great initiation because this allows them to self-generate as the deity. However, this is not a strict requirement.

It's very common in the East for laypeople to do nyung näs. Since many laypeople there don't know how to read, they can't read the text; they simply take the vows, do the prostrations and recite OM MANI PADME HUM all day long. As I've already explained, my mother couldn't read at all; she couldn't recognize even one syllable, not even OM or KA. But she did many nyung näs. Laypeople in the East often do nyung näs, even though on the second day many people collapse. In the break times, many of them are to be found lying on the gompa floor or outside on the ground, looking as if they've just lost World War III.

In the East, even though many people may recite prayers or read texts, it doesn't necessarily mean that they can meditate on what they are reciting. In the West, it's very different. Once something is translated into English, everyone knows the meaning of what is being said. Even someone who hasn't studied Dharma still has the intellectual capacity to understand the meaning of the words.

Blessing the Action Vase

In the action vase you put saffron water with an Action Tantra pill, which contains the twenty-five Action Tantra substances.[67] You can get these pills

---

[67] The twenty-five substances comprise five scents (white and red sandalwood, nutmeg,

from the Tibetan Medical Center in Dharamsala, the tantric colleges or some monasteries.

You also put a small branch from a tree in the vase. If possible, the tree should have some fruit on it. The text says to use a *milk tree*, but that's not always possible. If you can, use a small branch from a fruit tree or a tree with milky sap.

Blessing the Offerings

Eliminate interferers to the offerings by reciting the action mantra OM PADMANTAKRIT HUM PHAT and sprinkling water from the action vase. Visualize that millions of red one-face, two-arm Hayagrivas, a wrathful aspect of Chenrezig, are transformed from the syllable HRIH at your heart and chase away all the interferers abiding in the various offerings. (Or you can think that the drops of water you sprinkle become millions of Hayagrivas.) The interferers are chased away beyond the ocean and it is impossible for them to come back. The wrathful deities then dissolve back into the syllable at your heart, from where you transformed them.

Even if you don't do this particular meditation, you can just think that the offerings are blessed. Generating faith is important in tantric practice.

According to Kirti Tsenshab Rinpoche, when sprinkling water from the action vase in father tantra practices, sprinkle it toward the right side, and for mother tantra practices such as Cittamani Tara, Heruka, Vajrayogini and Gyalwa Gyatso, sprinkle the vase water toward the left as part of left-side conduct.

Also, Gomo Rinpoche explained that when you sprinkle the water, you can draw the Tibetan letter *chha* (ཆ) with the small branch, toward the right side in father tantra and toward the left in mother tantra. (Although Gomo Rinpoche didn't actually mention the sides, it accords with Kirti Tsenshab Rinpoche's advice.)

Whenever you offer water, flowers, light, food or any other offering, whether on an altar or somewhere else (you might see a beautiful flower in

---

camphor, Kashmiri saffron), five medicines (heart-leaved moon seed, Indian salamin, salep orchid, cuttlefish, white sweet flag root), five jewels (gold, silver, pearl, lapis lazuli, and coral or conch shell), five grains (barley, rice, wheat, lentils, sesame) and five outer nectars (honey, white crystal sugar, curd, milk, butter).

a garden or a forest or by the roadside, for example), you should first bless the offering with the mantra OM AH HUM and then offer it. OM signifies Buddha's holy body, AH signifies Buddha's holy speech and HUM, Buddha's holy mind; you are blessing the offering in the essence of Buddha's holy body, holy speech and holy mind.

If you don't recite OM AH HUM to bless the offering, different kinds of spirits, or interferers, who abide with each offering take the essence of the offering. There's a particular interferer abiding with water, flowers, light, incense and so forth. Also, if you make an offering without blessing it, various obstacles to the mind can arise. For example, if you offer a flower without blessing it, an interferer takes the essence of the flower so that it does not become a pure offering, and the interferer then causes you to develop desire. If you offer water without blessing it, your mind gets very distracted and you can't concentrate well.

When you offer anything, immediately bless the offering with OM AH HUM to stop the interferers.

Refuge and Bodhicitta

> I go for refuge, until I am enlightened,
> To the Buddha, the Dharma, and the Supreme Assembly.

In the refuge verse, the first two lines contain two types of refuge practice: causal refuge and resultant refuge. *To the Buddha, the Dharma, and the Supreme Assembly* contains the causal refuge and *until I am enlightened* contains the resultant refuge. You are practicing both types of refuge.

To achieve your ultimate goal of freeing all sentient beings from all their suffering and its causes and leading them to enlightenment, you yourself need to achieve enlightenment. In order to achieve enlightenment, you need to actualize the Dharma. By actualizing the Dharma, you then become a buddha, an omniscient being. Without actualizing the Dharma you can't be liberated from all the faults of the mind, all the obscurations; and without removing all the obscurations, you can't become a buddha. Actualizing the Dharma is what enables you to remove the obscurations. By actualizing the Dharma you also become Sangha. Your own Buddha, Dharma and Sangha are the resultant refuge, and this is the main refuge.

However, you can't accomplish this by yourself. For example, to become a qualified doctor, you have to depend upon learning from other experienced doctors. Like that, to achieve your own resultant refuge, your own Buddha, Dharma and Sangha, since you can't do it by yourself, you have to rely upon the external Buddha, Dharma and Sangha that are separate from your mental continuum. By relying upon them, you are able to actualize the Dharma and become Sangha and then Buddha.

To the Buddha, the Dharma, and the Supreme Assembly contains the causal refuge, which is possessed by the minds of others, and *until I am enlightened* contains the resultant refuge, your own future Buddha, Dharma and Sangha. *Sangha* usually means four fully ordained ones living in pure vows, but here the Sangha you become by actualizing the Dharma is the absolute Sangha.

There are absolute Buddha and conventional Buddha, absolute Dharma and conventional Dharma, and absolute Sangha and conventional Sangha. The absolute Buddha is the holy mind of dharmakaya. The conventional Buddha is the nirmanakaya or sambhogakaya form that sentient beings can see. The absolute Dharma is true path, the wisdom directly perceiving emptiness, and true cessation of suffering. Conventional Dharma is the scriptures that contain Buddha's teachings. Absolute Sangha is one who has realization of true path and true cessation of suffering. Anybody, whether ordained or lay, who has these realizations is absolute Sangha. But conventional Sangha have to be ordained, specifically four fully ordained ones living in pure vows.

> By my collections of generosity and so forth,
> May I become a buddha to benefit all migrating beings.

Here, *and so forth* refers to the rest of the six paramitas.[68] We dedicate all the merits we accumulate to achieving enlightenment in order to benefit *all migrating beings*, which means all suffering sentient beings. The Tibetan term used here is *dro wa*, which I prefer to translate as "transmigratory being" rather than "sentient being," as *transmigratory being* is very effective in causing compassion to arise. Hearing "transmigratory being" is a little different from hearing "sentient being," which is *sem chän* in Tibetan.

---

[68] Morality, patience, perseverance, concentration and wisdom.

There is no doubt that when you hear the word *dro wa*, or *transmigratory being*, and think of its meaning, compassion has to arise. Why? Because *transmigratory being* means that sentient beings have to migrate without choice. They have no freedom because they are totally controlled by karma and delusion, especially the ignorance not knowing the nature of the I. Because their consciousness is under the control of karma and delusion, they continuously have to migrate to another samsara, to another set of suffering aggregates, in one of the six realms, and then experience all the sufferings of that realm.

Because they are not free from what controls them, karma and delusion, they then die and are again reborn, either in the same realm or in another realm, where they have already reincarnated numberless times in the past. They again experience all the suffering of that realm and then again die. It goes on continuously like that. There's nothing new—they've already been born numberless times in each of those realms, experienced all the sufferings there numberless times and died there numberless times.

Until we actualize absolute Dharma—true path and true cessation of suffering—and become free from samsara, we have no choice. No matter how much we suffer from sickness, hunger, thirst, heat, cold, old age, birth, death, being separated from desirable objects, worry and fear about meeting undesirable objects, and not finding satisfaction even when we have found the objects we desire, we have to go through all these problems. For example, when we have a serious disease, particularly one that no medicine can cure, there's nothing we can do: we have to experience it. We have no choice. Since we have migrated into this samsara, since we have taken these aggregates, we have no choice: we have to go through these sufferings.

Until we become free from samsara, we have no freedom: we have to experience so many problems. We are like somebody who has to spend their whole life in prison being controlled and tortured by others. If we were free from samsara, we wouldn't need to experience these problems. Even if other people tried to harm us, we couldn't be harmed because we would have no cause to receive harm; we would be free from that cause.

It is the same with animals who are tortured by having to pull or carry heavy loads. They have no choice; they have to suffer because they have taken another samsara under the control of karma and delusion.

Sentient beings do not migrate with freedom but without choice, under the control of karma and delusion. They migrate to another samsara and again suffer. From there they again migrate to another samsara and again suffer. Like that, they go around and around continuously in the six realms. The word *transmigratory* means beings who are completely caught in the suffering of samsara. Transmigratory beings experience suffering that results from their past karma and delusion, but on top of that, while experiencing that suffering, they again create the causes, karma and delusion, to experience further suffering in the future. So, it goes on and on. This word *transmigratory* explains the entire suffering of samsara that sentient beings experience.

In this way we have been continuously suffering under the control of the root of karma and delusion and of suffering: the ignorance grasping the I, the false I, which doesn't exist. I'm not saying there's no I; there's an I that exists and there's an I that doesn't exist. There's an I that exists, but we don't realize that I. What is it? It is the I that exists in mere name, merely imputed, or labeled, by the mind. It can be said that because of not having realized that I, we have been reincarnating continuously in samsara, experiencing suffering and dying during beginningless rebirths. You could say that all this comes from not having realized the I that exists, the I that exists in mere name, merely imputed by the mind.

On the other hand, we totally believe in the I that doesn't exist, the false I. It's a false I, but we believe that it's true, that it really exists. That wrong concept is what has kept us in samsara during beginningless rebirths up to now. From that wrong concept, all the other delusions then arise, which then motivate karma, which then leaves karmic imprints on the mind, which produce future samsaric rebirth. This is how we've been experiencing all the sufferings of samsara numberless times during beginningless rebirths up to now.

When you think of the meaning of *transmigratory being*, there's no doubt that compassion has to arise because it expresses how sentient beings are suffering and how they have been suffering from beginningless time. It's not that their suffering began some eons ago. They have been suffering for time without beginning—that's what is most frightening. Sentient beings, including us, have been suffering from beginningless time.

The term *transmigratory being* gives the whole idea of how much sentient beings are suffering, totally trapped in so many wrong concepts and hallucinations, which then motivate karma, which then causes them to experience all those sufferings. It is continuously like that.

Thinking about sentient beings and how much they're suffering makes you think that you yourself must do something to help them. The best time to do that is now, in this life, while you have all the opportunities to practice Dharma. To be fully qualified to help others, you yourself need to actualize the path; you yourself need to be liberated and enlightened. The whole foundation is to practice Dharma.

This is why I always emphasize that this is almost the only life where we have all the freedom that enables us to be liberated from samsara and achieve enlightenment. Since we have this freedom, we should take the incredible opportunity that we have in this life.

Refuge and Bodhicitta is a short prayer but it has very deep meaning. It contains the whole graduated path to enlightenment: refuge, renunciation, bodhicitta, the six paramitas. If you recite this prayer while thinking of its meaning, you then generate bodhicitta. This practice alone makes the day meaningful. When we meet a friend, find a job or receive a gift, it makes us very happy; it makes our day. The practice in this one verse alone makes our day; it makes our day and our life meaningful. We accumulate infinite merit when we recite this prayer one time while meditating on its meaning and generating bodhicitta. It is because we generate bodhicitta, the thought to achieve enlightenment for the sake of infinite sentient beings, that we accumulate infinite merit. Each time we recite this prayer and generate bodhicitta we gain infinite merit. That's why it makes our day.

It's very important when we recite this prayer to meditate on its meaning.

If we also practice awareness that the merely labeled I is doing the merely labeled practice to achieve the merely labeled enlightenment, wisdom is also contained there.

Generating Bodhicitta

> With the thought wishing to liberate transmigratory beings,
> I shall always go for refuge
> To the Buddha, Dharma, and Sangha
> Until I reach the essence of enlightenment.

With the thought wishing to liberate transmigratory beings, I shall always go for refuge is particularly expressing taking Mahayana refuge. There are different ways of taking refuge according to the Hinayana, Mahayana and Vajrayana.

Invocation of the Merit Field

Next you invoke the merit field in front of you and then accumulate merit with the seven-limb practice, which begins with the limb of prostration, in which you prostrate to all the beings in the merit field.

You, as Chenrezig, emit beams from the HRIH abiding on the moon disc at your heart and invoke the Great Compassionate One and the rest of the merit field. In space in front of you, visualize an extensive thousand-petal lotus on a wide stem. Standing in the center of the lotus is Thousand-Arm Chenrezig. Above Arya Chenrezig are all the direct and indirect lineage lamas of the nyung nä practice. Around Chenrezig are all the deities of the four classes of tantra; then the Thousand Buddhas of the Fortunate Eon, the Thirty-five Buddhas, the Medicine Buddhas and other buddhas; then the bodhisattvas; the dakas and dakinis; and the Dharma protectors, who are around the edge of the lotus. You then make prostrations to this merit field.

If you can't visualize all the different deities in the merit field as described in the text, just think that Guru Chenrezig is the embodiment of the whole merit field: all the direct and indirect lineage lamas, the four classes of tantric deities, the buddhas, the bodhisattvas, the dakas and dakinis and the Dharma protectors. Just think that the whole merit field abides in each pore of Guru Chenrezig, then do the prostrations.

15. The Seven-Limb Practice

THE SEVEN-LIMB PRACTICE is essential to purify negative karma and accumulate merit. These seven important factors—prostrating, offering, confessing, rejoicing, requesting to teach, requesting to remain and dedicating—make it possible to achieve enlightenment. The seven-limb practice is a most important means to create the causes and conditions to develop the mind in the path to enlightenment. Since it comes here in nyung nä practice and in every other deity practice, it is important to know how to do the seven-limb practice.

Since you can't achieve enlightenment without the seven-limb practice, it is extremely important to do this practice as many times as possible every day. That's why the seven-limb practice always comes in Mahayana practices, especially in sadhanas. Meditation on any deity always has the seven-limb practice as a preliminary.

Every single prostration, offering and other practice done in relation to Buddha, by thinking of Buddha, becomes a cause of enlightenment. When you plant a seed in the ground, if all the minerals, water and other necessary conditions are present, even if you pray that the seed won't grow, it will still grow. It is the same with prostrating, offering, respecting and any other practice done in relation to Buddha. No matter how much you pray for it not to become a cause of enlightenment, everything becomes a cause of enlightenment. Generally, an action becoming a cause of happiness depends on the motivation, but prostrations, offerings and other actions done in relation to Buddha become causes of enlightenment even when done without a virtuous motivation. That is because of the power of the holy object. Even if the motivation for prostrating or making offerings to Buddha is one of anger, attachment seeking only the happiness of this life or another delusion, the action still becomes a cause of enlightenment because of the power of the holy object.

The seven factors of the seven-limb practice are like seven vital parts of a car, plane or other vehicle that enable it to function and take passengers to the places they wish to go. These seven important factors bring us success. The seven-limb practice, mandala offering and all the various other practices have incredible benefit in regard to bringing not only temporary but also ultimate happiness, especially the achievement of enlightenment. But to appreciate how important these practices are, you have to understand and have faith in karma.

The first law of karma you need to understand is that karma is definite to bring its own result. Any nonvirtue, as long as the negative karma is not purified, will definitely bring its own result of suffering. And any virtue, as long as there is no obstacle to it, will definitely bring its own result of happiness.

The second law of karma is that karma is expandable.

Another law of karma is that karma once created is never lost. No matter how long it takes—even eons or hundreds of eons—the result of karma will be experienced. Whether great or small, karma is never lost. Even though it might not be experienced immediately, after some time, when the time is right and the conditions have gathered, that karma will be experienced. Even negative things that are not purposely done create negative karma. It is still possible to experience the result of even small things that happened incidentally and many lifetimes ago. No matter how small a negative karma is, it doesn't get lost.

We should relate this to our own life, not only to this life but to our many past lives. We have created so many negative karmas. It is frightening to examine karma, because karma is related not only to this life but to beginningless rebirths. There are many things we have already finished experiencing, but there are so many things we have not yet finished experiencing.

The final law of karma is that unless we have created the karma, we don't experience the result.[69]

Limb of Prostration

The first of the seven limbs is the limb of prostration, which is a remedy to pride. When we have pride, we find it difficult to respect those we regard as lower than us.

---

[69] For more on karma, see appendix 4.

There are three types of prostration: body prostration, speech prostration and mind prostration. Body prostration is physically prostrating to Chenrezig, speech prostration is praising Chenrezig and the rest of the merit field, and mind prostration is devotion to Chenrezig. From these three, the most important one is mind prostration: devotion.

You are doing prostrations to the Great Compassionate One, in the center, and all the rest of the merit field surrounding him. If you aren't familiar with all the beings in the merit field, you can simply think that all the lineage lamas and all the multitudes of deities, buddhas, bodhisattvas, dakas and dakinis and protectors are all around Chenrezig. However, it might be more effective to think that Thousand-Arm Chenrezig himself is all the beings of the merit field: all the gurus, buddhas, Dharma and Sangha. Or think that the whole merit field is there in each pore of Chenrezig. With that concentration you then do the prostrations. As you prostrate you can mainly concentrate on Thousand-Arm Chenrezig, who is all the gurus, buddhas, Dharma and Sangha.

Or you can just think of Chenrezig, with a thousand arms and a thousand eyes, radiant and of the nature of light. Your own guru has manifested as Chenrezig to guide you by enabling you to purify your negative karmas and obscurations and to accumulate merit. By revealing these nyung nä practices to you, Guru Chenrezig is leading you to enlightenment. You can simply concentrate on Guru Chenrezig in that way.

Even if you can't visualize anything at all, simply prostrating to a statue of a buddha fulfills the meaning of prostration. As long as you're prostrating to a buddha, whether a statue or an actual living being, it becomes a prostration. Otherwise, it simply becomes good physical exercise. It might help somebody who has diabetes, relieving or curing the diabetes. If you have diabetes you need to walk because exercise is helpful, but some geshes do prostrations instead.

If you can't do the visualization, just think, "This statue of Chenrezig is all I can now see according to my karma. But later, when I have developed my mind and achieved the concentration of continual Dharma on the great path of merit, what I now see as a statue I will then see as an actual buddha. At that time the buddhas will appear to me as actual living beings."

You can think that strong nectar-beams, like sunbeams, come from the hearts of Chenrezig and the other beings in the merit field and purify you. You yourself are Chenrezig, but if you can, think that you and all your past lives in human form cover the whole earth and are doing prostrations to

Chenrezig and the rest of the merit field. If possible, also think that the bodies are as tall as snow mountains, the tallest you can imagine. There will then be more merit, because your bodies will cover more ground. There's much merit even in visualizing this. Think of all your past lives with the tallest possible bodies, and those who are qualified should visualize the bodies in the form of Chenrezig.[70]

You can begin the prostrations by reciting "OM NAMO MANJUSHRIYE, NAMAH SUSHRIYE, NAMA UTTAMA SHRIYE SVAHA" three times to multiply the prostrations. This mantra multiplies each prostration so that it becomes a thousand prostrations. It also protects you from obstacles and enables you to realize the path of seeing.

Limb of Offering

The practice of offering is a particular remedy to miserliness. If you are miserly, you should practice charity and make as many offerings as possible. From making offerings, you receive the inexhaustible perfect enjoyments of a buddha. These are the benefits, in brief, of the practice of making offerings.

Transform offering goddesses from your heart to make the eight offerings—drinking water, water for bathing the feet, flowers for the crown, incense for the nose, light for the eyes, scented water for the heart, food for the holy mouth and music for the holy ears—to Chenrezig and the merit field. In nyung nä practice we offer eight actually arranged offerings with mantras and mudras and we can also visualize other offerings. In this practice we make offerings many times, and each time we do we accumulate unbelievable merit.

The offering goddesses you emanate from your heart are youthful and extremely beautiful, as beautiful as you can imagine, with all the good qualities. Even each of the goddesses becomes an offering of the six sense objects to the merit field, generating much bliss in their holy minds. If it's difficult for you to transform the offering goddesses carrying the offerings one by one, you can transform them all together.

In Action Tantra the offering mudras are regarded as very important. It is emphasized to not miss doing the mudras when you make the offer-

---

[70] That is, those who have had the appropriate initiation.

ings. In Highest Yoga Tantra practice, you don't transgress the samaya if you don't do the mudras. Of course, by doing the offering mudras you create more merit, but you do not transgress your samaya by not doing them. In Action Tantra, however, doing the mudras is part of the samaya and shouldn't be left out. You must learn the mudras and make the mudra offering to the merit field. You must do the mudras when you do a nyung nä, and you must do them precisely.

To make the offerings, first meditate well on emptiness. Highest Yoga Tantra talks about the transcendental wisdom of nondual bliss and voidness, but here in Action Tantra practice, the creator of everything is the transcendental wisdom of nondual clarity and profundity, where *profundity* means emptiness.

You, Chenrezig, are empty of existing from your own side. The wisdom of emptiness manifests in the form of Chenrezig. This wisdom focuses on the clarity of Chenrezig and at the same time is aware of the nature of Chenrezig, that Chenrezig is empty of existing from his own side. It is similar with the offering goddesses and also all the offerings. The offering goddesses are manifestations of your wisdom, as are the beings in the merit field. All these are the transcendental wisdom of nondual clarity and profundity. You yourself are also the result-time actual buddha Chenrezig.

Or you can meditate that you are the result-time Chenrezig, your mind has become dharmakaya, and everything is a manifestation of that dharmakaya. You yourself, the offering goddesses, the offerings—everything is a manifestation of your own dharmakaya, your own wisdom. Your mind's wisdom of emptiness manifests in the offering goddesses.

The dharmakaya wisdom is aware of the absolute nature, the emptiness, of the subject, the offerings and the object of offering, the merit field, as well as aware of their dependent arising. While you are making the offerings, mostly concentrate on emptiness or on dependent arising, that everything is merely labeled, which comes to the same conclusion, emptiness.

As you visualize the offering goddesses coming from the syllable HRIH at your heart and making the offerings, think that the I who is making offerings to the merit field is merely labeled, the action of offering is merely labeled, and the offerings themselves are merely labeled. If you think in this way, what Lama Tsongkhapa says in the *Three Principles of the Path* will become very real and very clear to your mind.

If thinking that all these things are empty or merely labeled isn't effective for your mind, at least think, "I'm making offerings in a dream." It is the most basic instruction for meditating on emptiness. There's a big difference between "in a dream" and "like in a dream," but to think something is "like in a dream" might be a little too hard, so just think, "I'm making offerings in a dream." When you think that you're dreaming, your solid belief in you yourself, the offerings and the merit field as existing from their own side automatically becomes weaker. Thinking this is helpful as it weakens the object of ignorance. Your belief that these things exist from their own side is harmed.

Whatever appears to you now appears to be truly existent and you believe this to be the way things exist. But the truly existent you, the truly existent offerings and the truly existent object of offering do not exist at all. Not even an atom of them exists. You are making offerings to Chenrezig and the rest of the merit field in a dream. None of these three—truly existent I, truly existent action, truly existent object—exists. Just as none of the things you see in a dream exist, the truly existent I and the truly existent Chenrezig statue you see in the daytime don't exist. You can't say that the truly existent *appearance* doesn't exist; it exists. But the truly existent I, truly existent action and truly existent object do not exist. The appearance of true existence exists, but the truly existent things do not exist.

You have to apply the example of a dream to the appearances of these truly existent objects: the truly existent you, the truly existent action of offering, the truly existent merit field. You believe that they truly exist, but if you think, "This is a dream," it at least gives you the feeling that they are not real.

When you transform the offering goddesses carrying the offerings, snap your fingers outwards. The sound of the fingers snapping signifies dependent arising as the sound happens in dependence upon your intention and your effort to make your two fingers meet. It reminds you that since the sound is a dependent arising, it is empty. It reminds you that the three things—you yourself, the action of offering and the object, Chenrezig—are empty and dependent arisings. It reminds you of the unification of emptiness and dependent arising.

When you hear the sound of your fingers snapping, it seems as if the sound exists completely from its own side without depending on your fingers, your intention or your effort. It appears to your mind as though the sound exists only from the side of the sound. In reality, however, the sound exists in dependence upon all these conditions. The sound is merely labeled by thought on this base, the gathering of these conditions. How the sound appears to you and how it actually exists are completely contradictory. The sound doesn't exist from its own side at all. It exists in dependence upon its base, the gathering of these conditions.

It is similar with making the offering. You yourself, the action of offering and the offering—even though they all appear to exist from their own side, in fact they exist by being merely labeled. To remind you of the emptiness of these three things, you snap your fingers. With this awareness that subject, action and object are empty, with awareness of emptiness and dependent arising, you then make the offerings.

You offer to the merit field—Guru Chenrezig surrounded by all the other beings of the merit field—all the offerings you have arranged on the altar, as well as the whole sky filled with various offerings. Meditate on the offerings as manifestations of wisdom, of emptiness, and then offer them one by one as you recite the offering mantras. Also think that all these offerings generate uncontaminated great bliss in the holy minds of the merit field. They are extremely pleased. Each time we make an offering, it's extremely important to think that great bliss is generated in the holy minds of the merit field. That's the essence of the offering. We should remember this not only here, but also in our everyday life whenever we make offerings, whether *tsog* offerings or offerings in sadhanas or on our altar.

Each time we make an offering, whether a tsog offering, inner offering or any other offering, we should think that it causes extraordinary, inconceivable great bliss to be generated in the holy minds of the merit field. It is extremely important to remember that every time. When you offer the inner offering to each of the lineage lamas in Highest Yoga Tantra practice, you might not be able to visualize clearly how he is sitting, how he is wearing his robes, whether he is wrathful, whether he has a beard, or what kind of nose he has. Mainly remember the aspect. If it is a lay lama, visualize a lay form; if it is a monk, visualize the form of a monk. Then make the offering to each one as you recite his name, thinking that he generates great bliss in his holy mind. That is the most important point. My guess is that by doing this practice, sooner or later in this life we will be able to have that experience, that level of mind. We will be able to generate the actual experience that we imagined being experienced in the holy minds of the merit field.

There's no inner offering here in nyung nä practice, but Highest Yoga Tantra has a lot of explanation about the inner offering. When you offer the inner offering, if you're offering according to Gyüme, the Lower Tantric College, offer with your palm facing downwards, whereas, according to Gyüto, the Upper Tantric College, offer with your palm facing upwards. Again, there are references for these practices, but I haven't yet seen them. The Lower and Upper Tantric Colleges have different ways of doing many things, which can usually be traced back through the lineage to the lama who founded the monastery. The founding lama initiated the practice, and since then it has been preserved. It's not that somebody just made up these things. The practices have been preserved very precisely and can be traced back to the great lamas, the great enlightened beings, who founded the monasteries.

It is the same when we offer tsog. The question often arises as to how to offer tsog, and this is the very essence of the Highest Yoga Tantra way of blessing tsog. You accumulate extra good karma if you visualize as nectar the tsog substances, the food and other offerings, those you have actually arranged and the ones you have visualized. However, each time you say the offering prayer, think that you are generating extraordinary, inconceivable bliss in the holy minds of the merit field. They don't need it. It's not that they haven't completed their bliss; it's not that they have further bliss left to achieve. When one becomes a buddha, one has perfect enjoyments—there is no further enjoyment to be experienced. You could say that arhats and bodhisattvas have still not completed their happiness, but buddhas have no higher happiness to experience. We do this visualization to accumulate merit ourselves.

I think that by doing a lot of practice in this way, sooner or later you will be able to have the tantric mahamudra experience in this life. You will have the experiences of clear light that are talked about so much in Highest Yoga Tantra. By attaining enlightenment, you will also be able to have perfect enjoyments in this life. This is just my guess about the results of doing this meditation. I think this is probably why the inner offering comes so many times in every Highest Yoga Tantra sadhana, with offerings to all the indirect and direct gurus. I think that by doing this practice of offering bliss to the merit field every day, you will be able in this life to have the actual experience of tantric mahamudra, of the completion stage of Highest Yoga Tantra. That is why it is very important not to let your mind wander during the practice.

Remembering emptiness, you then make the offering. When you snap your fingers outwards, you, as Chenrezig, manifest from your heart not just one but numberless offering goddesses completely filling the whole sky, who make the offerings. Everything should be as beautiful as possible. With awareness of how everything is merely labeled, transform the offering goddesses and offerings. For each offering, think that the whole sky is completely filled with offering goddesses. Don't transform just one offering goddess. Since the visualization doesn't cost anything, think that the whole of space is filled with each offering. The clearer and more elaborate your visualization and the better the quality of your offerings, the more merit you accumulate. Transform numberless goddesses carrying each of the offerings so that they fill the whole of space.

As mentioned at the beginning of the nyung nä sadhana in *Blessing the Offerings*, the offerings are empty in nature and grant extraordinary bliss. Their aspect is the various offerings, their nature is empty, and their particular function is to generate extraordinary bliss in the holy minds of the merit field.

After snapping your fingers and before doing the offering mudra, do the lotus-turning mudra at your heart. When you begin the lotus-turning mudra, snap your fingers to remind yourself of emptiness, of the ultimate reality of you yourself, the action of offering, the object to whom you are offering and the offerings. However, even though they are all empty, they exist in mere name, so all the functions are happening in mere name. Seal with emptiness the person who is doing the offering, the action of offering, the objects to whom you are offering and also the offerings. There is unification of emptiness and dependent arising.

Start the lotus-turning mudra with your right hand on top and your left hand below. As your right hand goes down, your left one comes up. This means that you are transforming the offerings out of the wisdom realizing emptiness of your own mind, which is Chenrezig's holy mind.

The nyung nä practice is lower tantra. Highest Yoga Tantra has father tantra and mother tantra. In father tantra, turn to the right side first; in mother tantra, turn to the left side first. Here, turn from the right side to the left side three times, but in Vajrayogini, Cittamani Tara or any other mother tantra practice, turn from the left to the right side three times.

After you have done the lotus-turning mudra, do the mudra for ARGHAM, for offering water to drink. As you do the mudras, keep your fingers together, not separate, as this creates good karma. I think it might be similar to keeping your fingers together when you do prostrations, which creates the good karma to achieve webbed fingers, one of the holy signs of the nirmanakaya aspect of a buddha needed to guide sentient beings.

Some of the Action Tantra mudras are different from the Highest Yoga Tantra ones, and some Action Tantra mudras from other lamas and other traditions could be different. If you are going to judge one guru as being right and another as being wrong, you will only destroy yourself; you will only destroy your own enlightenment. Doing this blocks your own realizations. Someone explained to me that one of the very first problems at Manjushri Institute[71] was related to mudras.

His Holiness Song Rinpoche's way of doing the mudra for ARGHAM was with the index finger a little bent, similar to the NAIVIDYA mudra for offering food. However, when giving the Mitra Gyatsa initiations at Tushita Retreat Centre, Kirti Tsenshab Rinpoche explained that another mudra is the actual Action Tantra mudra for ARGHAM.[72] There were abbots, including the abbot of Namgyal Monastery, as well as other high lamas there. The way Rinpoche presented it was by saying it was not a new mudra that he had made up but an old mudra from the past.

After you have done the meditation and mudra of offering for ARGHAM, then snap your fingers inwards, and all the offering goddesses, having finished making the offering, are absorbed back into your heart, from where you transformed them. There is a special reason related to Highest Yoga Tantra for doing this: it helps you to achieve clear light, to create the direct cause of dharmakaya.

Then snap your fingers outwards again and transform the next set of offering goddesses, who offer water for bathing the feet. Some say that when you snap your fingers you have one hand facing out and the other fac-

---

[71] A Dharma center in England; formerly an FPMT center.
[72] For a description and a photograph of Kirti Tsenshab Rinpoche doing this mudra, see page 68 of the 1995 edition of *Nyung Nä*.

ing in, which means that some offering goddesses who have already offered are being absorbed back at the same time as other offering goddesses carrying offerings are being emanated.

With the mudra for PADYAM, water for bathing the feet, gradually release the fingers of your right hand. It is the same mudra as in Highest Yoga Tantra. As you make the offering, remember Guru Chenrezig and the rest of the merit field. If you can't think of all of them, just think of Guru Chenrezig.

The Action Tantra mudra for PUSHPE, offering flowers, is different from the one in Highest Yoga Tantra. During nyung näs, some people do this mudra in the Highest Yoga Tantra way, but I haven't seen any high lamas or any of my gurus do it that way. With PUSHPE, you again generate great bliss in the merit field, and the offering goddesses are then absorbed back into your heart.

Pure morality is the result of offering incense, DHUPE.

The mudra for ALOKE, offering light, looks like the wick of a butter lamp.

The particular benefit of offering light is wisdom. Making as many light offerings as possible helps very much to develop wisdom, now and in the future, and to achieve clairvoyance, enabling you to actualize the path. The ultimate benefit is enlightenment.

It's very important to make as many light offerings as possible. Various tantric teachings advise making hundreds or thousands of light offerings. In Tibet there was a common tradition of offering a hundred or a thousand lights as advised in tantric texts. It is similar with flower offerings.

With GANDHE, you offer scented water at the heart.

The mudra for NAIVIDYA, the food offering, is the same as in Highest Yoga Tantra.

SHAPTA is offering music. According to His Holiness Serkong Tsenshab Rinpoche, the mudra for SHAPTA has been lost. Even though we do a particular mudra for SHAPTA, Rinpoche said the actual mudra is something else.

When you offer music, SHAPTA, you can use a bell or anything else that has a good sound to make the offering. This way you accumulate more merit. But the most important thing is that in your mind you think that you are offering the music to Guru Chenrezig. You then collect much merit.[73]

---

[73] See appendix 4 in *Nyung Nä* for the offering mudras.

Offering music (or any other offering) by thinking of Buddha collects infinite merit. Offering a bell to a stupa creates the karma to achieve the qualities of a buddha's holy speech. As well as the specific temporary benefits of offering music, such as a sweet voice, the ultimate benefit is that you quickly achieve enlightenment.

It is very important when we use musical instruments that we don't just play them mindlessly. The essential point is to think, "I'm offering music to Buddha." It is very important to have that awareness whenever we play music. This is the way to accumulate extensive merit. If we think of offering the music to Buddha, every single time we play the cymbals or any other instrument it becomes a cause of enlightenment. That is the ultimate goal.

In the sadhanas of various tantric deities, there are many places where you use bells and other instruments to make music offering and where you make other offerings. Many offerings come in each sadhana, and each time you make the offering, you collect inconceivable merit.

If we make offerings as much as we can during this time of Guru Shakyamuni Buddha's teachings, or even rejoice in other people accumulating merit in this way, even if we don't achieve liberation or enlightenment during this time, when Maitreya Buddha descends on this earth we will be able to see Maitreya Buddha. We will be born as the very first disciple of Maitreya Buddha, and by receiving teachings we will then be liberated from samsara.

Mandala Offering

In the case of the mandala offering, the meaning of Samantabhadra offerings is as explained in the sutras.[74] Beams emitted from each atom of the mandala carry a mandala, and beams carrying a mandala are emitted from each atom of each mandala. In that way, mandala offerings fill the whole of space.

There are other visualizations. You can put your palms together and visualize that beams are emitted with bodhisattva Samantabhadra, with his palms together, on a lotus on the tip of each beam. Again, beams are emitted from his hands, carrying many offerings, and from them, beams are

---

[74] The Samantabhadra offering in *Guru Puja* has a different meaning.

again emitted with many offerings. This visualization of Samantabhadra offerings is according to sutra.

Auspicious Prayer is usually recited after the long mandala offering, but you can also recite other verses, such as:

> Due to the merit of having offered this mandala to Chenrezig and the rest of the merit field, may bodhicitta be generated within my mind and within the minds of all sentient beings. May those who have bodhicitta develop it.
>
> Due to the merit of having offered this mandala to the Great Compassionate One and the rest of the merit field, please grant me and all sentient beings blessings to be able to practice exchanging self for others as our heart practice, because cherishing the self is the source of all shortcomings and cherishing others is the basis of all qualities.
>
> Due to the merit of having offered this mandala to Compassion Buddha and the rest of the merit field, may I and all sentient beings, in all our lifetimes, be born of noble caste, have clear minds, have great wisdom, be free of pride, have great compassion, have devotion to the virtuous friend and always abide in the samaya of the virtuous friend.

To *always abide in the samaya of the virtuous friend* means to always live in the vows that are particularly related to the virtuous friend, which becomes the root of all success in actualizing the whole graduated path to enlightenment. Without this practice of living in the samaya of the virtuous friend, there can be no realization of the path to enlightenment, so then there's no enlightenment. You cannot then do perfect works for all sentient beings, bringing them to enlightenment.

> Due to the merit of having offered this mandala to the Compassionate-Eyed One and the rest of the merit field, may I and all sentient beings become only like you, Compassionate-

Eyed One, with your holy body, your retinue and your supreme holy name.

Becoming like the Compassionate-Eyed One means to cease taking rebirth in samsara—in the lower realms and even in the deva and human realms—and to cease being bound to even the lower nirvana, the blissful state of peace. It means to cut off reincarnating again in samsara and even being bound to the lower liberation. We want to become only like Compassion Buddha, with the same qualities, to be able to perfectly guide all sentient beings.

Also, if you like, you can recite *Request for the Three Great Purposes*:

> I prostrate and go for refuge to the Guru-Three Rare Sublime Ones.
> Please bless my mental continuum.
> I am requesting you to immediately pacify all wrong conceptions, from wrong conceptions toward the virtuous friend up to the subtle dual view, that are in my mind and in the minds of all sentient beings.
> I am requesting you to immediately generate all the right realizations, from guru devotion up to the enlightenment, in my mind and in the minds of all sentient beings.
> I am requesting you to pacify all outer and inner obstacles.

Limb of Confession

Next we make confession and then do prostrations to the Thirty-five Buddhas. Confession is a remedy to the three poisonous minds. You could also say that it is a remedy to obscurations. It enables us to achieve the cessation of delusions, which means it enables us to achieve the dharmakaya. (In the seven-limb practice, the general result of each of the practices is the same, achievement of the two kayas, but a specific result for each one is also mentioned.)

When you confess your past negative karmas, it actually means that from now on you are going to try to practice virtue.

You and all sentient beings, who surround you, confess with regret, or repentance, all the negative karmas and downfalls you have accumulated in the past. The stronger your regret, the thinner your negative karmas become.

You should feel much regret, as if you had swallowed deadly poison. If you swallow a deadly poison, if you don't immediately do something you will definitely die. In a similar way, if you don't do something about all your negative karmas, you can be born in the lower realms, even in the Inexhaustible Suffering Hell.

Poison is used as an example to give you an idea of how strongly you should feel about the dangers of negative karmas. You can't stand to have negative karmas, which are like poison, for even a moment. You want to purify them right this second.

Then make the determination not to commit negative karmas and downfalls again, even if it endangers your life. With this determination, then recite the verse of confession:

> I confess individually every negative karma I have accumulated with my body, speech and mind under the control of attachment, anger and ignorance.

As you say this verse, think that all the negative karmas and obscurations in your mental continuum become nonexistent. Your mental continuum becomes completely pure.

You can also think of the emptiness of the negative karma. When doing confession, when you think of the delusions, negative karmas and obscurations, it looks as if they are real. There *are* negative karmas and obscurations, but there are no *real* negative karmas and obscurations, as they appear to us and as we believe them to be. What appears to us, what we think is real, is empty. That is the ultimate nature, the emptiness, of the negative karmas and obscurations. They are merely imputed by the mind in dependence upon the function of the imprint or thought, whether it is harmful.

Think that all the negative karmas and obscurations become empty. Look at their nature, which is emptiness. They all become nonexistent; they don't exist even in name. Think that they are all purified.

It's very good to think of the emptiness of the negative karma when you do confession. It then becomes very powerful confession, bringing powerful purification.

Meditating for just a few seconds, or even one second, on emptiness purifies unbelievable past negative karmas. Even having the wish to meditate on emptiness purifies the heavy karma of the five uninterrupted negative karmas, as well as the ten nonvirtues and many other negative karmas. Since generating a wish to meditate on emptiness has so much power to purify, there's no doubt about the power of actually meditating on emptiness, even for one second.

The Practice of Prostrations to the Thirty-five Confession Buddhas

Even though prostrations to the Thirty-five Buddhas are normally done in the limb of confession, I sometimes do them at the beginning of the nyung nä session. You then don't need to do them later. In some ways it's easier if you do the prostrations before you sit down. Of course, generally, the harder practice is, the greater the purification it brings. The harder you find nyung nä practice, the greater purification it becomes. However, that doesn't mean it's bad if someone finds nyung näs easy. It is different for different people. Some people find nyung näs very, very hard; others find them very easy. It depends on a person's mind and karma. If you find nyung näs very difficult, it might be due to heavy karma, so if you do them, perhaps it means you perform great purification of that heavy karma.

The practice of the Thirty-five Buddhas is emphasized in the Lama Tsongkhapa tradition. Lama Tsongkhapa himself did many hundreds of thousands of prostrations to the Thirty-five Buddhas in a cave in Tibet. At first Lama Tsongkhapa recited the name of each buddha alone, without the epithet *De zhin sheg pa*, which means *Tathagata*, or *Gone As It Is*. He then had a vision of the Thirty-five Buddhas without heads. After adding *De zhin sheg pa* to the recitation, he then saw all the Thirty-five Buddhas with complete holy bodies. This is why *De zhin sheg pa* is recited in the Lama Tsongkhapa tradition—the other traditions don't recite it. By doing those many hundreds of thousands of prostrations to the Thirty-five Buddhas, Lama Tsongkhapa achieved many realizations of the graduated path to enlightenment.

To purify any negative karma or degeneration of a vow that happened during each day, Lama Tsongkhapa recited each of the Thirty-five Buddhas' names thirty-five times at the end of the day. He would then go to bed with a very comfortable mind. If you are ordained and practice this way, you don't go to bed with the vices of having degenerated vows and you don't continue the vices into the next day. Before going to bed, you purify whatever vices you have accumulated that day; there is then no continuation to the next day. This is another way to live purely in vows, besides living in them purely by not breaking them at all. Since the branch vows are especially difficult to keep, it is very easy to accumulate vices, but by purifying vices the same day in this way, you remain pure.

When you create some negative karma in the future, feeling much regret, you can immediately recite the names of the Thirty-five Buddhas or do Vajrasattva practice and purify with nectar. This is how Lama Atisha and many Kadampa geshes practiced.

Before reciting the prayer, think that in front of you is Chenrezig in the center, surrounded by the deities of the four classes of tantra, then the sutra buddhas, including the Thousand Buddhas of the Fortunate Eon. In this nyung nä practice, you visualize the Thirty-five Buddhas and seven Medicine Buddhas in that line of sutra buddhas. But normally when you do the practice you just visualize the Thirty-five Buddhas in front of you.

The simplest visualization of the Thirty-five Buddhas is to visualize them in the aspects of the five types of buddhas. First visualize Shakyamuni Buddha up in space. Out of compassion Shakyamuni Buddha emits beams from his heart, and on the tips of the beams are the other thirty-four buddhas, each seated on a lotus, sun disc and moon disc on a throne lifted up by elephants, not by snow lions. Since an elephant is a very powerful animal, visualizing an elephant helps to bring powerful purification. There are also pearl decorations on the elephants. Since pearls are white, visualizing pearls brings stronger purification.

In the first row there are six buddhas in the aspect of Akshobhya, blue in color and in the same aspect as Shakyamuni Buddha. However, while King Lord of the Nagas' holy body is blue, he has a white face and a different mudra from the other five. There are then four lines with seven buddhas in each one. The seven buddhas in the second line are white and in the aspect of Vairochana, with hands in the mudra of supreme enlightenment. The third line has seven yellow buddhas in the aspect of Ratnasambhava, with the right hand in the mudra of granting sublime realizations. The next seven buddhas are red, in the aspect of Amitabha, with their hands in the mudra of concentration. The final seven buddhas are green and in the aspect of Amoghasiddhi, with the mudra of giving protection.

Visualize the Thirty-five Buddhas like this in front of you and think that nectar-beams are emitted from the Thirty-five Buddhas in all ten directions, purifying you and all sentient beings. When there isn't enough space to physically do prostrations—in an airplane, for example—just recite the names and do the visualization of purifying nectars coming from the Thirty-five Buddhas. Think that the nectars come from all the directions and enter your body and mind, completely purifying them, like cleaning a glass under a tap.

Even if there's no space to physically do prostrations, if you visualize doing the prostrations, the benefit is the same. If you visualize one body doing prostrations, the benefit is the same as your body actually doing prostrations. Visualize the tallest body you can, with it covering the whole ground. If there are statues, think that all the ground surrounding the statues is completely covered by your body. In this way you collect the same merit as your body having actually covered the ground and done the prostrations.

It's very good to memorize the names of the Thirty-five Buddhas so that you can then say them any time. While you're walking or traveling you can then do the Thirty-five Buddhas practice.

When you prostrate, you can think that every holy object in the gompa, every single buddha statue, is the Thirty-five Buddhas. Even if you don't know the particular details of how to visualize the Thirty-five Buddhas, just think that each statue is Buddha, then prostrate to that. As long as you are prostrating to Buddha, all the benefits of prostrations are there.

If you know how to visualize the Thirty-five Buddhas, it's good if you do. If not, just think that Thousand-Arm Chenrezig is the Thirty-five Buddhas; the Thirty-five Buddhas are abiding in each pore of Chenrezig and you are doing prostrations to them.

Begin the prostrations with the buddha's name and mantra that multiples the prostrations 100,000 times. Recite them each seven times:

CHOM DÄN DÄ DE ZHIN SHEG PA DRA CHOM PA YANG DAG PAR DZOG PÄI SANG GYÄ RINCHHEN GYÄLTSHÄN LA CHAG TSHÄL LO

OM NAMO BHAGAVATE RATNA KETU RAJAYA /
TATHAGATAYA / ARHATE SAMYAK SAMBUDDHAYA /
TADYATHA / OM RATNE RATNE MAHA RATNE RATNA
BIJA YE SVAHA

Then recite three times the mantra that multiplies each prostration one thousand times:

OM NAMO MANJUSHRIYE / NAMAH SUSHRIYE / NAMA
UTTAMA SHRIYE SVAHA

As you do the prostrations, repeat the name of each buddha as many times as possible because simply reciting each name purifies many thousands of eons of different negative karmas. You make a great profit by doing this practice. Reciting well the Thirty-five Buddhas' prayer from the beginning to the end even once is very powerful.

Stand up straight when you finish each prostration, before you do the next prostration. It's not correct to be bent over, and it also makes doing the prostrations difficult. When you come down, put your knees down first and then lie down; it's easier to do it that way. You should also place your hands down flat. Another point is that when you do prostrations, your feet should point straight back, not be stretched out to the side. When you lie on your bed to relax, you can stretch your feet out as much as you like, but not when you do prostrations.

Certain things are disrespectful. Even though there's no bad intention, it becomes negative karma because of the power of the object. For example, when an insect or an animal walks over a Dharma text or a statue, it happens out of ignorance, not purposely, but they still create negative karma just because of the power of the object. Showing respect and acting correctly in relation to holy objects or actual living holy beings have incredible benefit because of the power of the object. Even if you have no thought of disrespect in your mind, if you perform even a small disrespectful action due to ignorance, the shortcomings are great because of the power of the object.

When we do prostrations, we have to do them properly. The teachings emphasize very much how to do prostrations respectfully. It feels a little uncomfortable to see mistakes, even small ones. Since you are going to do prostrations many times, not just during a nyung nä but also in the future, it is good to do them correctly.

If your mind wanders, even though you are physically doing prostrations, they don't become proper prostrations. Doing a similar action toward a table doesn't become a prostration; it doesn't purify negative karma or accumulate merit. Without depending on even a virtuous motivation, however, a prostration done to Buddha becomes virtue by the power of the holy object.

At the end of the prostrations, think, "All the negative karmas and obscurations I have accumulated with my body, speech and mind during beginningless rebirths have been completely purified—not even the slightest remains. No negative karma or obscuration exists within my mental continuum." Generate strong faith in this. Try to feel this in relation to yourself as well as all other sentient beings. You and all other sentient beings have been completely purified by the strong nectar beams emitted by the merit field entering your body and mind. Think, "Now there isn't the slightest cause to be born in the lower realms left within my mental continuum."

Rejoicing in Virtue

The third of the seven limbs is rejoicing, which is a particular remedy to jealousy. If you feel a lot of jealousy, you should practice rejoicing. It's very difficult to rejoice in the good qualities of someone of whom you are jealous, but you should practice rejoicing particularly in relation to anyone of whom you feel jealous by remembering their good qualities. The result of rejoicing is that you achieve a buddha's holy body, which has no ugliness, only beauty. It's perfect as a result of the practice of rejoicing.

To practice rejoicing is very enjoyable, because your mind is happy when you rejoice. It is easy for your mind to get upset, angry or jealous when you don't rejoice in your own merit and good things and in other people having good things. If you don't rejoice, your mind is unhappy, but if you rejoice, you naturally have a happy mind.

Rejoicing is something you can practice while you are eating, while you are walking, while you are working, while you are lying down. You can do it even when your body is engaged in doing something else. It is a very important practice—you should rejoice as many times as possible every day, as it's the easiest way to accumulate merit. If you do this practice, you collect merit as infinite as space. It makes merit increase, like investing $100 then getting interest all the time until you have thousands, tens of thousands, hundreds of thousands, then millions of dollars. When you rejoice, your merit increases greatly.

In *A Brief Account of My Spiritual Life* (*Rang gi tog pa jö pa do zam du tän pa*), Lama Tsongkhapa says that among all virtues, rejoicing is the best. In other words, if you want to create good karma, good luck, rejoicing is the best way. People usually think that luck is something that comes from its own side. That's completely wrong. It is not that luck suddenly comes from outside, without our having to create it. Luck comes from our mind. If we experience good luck, it's luck that we have created with our mind; we must have created it. There is no way we can experience luck that other people have created or independent luck, with no creator.

We create so much luck, so much good karma, by having faith in karma and by knowing how to practice Dharma. We create so much good luck with the seven-limb practice, mandala offering, generating bodhicitta, meditation on emptiness and the various other practices, as well as with Vajrayana practice.

Among the virtues, rejoicing is the best because it is the easiest one to practice. It simply involves your mind thinking in a particular way, and the merit you accumulate is infinite. The practice of rejoicing is incredibly easy; if you are not lazy and do the practice, in each second you accumulate merit equal to infinite space.

A king once asked Nagarjuna for advice. The king explained, "I'm so busy that I can't meditate and I don't have time to go to an isolated place to do retreat. So, how should I make my life meaningful?" Nagarjuna told the king three ways to make his life meaningful. The first way was to practice bodhicitta, the second to practice rejoicing and the third to do dedication.

With the practice of rejoicing, it's not enough just to say the words. Simply saying the words without contemplating their meaning doesn't become the practice of rejoicing. With the seven-limb practice, it is extremely important to remember to meditate on the meaning of the prayer and not let your mind wander. It doesn't become a practice of the seven limbs unless you have the right attitude. If you chant the prayer, it perhaps becomes an offering to the merit field, but otherwise, if you don't contemplate the meaning, it doesn't become practice of the seven limbs. If you want to recite the words, recite them, but the most important thing is to spend a little time meditating on the meaning of rejoicing. Since it's extremely easy to do and creates infinite merit, don't miss the opportunity.

It is actually better if you just meditate without saying the words. Every time you do the seven-limb practice, whether you say the words or not, don't miss doing the meditation. The seven-limb practice is an essential method to accumulate merit and to purify negative karma. If this most important practice becomes just words, it will be difficult to have quick development of your mind. You should just read one verse then stop to meditate, then read another verse and stop to meditate. Or don't read them at all or just read them to yourself and meditate.

It's very important to meditate each time you practice the *Four Mandala Offerings to Cittamani Tara*, where the seven-limb practice comes again and again, and in other practices with the seven limbs. When you are doing a public puja, of course, you don't have any choice; you have to go straight through the puja, so you can't take the time to meditate. But when you are doing the practice alone, you have the freedom to spend some time on the seven limbs. When I do the seven limbs, I'm normally not satisfied if I just say the words of the prayer. I feel that if I don't meditate I'm losing a great opportunity. One problem that then happens is that while I'm trying to think of the meaning, other people have reached the next part of the prayer.

If we rejoice in our own merit from doing a virtuous action, we accumulate more merit than we accumulated by actually doing the action. When we rejoice in the merit of other sentient beings, if their level of mind is lower than ours, we accumulate more merit than they did, but if their level of mind is higher than ours, we get half or a quarter of their merit. As Pabongka Dechen Nyingpo explains in his lam-rim notes, if we, who are not bodhisattvas, rejoice in the merit that one bodhisattva accumulates in one day, we accumulate half or a quarter of that amount of merit. If we wanted to accumulate the merit that one bodhisattva accumulates in one day, it would take us 15,000 years without practicing rejoicing, but by rejoicing we can accumulate in a few seconds the merit that would otherwise have taken us 15,000 years to create.

Generally in our life we should practice rejoicing as much as possible.

We should rejoice whenever we see good things happening to other people. When other people develop their Dharma practice and have realizations, or have education, wealth, happy families or many friends, we should always think, "How wonderful it is!" When somebody succeeds in business or any other good thing happens to them, we should always rejoice, thinking, "How good it is! How wonderful it is!" It then becomes the best business for us. Why? Because by rejoicing we are creating the cause for our own success—success in our Dharma practice, in benefiting sentient beings and the teachings, and success in even the ordinary works of this life. By rejoicing, we are creating the best cause for success. But if we feel jealous of other people's success, which is the opposite of rejoicing, we are creating obstacles to our own success. It is important to understand this and to practice rejoicing.

Rejoicing in your own merit

There is no way to experience happiness without good karma. That is natural—a dependent arising. Without good karma, there is no way to experience happiness or success at all. All happiness, up to the happiness of enlightenment, comes only from good karma; therefore, good karma is extremely precious. You should feel as happy at having the opportunity to create good karma as a beggar who has unexpectedly found a million dollars in the garbage. You can't believe it. It's like a dream.

With this awareness, you should first rejoice in your own merit of the three times: past, present and future. You can then rejoice in the merit of the three times of all ordinary sentient beings, bodhisattvas and buddhas of the ten directions. It is very good to remember all the arya beings, all the bodhisattvas and all the buddhas. The verse says,

> I rejoice in all positive potential
> Of the buddhas and bodhisattvas in ten directions,
> Of solitary realizers, hearers still training, and those beyond,
> And of all transmigratory beings.

Think, "Without good karma, without merit, there's no way at all for me to experience happiness. I have accumulated merit numberless times in the past, I am accumulating it in the present, and I will also accumulate it in the future. This will result in so much temporary and ultimate happiness, including enlightenment."

From the very depths of your heart feel, "How wonderful it is that I've accumulated so much merit in the past, in the present and in the future." Count twenty-one repetitions of "How wonderful it is!" It's very good to count the repetitions on a mala.

Rejoicing in the merit of ordinary sentient beings

Then rejoice in all the merit of the three times of all ordinary sentient beings. Happiness comes only from good karma; without good karma, it's impossible to experience happiness. Rejoice in others' merit of the three times, with awareness that that merit results in so much happiness, temporary and ultimate, up to enlightenment. Think, "How wonderful it is!"

Normally, sentient beings create much negative karma, and it's very difficult and very rare for them to create good karma. You should feel much happiness about the good karma they have created, because it is only through their own good karma that they can experience happiness. We should cause them to accumulate merit, but how wonderful it is that they are putting effort into accumulating merit from their own side.

When you rejoice in the merit of other sentient beings, if it is more comfortable for your mind, rejoice first of all in those to the east, then to the south, the west, the north, then up and down.

Or you can rejoice in all the people in Tibet who have accumulated merit in the three times. After that, rejoice in all the people in Nepal who have accumulated merit in the three times. Then rejoice in all the people in India who have practiced virtue and accumulated merit in the three times. Think, in particular, of Dharamsala, where His Holiness the Dalai Lama lives, where so many people, lay and ordained, are practicing Dharma. Then think of all the people in all the other Buddhist countries and rejoice in all their merit of the three times. Then think of all the sentient beings in the whole world.

Being more specific makes it even easier to rejoice, because you relate to particular people in each country. Many people, lay and ordained, are intensively accumulating much merit day and night by living in Dharma, experimenting on the path and so forth. Think of the countries you have been where you have seen this happening. It then becomes more real, and it is easier for you to rejoice because you have been there and seen people accumulating merit.

Also, there is no sentient being who hasn't accumulated merit and there are numberless sentient beings. Pray, "For the benefit of each sentient being, may I be able to accumulate as much merit as other sentient beings have accumulated."

Rejoicing in the merit of bodhisattvas

Then rejoice in all the merits of the three times of all the bodhisattvas, who are uncountable in number. I mentioned before the great profit that comes from rejoicing in the merit one bodhisattva accumulates in one day.

Rejoicing in the merit of buddhas

Then rejoice in all the merits of the three times of all the buddhas. They create so much merit in the three times, which results in so much happiness, including the achievement of enlightenment. Again think, "How wonderful it is! How wonderful it is! How wonderful it is!" Count your repetitions.

Rejoicing in the merit of ordinary sentient beings, bodhisattvas and buddhas together

If you're short of time, you can think of all the ordinary sentient beings, bodhisattvas and buddhas in all the ten directions and rejoice in their merit together. Or you can start by rejoicing in the merit of the three times of all the ordinary sentient beings, bodhisattvas and buddhas to the east. Remembering that those merits will result in the experience of unbelievable happiness, feel great happiness in your heart. Think, "How wonderful it is!"

Then think of all the ordinary sentient beings, bodhisattvas and buddhas in the south who have accumulated merit in the three times and how this will result in incredible happiness. Think, "How wonderful it is!"

Rejoice in the same way in all the merit of all the numberless ordinary sentient beings, bodhisattvas and buddhas in the west and then in the north.

Rejoice also in the inconceivable temporary and ultimate happiness that will result from this merit. Think, "How wonderful it is!" Also rejoice in the same way about those who are up and down and in other directions.

It might be good to rejoice in your own merit in one session and then rejoice in the merit of others in the next session. Or in the first session you could rejoice more in your own merit, then rejoice in others' merit one time at the end; in the second session you could rejoice more in others' merit, then rejoice one time in your own merit. You can do it in different ways.

Requesting to Turn the Wheel of Dharma

The limb of requesting the merit field to turn the Dharma wheel is a particular remedy to ignorance and purifies the heavy negative karmas we have created by avoiding holy Dharma, such as disrespecting Buddhist scriptures by throwing them in the garbage and criticizing the different types of Buddha's teachings. For example, Gelugpas criticizing Nyingmapas, Nyingmapas criticizing Gelugpas or Kagyüpas criticizing Sakyapas is avoiding Dharma, as is Theravadins criticizing the Mahayana teachings or people who believe themselves to be Mahayanists criticizing and putting down the Theravadin teachings. Since all those different teachings were revealed by Buddha, criticizing any of them is avoiding Dharma. I saw in one Tibetan text by Je Drubkhangpa that even judging your guru's teachings by saying, "This isn't a skillful way of teaching" becomes avoiding Dharma.

Requesting to turn the Dharma wheel creates the cause to achieve a buddha's holy speech in the future and creates the cause for you to teach Dharma to other sentient beings as well. The particular result of this practice is achieving a buddha's perfect holy speech. It also becomes a cause in the future for other sentient beings to ask you to give teachings. One of the results is that you yourself turn the Dharma wheel for other sentient beings.

When asking the merit field to turn the Dharma wheel, visualize offering a thousand-spoked golden *dharmachakra* to Guru Chenrezig, the indirect and direct gurus and all the rest of the merit field. Think that the dharmachakra is large and radiant. Visualize that you are not just one but numberless, and every one of your replicas is holding a dharmachakra. Then ask the merit field to turn the Dharma wheel. Offering a dharmachakra to persuade the holy mind to teach Dharma collects so much merit. The more you can visualize, the more merit you collect.

Then think that the merit field accepts your request to turn the Dharma wheel whenever you need. There are two ways in which they can accept. The dharmakaya way of accepting is to agree in silence. The rupakaya way of accepting is by saying, "Yes, yes. Why not?"

If you have a mandala top, you can hold and offer it as the dharmachakra.

Requesting the Guru to Remain

The limb of requesting the guru to have a long life purifies the heavy negative karmas of having criticized or given up the guru or having disturbed his holy mind, making the guru unhappy. It also naturally becomes a cause for your own long life, even if that is not your intention. The result of this practice is that you achieve the immortal, indestructible vajra holy body of a buddha.

You ask the merit field to have long life and to not pass away until samsara ends. As it says in the verse, request them not to enter parinirvana, which means not to show passing away into the sorrowless state. Visualize that you are holding a golden throne decorated with jewels and offering it to Guru Chenrezig and the rest of the merit field. The throne has a variegated double vajra in front and is raised up by four or eight snow lions, like Guru Shakyamuni Buddha's throne. Visualize numberless replicas of yourself offering a throne.

This golden throne then absorbs into the thrones of Guru Chenrezig and the merit field. Then think that they have accepted to turn the Dharma wheel whenever we need and have also accepted to live long.

Dedicating

Then dedicate all the merit you have accumulated to achieving enlightenment for the sake of all sentient beings. Dedication is a particular remedy to heresy. Its specific result has to do with achieving the qualities of a buddha's holy body, holy speech and holy mind, as Jetsün Pabongka mentions in his notes to the lam-rim teachings.

Again, as with the offerings, remember that the merely labeled I is dedicating the merely labeled merit to the merely labeled enlightenment for the merely labeled sentient beings. We are dedicating all the merits we have just accumulated by doing prostrations, making offerings, confessing and so forth, as well as all the merits of the three times.

The Mantra of Pure Morality

Next, recite this mantra twenty-one times: OM AMOGHA SHILA SAM-BHARA [SAMBHARA] / BHARA BHARA / MAHA SHUDDHA SATTVA PADMA VIBHUSHITA BHUJA / DHARA DHARA / SAMANTA AVALOKITE HUM PHAT SVAHA.

Prayer to Keep Pure Morality

Then recite,

> Due to all the merits of the three times accumulated by me and by all other sentient beings, may I and all sentient beings complete the paramita of morality by keeping it purely and without pride.

Four Immeasurables

You can do tong-len practice with the prayer of the four immeasurables. With the first one, immeasurable loving kindness, you can do the practice of giving, giving all good things to others. When you generate immeasurable compassion, you can take on the sufferings of others. With immeasurable joy, you can again practice giving, and with immeasurable equanimity, you can practice taking. In this way there's more merit. Generating each of the immeasurable thoughts accumulates merit equaling infinite space, but especially if it's combined with tong-len. There is much more merit, twice the merit, so you accumulate another lot of infinite merit by doing the tong-len practice.

> May all sentient beings have happiness and the causes of happiness.

First of all, think of those who are devoid of temporary pleasure, and then think of those who are devoid of ultimate happiness. Otherwise, the inspiration to practice giving won't arise.

> May all sentient beings be free from suffering and the causes of suffering.

With the generating of immeasurable compassion, you can do the meditation of taking all the undesirable things upon yourself. Remember the different sufferings of sentient beings so that your compassion becomes strong. Just in one moment they all become free of suffering and all the suffering comes from all the directions and is absorbed into the self-cherishing thought in your heart. Your self-cherishing thought becomes nonexistent, as does your wrong conception of a truly existent I.

> May all sentient beings never be separated from the happiness that is without suffering.

With immeasurable joy, you can again do the meditation of giving.

> May all sentient beings abide in equanimity, free from discriminating others as close and distant through attachment and anger.

With immeasurable equanimity, you can do the meditation of taking others' attachment and anger, as well as all the problems that arise from those two discriminating thoughts. Take all the attachment and anger, the cause of problems, and all the confusion that results from them into your heart, absorbing it all into your self-cherishing thought.

You can take the whole of samsara, because all the problems, all the sufferings of the whole of samsara, actually come from attachment. The whole world is filled with this major problem of attachment and there is so much suffering from it. So, take everything upon yourself. Take both the cause and the result into your own heart, onto your self-cherishing thought, which becomes nonexistent.

Departure of the Merit Field

Then, the merit field, which you have invoked from its natural abode, the dharmakaya, returns to its natural abode.

Next comes the actual body of the practice, with meditation on the self generation.

Part Three

The Actual Ritual

Meditate on the self generation and recite the heart mantra,
Establish the front generation, then recite the long dharani,
Make offerings and praise, and offer the tormas:
These are the six practices of the actual body.

16. Meditation on the Self Generation

Next you have to generate yourself as Chenrezig, which is the actual body of the meditation. You can't generate yourself as Chenrezig without having first received a great initiation. Otherwise, it becomes revealing secrets. Even if you haven't received a Chenrezig great initiation, if you have received a Highest Yoga Tantra initiation you can visualize yourself as Chenrezig.

Meditating on the six deities is the most important practice of Action Tantra, and the first of them is meditating on the ultimate deity, or the deity of absolute nature. Until you have received a great initiation, you can just meditate on the emptiness of the I, the deity Chenrezig and all other phenomena.

1. The Ultimate Deity

If you have already had some experience of emptiness, this meditation is easy. Instantly recall that experience of emptiness and think, "This is the absolute nature of Chenrezig," and meditate on that. This is not exactly the same as the dharmakaya meditation in Highest Yoga Tantra, with its four characteristics, but I think it could be a substitute for that. It doesn't have all the qualities of the dharmakaya meditation.

If you haven't experienced emptiness, you can't suddenly see emptiness, or absolute nature.

> OM SVABHAVA SHUDDHA SARVA DHARMA SVABHAVA SHUDDHO HAM
> Myself, the meditational deity and all phenomena become of one taste in emptiness.

When you meditate on the ultimate deity, the natures of you, the meditational object (the deity) and all dharmas (all things and events) become of the same essence, the same taste, in emptiness, like having put a drop of water into the ocean. When many streams come from different directions to mix in the ocean, there is nothing to differentiate them. It is like that with the emptiness of all these things: everything becomes of one taste.

If you don't get much feeling from this, think that this I, the meditator, is merely imputed to its base, the aggregates. Therefore, this I is empty; it doesn't exist from its own side. What appears to exist from its own side is empty from its own side.

Stop there and meditate for a little while.

A brief meditation on emptiness

As beginners, we haven't had any experience of emptiness; we haven't even recognized the object to be refuted. To get some idea of emptiness, first of all we have to get some idea of what it is that we have to see as empty. In order to recognize the emptiness of the I, we have to know about the object to be refuted, the thing that we have to see as empty. We have to recognize that the object to be refuted, which is on the I, doesn't exist.

One simple way to recognize the object to be refuted is to meditate in the following way. First of all think, "The I is merely labeled." Remember the base on which you label "I": the five aggregates, the association of the body and the mind. Try to have the aggregates on which you label "I" become the object of your mind. Then think, "My mind has merely labeled 'I' on this. There is no I existing on this at all, except the I that has been merely labeled by my mind."

It is good to take your time in thinking about this.

Then check the result in your mind. Is there any change in your experience when you think this? When you hear and think of the meaning of the word *except*, it becomes very clear that not the slightest I exists from its own side on these aggregates. It is very good if you experience this as it means you have either already been able to recognize the object to be refuted or will soon be able to do so.

A more elaborate meditation on emptiness

I will now explain a more elaborate way to meditate on emptiness. If you don't recognize what doesn't exist, there's no way you can meditate on emptiness. You first have to recognize what exists and what doesn't exist. To really know how the I exists you have to know the I that doesn't exist. It is only by realizing the emptiness of the I that you can realize how the I exists. Before realizing the emptiness of the I, you have no way of realizing how the I exists.

The association of the body and the mind comprise what are called *the aggregates*. There are five aggregates: form; feeling; discrimination, or recognition; the compounding aggregates; and consciousness. First of all, we need to know the definition of the I, the person, the being. What is the definition of the I? What are the characteristics of the I? The I is that which is merely imputed in dependence upon the base, one of the five aggregates. As human beings, we have all five aggregates, but beings in the formless realm don't have a body, a form, and have only consciousness. To include beings in the formless realm, the general definition mentions *one of the five aggregates*. For us, however, the I is merely imputed in dependence upon the base, the group of all five aggregates.

So, the I is that which is merely imputed in dependence upon the base, the group of the five aggregates or one of the five aggregates. That is what the I is. From this definition it is clear that the mind is not the I, the body is not the I, each of the five aggregates is not the I and even all five aggregates together are not the I. There is no I anywhere on these aggregates.

Nothing of this is the I. Neither the body nor the mind is the I; none of the five aggregates is the I and even the whole group of the aggregates is not the I. The I is neither inside the body nor outside it. The reality is that you can't find the I anywhere on this base, but that doesn't mean that there's no I, that the I doesn't exist. There is I. As mentioned in the definition, the I is that which is merely imputed in dependence upon the base, the five aggregates or one of the five aggregates. Even though we may think that the body is the I or the mind is the I or even the association of the body and mind is the I, that is completely wrong.

The I exists, but what is it? The I exists, but it exists as a mere imputation by the mind. What the I is is extremely subtle, extremely fine. Compared to our previous belief in a real I, the I that appears to us and we hold to be true, it's like the I doesn't exist. It's not that it doesn't exist, but it's *like* it doesn't exist compared to that other real I. It's not nonexistent but it's like it doesn't exist. Saying the word "like" makes a huge difference. You can't say that the I doesn't exist, but what exists is unbelievably subtle.

It is just because the aggregates, and basically the consciousness, are here now in this room that the mind has merely labeled, or imputed, "I am here in this room," and believed in that. That's all it is—just an idea.

Even though this is what the I is, we think the I is completely something else. Day and night we think the I is here inside our body, somewhere inside our chest. We think we can find a real I inside our chest, where there is no I at all. Our normal belief that the I exists inside our body is a complete hallucination. Our thinking there is an I where there is no I is like believing we have a million dollars in our hand right now. It's a complete hallucination. How we normally think of the I has nothing to do with the reality of the I. The reality is something else completely.

Even though the I is merely labeled, it doesn't appear to us that way. It appears to be independent, unlabeled, real from its own side. It is the same with a mala. When we look at a mala, it appears to be a real mala. Even though the mala is merely labeled by our mind, it doesn't appear that way. It appears to be something independent, unlabeled, real from its own side. We label this object "mala" in dependence upon its shape and function. Our mind merely imputes "mala," but it doesn't appear that way to us. The mala we have merely labeled appears to us in the wrong way, as an independent mala, an unlabeled mala, a real mala from its own side. Again, that real mala from its own side doesn't exist; it's empty, completely empty, just like the I. The real I from its own side that you feel is inside your chest is also completely empty.

When you are sitting on a cushion on the floor, there's a cushion from its own side and a floor from its own side. Again, in reality, our mind merely imputes "cushion" and "floor." But where you are now sitting and where you are going to do prostrations don't appear that way. An unlabeled, independent, solid, concrete cushion and floor appear to you. Again, they are completely empty from their own side.

The real I doing prostrations and doing Chenrezig retreat, the real body, the real mala, the real floor and the real room are like things in a dream. While you are awake, you don't call what you are experiencing dreaming, but it's like a waking dream. When you are asleep, the things in your dreams don't exist. There are also daytime dreams when you are awake. All these daytime dreams are hallucinations. If you label these real things as dreams, it's very helpful for meditation on emptiness. When you think this real I, this real body, this real mala, this real floor and this real room are all things in a dream, you then know that it means that even though they appear to be real, they're not real; they don't exist in that way in reality.

When you think all these things are like things in a dream, it means that they're not true, that they don't exist. These real things do not exist from their own side. That is the ultimate nature of things. You then concentrate on this ultimate nature, this emptiness, for a little while, without allowing your mind to become distracted.

(I can't explain exactly what you meditate on at this point because it has to do with tantric meditation, but what I have just explained is the foundation for meditating on emptiness.)

Meditating on the ultimate deity

Think, "During beginningless rebirths until now, my mistake has been believing that the I exists—in other words, that there is a truly existent I, a real I. The way I have believed the I to exist is actually a complete hallucination. That real I, that truly existent I, doesn't exist. In reality, the real I is completely false, completely empty."

Just focus on that.

"In emptiness, there's no such thing as subject, action, object. There's no me, no deity, no phenomena. There are no such things."

"Everything is of one taste in emptiness. In emptiness there's no such thing as, 'This is my emptiness and this is the deity's emptiness.' It's of one taste, like having put a drop of water into the ocean."

This way of meditating on the absolute deity is like an atomic bomb, the weapon that gives the greatest, quickest harm. You then do the meditations on the rest of the six deities by continuing this awareness of emptiness.

2. The Deity of Sound

This emptiness now manifests in the sound of OM MANI PADME HUM, which pervades the whole of space. This is the deity of sound.

3. The Deity of Syllables

Your mind, the inseparable absolute nature of yourself and the deity, becomes a moon disc. The mantra in space is decorated around the moon disc as if the syllables have been written with pure liquid golden sounds.

The moon disc and the sound of the mantra are actually both manifestations of your absolute nature, which is oneness with the absolute nature of Chenrezig. First you think of the sound. Afterwards, when you've transformed the moon disc, the sound appears actualized in the letters decorated around the moon.

Concentrate on this, which is the deity of syllables.

4. The Deity of Form

The peaceful red face on the crown is that of Amitabha, signifying that Chenrezig became enlightened in the essence of Guru Amitabha. Having Amitabha on his crown means that even after having achieved enlightenment, Chenrezig still respects and prostrates to Amitabha, to the guru.

When time is short, instead of going over all the details of the aspect, you can abbreviate the description of the aspect to "Chenrezig with a thousand arms and a thousand eyes." Other parts of the practice can also be abbreviated when you want to do it quickly.[75]

---

[75] See chapter 19 for more details.

5. THE DEITY OF MUDRA

After you become Thousand-Arm Chenrezig, there is the deity of mudra, in which you bless the five places with the commitment mudra and OM PADMA UDBHAVAYE SVAHA. With your hands in the mudra of the lotus family, first touch your heart, then the point between your eyebrows, your throat and then your two shoulders.

6. THE DEITY OF SIGN

The last of the six deities is the deity of sign. Meditate here on the meaning of the transcendental wisdom of nondual clarity and profundity.

First invoke the transcendental wisdom beings and then the empowering deities. After finishing the initiation, visualize the transcendental wisdom being at your heart.

Focusing your mind and meditating on yourself clarified in the holy body of the deity without being distracted is meditation on the deity of sign. There are two ways of doing this. One way is to go through the details of the aspect one by one. After doing that analytical meditation, then do fixed meditation, one-pointedly concentrating on the general view of yourself generated as Thousand-Arm Chenrezig.

The way to stabilize single-pointed concentration on yourself as Chenrezig is not to let the wind go out through the pores of your body but to keep it inside so that there's no air going out. Block the air coming in and out. Since the wind doesn't go out through the pores, the mind, which rides on the wind, doesn't go out, and your single-pointed focus on yourself as the deity will last longer. Try to have clear meditation with intense remembrance and awareness that you are Chenrezig. You have to stop sinking thought and attachment-scattering thought from arising. Hold the strong divine pride, "I am actually Chenrezig. This Chenrezig I have clarified is me."

Keep the air inside, without letting it go out. Keeping the wind inside by thinking that you have closed your pores helps your mind not to wander. Think, "This pure base, this pure body and mind clarified as Chenrezig, is my result-time Chenrezig, with a thousand arms and a thousand eyes. This pure base to which 'Chenrezig' is merely imputed is not somebody else—this is me. I am Chenrezig."

Hold the strong divine pride, "I am Chenrezig," combined with the clear appearance of yourself as Chenrezig. Unify these two.

You have the intense divine pride that you actually are Chenrezig combined with the clear appearance of yourself as Chenrezig. However, even though this divine pride appears as if it exists from its own side, it's actually merely imputed to the base by thought. It is empty. As well, the Chenrezig that appears to exist from its own side is empty from its own side. It is merely imputed to this pure base. Your previous impure aggregates became empty; then, out of emptiness, pure aggregates with one thousand arms and one thousand eyes were generated. There is a combination of wisdom and appearance, which means Chenrezig's holy body. Think, "I, Chenrezig, am merely imputed." It is like the reflection of your face in a mirror: even though the reflection appears as a face, it's empty of being a face. There's an appearance of a face, but it is not a face. There's an appearance, but it's empty.

Meditate on Chenrezig with this divine pride, but with no clinging to a truly existent I, a truly existent Chenrezig. Meditate on Chenrezig in the meaning of vajra, the unification of method and wisdom, of clarity and profundity. This is the transcendental wisdom of nondual clarity and profundity, the very essence of the meditation of lower tantra.

There is Chenrezig on this pure base, but there's no Chenrezig from its own side. There is unification of the absolute truth and the conventional truth. Chenrezig is empty of existing from its own side, but it's a dependent arising, merely imputed to its base. So, it unifies the two truths.

The way you hold the strong divine pride of yourself as Chenrezig, as well as your focus on Chenrezig, is like seeing a mirage. Even though water appears to your eyes, at the same time you know that there is no water there. In the same way, even though Chenrezig appears from its own side, you know there is no Chenrezig from its own side. Chenrezig is merely imputed to this pure base, and it appears to the wisdom that is aware of absolute nature that Chenrezig is empty from its own side. This is the yoga of nondual clarity and profundity. Your mind focusing and meditating on the aspect of yourself as Chenrezig is the clarity. That same mind is aware that while there is no Chenrezig from its own side on this base, there is a merely labeled Chenrezig on this base. That same mind being aware that Chenrezig is a dependent arising and is empty of existing from its own side is the profundity.

That one mind is creating the cause of dharmakaya and rupakaya together. The mind focusing on the aspect of Chenrezig is method, and that same mind being aware of the absolute nature, that it's empty of existing from its own side, is wisdom. Profundity, the awareness of emptiness, is the cause of dharmakaya, and clarity, the clear appearance of Chenrezig that the wisdom is focusing on, is the cause of rupakaya. This meditation accumulates both the merit of wisdom and the merit of method, enabling you to achieve the unification of dharmakaya and rupakaya, or enlightenment. This meditation makes enlightenment happen quickly on your mental continuum.

Whenever you meditate on a deity, if your one mind can meditate on profundity and clarity, your meditation on the deity unifies wisdom and method. When you do deity yoga meditation, if the one mind does this deity yoga with inseparable method and wisdom, it becomes practice of Vajrayana. *Vajra* means inseparable method and wisdom and *yana* means vehicle. It becomes a quick vehicle to enlightenment, to achieve rupakaya and dharmakaya. If either method or wisdom is missing, however, your practice of deity yoga doesn't become Vajrayana. Since most of the time wisdom is missing, our practice doesn't receive the name "Vajrayana."

Offerings to the Self Generation

Blessing the Offerings

Now bless the eight offerings to the self-generation Chenrezig. First, with OM PADMANTAKRIT HUM PHAT, dispel the interferers abiding in the offerings to the self generation.

The offerings to the self generation, to you as the deity, start from your right side. The offerings to the front generation start from your left side, which is the right side of the front-generation deity.

Presenting the Offerings

When you say the offering mantras OM ARYA LOKESHVARA SAPARIVARA ARGHAM (PADYAM, PUSHPE, DHUPE, ALOKE, GANDHE, NAIVIDYA, SHAPTA) PRATICCHA SVAHA, transform offering goddesses from your heart, and they make the offerings. At this point you are making the offerings to yourself as Chenrezig. With each offering, it is good to think, as you did earlier with the merit field, that the offering generates extraordinary, immeasurable bliss within you, the deity Chenrezig. You should feel that bliss.

The bliss that you experience in Action Tantra is not the same as the great bliss of Highest Yoga Tantra, but there is a level of great bliss that accords with this tantra. It is good to generate this experience of bliss, produced by the condition of the offerings.

Blessing the Rosary

To bless the mala, which you hold in your hands at your heart, recite OM GURU SARVA TATHAGATA KAYA VAK CITTA VAJRA PRANAMENA SARVA TATHAGATA VAJRA PADA BANDHANAM KAROMI once, and then OM VASU MATI SHRIYE SVAHA seven times.

According to the commentaries to Chenrezig practice, you should hold the mala in your right hand, with it hanging over your ring finger. But if you cannot do that, you can hold the mala in the usual way. If you're going to practice pacifying actions, the mala should be either bodhi seed or crystal. Bodhi seed and crystal, or glass, malas are suitable for all four tantric actions.[76]

Mantra Recitation

After the introduction to the meditation, recite the mantra. It is said that in Action Tantra mantras are counted using the right hand.

While you recite the mantra, send beams from the mantra at your heart, illuminating your whole body and pacifying all your negative karmas and obscurations, all the causes of your suffering. By the way, your suffering is pacified. The power of the mantra and that meditation can help to pacify suffering.

Then emit Chenrezigs from your heart, and a Chenrezig comes above the crown of each sentient being. Nectar flows down and purifies all the negative karmas and obscurations of each sentient being, and they are led to Chenrezig's enlightenment. All the Chenrezigs are then absorbed back into the syllable HRIH from where you transformed them.

Padmasattva Mantra

Each time you recite the hundred-syllable mantra in a sadhana, you *must* ring the bell, because it signifies wisdom, or emptiness. By remembering the absolute nature of all negative karmas and obscurations you purify them, and you ring the bell to remind yourself of this. His Holiness Trijang Rinpoche advised that you should ring the bell whenever you recite this mantra in sadhanas or in pujas.

When we recite the Padmasattva mantra after the mantra recitation, the vices of having recited extra mantras or recited mantras incorrectly are purified. So during this time you must ring the bell. The vajra represents method, and the bell, wisdom. What is that wisdom? The wisdom of emptiness. The sound of the bell signifies emptiness; it means that all three—subject, action, object (the negative karmas and vices you have accumulated)—are empty, that they don't exist from their own side. Meditate by remembering the meaning of the sound of bell. What it's saying

---

[76] Pacifying, increasing, controlling and wrathful.

is, "Everything is empty." Meditate, in particular, that I, action and object (negative karmas and vices) are empty. Remembering emptiness again in this way brings incredibly powerful purification.

Do the same thing each time you recite the Padmasattva mantra. You can understand the particular context from what comes before the recitation of the Padmasattva mantra—the meditation is then the same.

Also, you can do the Padmasattva visualizations in relation to either yourself or other sentient beings, whom you have visualized as the deity.

17. Meditation on the Front Generation

NEXT IS GENERATING the mandala and the front-generation deity. Dispel the interferers at the site of the mandala with OM PADMANTAKRIT HUM PHAT, purify the mandala in emptiness with OM SVABHAVA SHUDDHA SARVA DHARMA SVABHAVA SHUDDHO HAM, then generate the mandala. Even if the mandala is physically somewhere else, you can still generate it in front of you; you don't have to generate it in the place where the mandala is.

Also generate the buddhas of the five types inside the mandala. Visualize Thousand-Arm Chenrezig with Amitabha on his crown in the center of the mandala, and Akshobhya, Ratnasambhava, Vairochana and Amoghasiddhi around Chenrezig in the four cardinal directions.

INVOCATION

After you have generated the mandala and the deities inside, invoke the transcendental wisdom Chenrezig, who absorbs into the deities generated in the mandala.

Think that in front of you is the mandala, with Chenrezig in the center and the four buddhas around Chenrezig. Then invoke Chenrezig, surrounded by all the buddhas and bodhisattvas, from the pure land of Potala, which is to the south.

EMPOWERMENT

Invoke and make offerings to the empowering deities, who then initiate Chenrezig.

Blessing the Offerings

Next bless the offerings and then make the offerings to the front-generation Chenrezig and the other mandala deities.

There are offering mudras for the five sense objects.[77] With OM RUPA AH HUM, offer forms with the mudra of a mirror, with the left hand forming the handle of the mirror. Then offer sounds with OM SHAPTA AH HUM and scents with OM GANDHE AH HUM and the mudra for offering scented water. With OM RASA AH HUM, offer tastes. With OM SPARSHA AH HUM, offer scarves as tangible objects.

Presenting the Offerings

When you present the offerings in the short way, recite just the mantras and not the verses of offering: OM ARYA LOKESHVARA SAPARIVARA ARGHAM (PADYAM, PUSHPE, DHUPE, ALOKE, GANDHE, NAIVIDYA, SHAPTA) PRATICCHA SVAHA. Then offer the five sense pleasures: OM ARYA LOKESHVARA SAPARIVARA RUPA (SHAPTA, GANDHE, RASA, SPARSHA) PRATICCHA SVAHA.

Next offer robes or divine dress, ornaments and a jewel vase to the merit field. With the vase water you also purify the sentient beings of the six realms and generate bodhicitta in their minds.

In Mongolia I met an old monk, eighty or ninety years old, who had been a monk before the Communists came to Mongolia. He disrobed, and I think he later took the five lay vows when His Holiness the Dalai Lama came to Mongolia. He wore robes, though, so I'm not sure . . .

I meet him every time I go to Mongolia and he offers me different things. One time he gave me a nyung nä text compiled by some great Mongolian lamas. In that text there are additional offerings. I thought it would be very good to add them, so I took the verses for offering the seven signs of royalty, eight auspicious signs and eight substances from the Chenrezig great initiation. It would be very good to offer them after offering the vase.

---

[77] See *Nyung Nä*, appendix 4.

Offering the twenty-five substances

The twenty-five substances comprise five sets of five: five medicines, five grains, five jewels, five scents and five essences, or nectars.[78] It's good to set up these twenty-five substances on the altar to collect extensive merit and achieve enlightenment more quickly. There are different benefits from offering each set.[79]

> The savior of us transmigratory beings abides magnificently,
> Having achieved the five holy bodies and wisdoms,
> And with the compassion that benefits others,
> Manifests in whatever aspect subdues us:
> May we transmigratory beings achieve the five holy bodies and wisdoms.
>
> OM PANCH PANCH VIMALA PUNDZA MEKA AH HUM

Offering the seven signs of royalty

> By offering the seven precious signs of royalty,
> May I be victorious in the war with the four maras
> And achieve the complete power to propagate the Mahayana teaching,
> To quickly lead transmigratory beings to everlasting supreme happiness.

Offering the eight auspicious signs

> Just by being touched, seen, heard or remembered,
> These eight auspicious signs blessed by the Victorious Ones
> Eliminate all inauspiciousness and grant perfect sublimeness.
> By this virtue, may I quickly and effortlessly achieve
> The collections of the qualities of cessation and realization and the works for others.[80]

---

[78] See note 67.
[79] For more, see *Teachings from the Mani Retreat*, pp. 68–72.
[80] For more, see ibid, pp. 76–79.

Mandala offering

After that, offer a mandala. Here you can offer a short mandala.

Brief Praise

Next offer praise to Thousand-Arm Chenrezig, then to the five types of buddhas.

Blessing the Vase Water and Reciting the Mantra

After the front generation, bless the vase water with nectar coming from Chenrezig's hand. If you have generated yourself as Chenrezig, visualize that nectar flows from your own palm, as Chenrezig, and from the front Chenrezig's palm and enters the victory vase on the altar, which becomes filled with transcendental wisdom nectar that can purify all your negative karmas and obscurations and those of all sentient beings. The water in the vase becomes, in essence, the transcendental wisdom of the Great Compassionate One, and, in aspect, nectar that has the power to purify all diseases, all spirit harms and all the negative karmas and obscurations accumulated with body, speech and mind. Each atom of the water has this power. Everything can immediately be purified with the nectar. You and all sentient beings are then able to generate all the realizations of the graduated path to enlightenment, especially bodhicitta.

If you haven't generated yourself as Chenrezig, visualize that nectar flows into the vase from the palm of just the front Chenrezig.

Here you recite the long Chenrezig mantra while doing the meditation of blessing the water.

Many years ago in Taiwan we did a Chenrezig retreat for seven or ten days, upstairs in a large Chinese monastery. At the beginning, to mark the borderline of the retreat, we made torma offering, put a syllable and visualized the protector there. One girl who had been possessed by a naga told us that there were numberless pretas outside the retreat place, like trees in a forest. There were also three monks just outside the retreat boundary. One monk didn't have a head and another had something wrong with his arms; they were pretas, and, it seems, in unimaginable suffering. As she was coming into the retreat room she saw a protector, who kicked her in the head, but she was still able to come inside. She had a pain in her head where the protector had kicked her.

She came to me during a break. Because she was possessed by a naga, even though she could walk, her legs were kind of stuck together so that she couldn't move quickly. She asked me to give her refuge.

At the end of the session the blessed water was passed around and when it reached her she didn't drink much. She said that the water was needed outside for the forest of pretas. I then prepared three buckets of water from the vase water and also chanted additional mantras. I gave them to Thubten Drolkar, a Taiwanese nun, but she was too scared to go outside. One man, the possessed girl's friend, who was very familiar with the situation, took the buckets and sprinkled the water all over the ground outside. It seems that the water benefited the pretas outside greatly. Even though we don't see them, there are so many beings, including spirits, all around us. Since the water had the power to purify the pretas' negative karma, it was of unbelievable benefit. Since the vase water becomes blessed through Chenrezig, it has great benefit.

My main purpose in telling this story is to show you that the water you bless during a nyung nä has a lot of blessings. People should drink it and it should also be sprinkled outside. It's very good for purifying the spirits, but you can also think that you are purifying the sentient beings of the six realms.

When you are doing many nyung näs, don't put all the water outside. Keep the continuation of the same water and add to what is already there. It then becomes more and more powerful. After you have done many nyung näs, the blessed water can be given to people who are sick or dying to purify their minds. You can give it to many other people to purify and bless their minds, their hearts.

Absorption of the Exalted Wisdom Beings

The transcendental wisdom of the self generation absorbs into the front-generation Chenrezig.

The Principal Practice of Praise

Again, here, we do prostrations. We do twenty-one praises with prostrations to Thousand-Arm Chenrezig.

Above your crown on a lotus and moon disc is Bhikshuni Lakshmi, in the aspect of a renunciate, with her two hands together in the mudra of prostration, recommending you to Chenrezig. Remember that Bhikshuni Lakshmi received this nyung nä practice from Chenrezig and actually attained Chenrezig, becoming enlightened in the essence of Compassion Buddha.

You as Chenrezig are bigger than a mountain. The taller you visualize yourself, the more merit you accumulate. You can also visualize all the bodies of your past lives in the form of Chenrezig and all sentient beings around you doing prostrations. You are surrounded by all the mother sentient beings and you do the prostrations together.

As well as body prostration, there are speech prostration, which means singing the praise, and mind prostration, which means strong devotion to Chenrezig. Your body does physical prostrations to Chenrezig, your speech praises Chenrezig and your mind has strong devotion to Chenrezig.

If you want, you can also generate a motivation of bodhicitta to do the prostrations.

As much as possible without a distracted mind, prostrate to Thousand-Arm Chenrezig, inseparable from your guru. This accumulates the most merit.

Because of the power of the object, doing prostrations to Chenrezig brings purification. Since we have accumulated so much negative karma, it's good to think, "By my doing this prostration to Chenrezig, Chenrezig is guiding me, saving me. Because of Chenrezig, this prostration becomes a method of purification. Chenrezig is saving me from the lower realms—from the hell sufferings, preta sufferings and animal sufferings—by purifying my negative karma to be born in the lower realms."

If we don't purify our negative karma, Chenrezig cannot guide us. Somebody giving us money, food or clothing alone cannot save us from the lower realms. To be saved from the lower realms we have to purify our negative karma to be born there. Think, "I create the negative karma to be born in the lower realms so many times in one day, but Chenrezig is saving me from the lower realms."

Each time the desire comes to be warm, for example, that attachment to warmth creates the cause to be in the hot hells. Each time the desire comes to be cool, that attachment to coolness creates the cause of the cold hells. Similarly, desire for food and drink creates the cause to be born in the preta realm, where those sentient beings pass their lives with intense suffering of hunger and thirst. The ripened aspect result of anger is rebirth in the hells. Ignorance causes one to be born in the animal realm, among those foolish suffering beings. (This is just to give you a general idea.)

Also think, "Chenrezig is saving me from samsara by purifying my disturbing-thought obscurations. Chenrezig is also saving me from the subtle obscurations, the obscurations to knowing, which prevent my achievement of omniscient mind. Chenrezig is guiding me away from the lower realms and away from samsara. Chenrezig is also guiding me away from the lower nirvana."

With awareness that Chenrezig is guiding you by purifying your obscurations, make prostrations. Again, this is extremely effective for the mind. You get so much feeling for Chenrezig. You feel Chenrezig is very close to you; you don't feel any distance between you and Chenrezig.

Also, you can sometimes think, "Even if I die today by fasting and doing prostrations, bearing hardships to practice Dharma is a very worthwhile way to die. I have died numberless times in beginningless lifetimes for meaningless things. I have died so many times while creating negative karma. I have died so many times for material possessions and for other meaningless things. I have died so many times in wars or while climbing mountains, trekking, sailing, surfing or skiing for pleasure. But I have never died for Dharma; I have never died working for sentient beings. If I die today, it's extremely worthwhile." You should think like this especially at the times when you feel exhausted and your mind is so discouraged that you don't want to do anything.

A Guide to the Bodhisattva's Way of Life says that it's regarded as better for a person to have a limb cut off than to be killed.[81] Like that, no matter how exhausted you feel when you practice Dharma, and even if you

---

[81] Ch. 6, v. 72:
Why is a person condemned to death not fortunate
If they are released after having a hand cut off?
Why am I who am experiencing human misery not fortunate
If by that I am spared from (the agonies of) hell?

get sick, it's much better than experiencing the results of all your negative karmas. Experiencing suffering during a nyung nä is much better than not doing any purification and experiencing all the undesirable results of negative karma. We don't need to talk about the lower realms but just about the human realm. Even if we're born again as a human being, we have to go through problems again and again. Even in one life we go through hunger, being unable to find a job, running out of money, disharmony in relationships, fighting and other difficulties so many times. We take rebirth again and again and experience this kind of life again and again, going through the same problems. Without needing to talk about the sufferings of the lower realms, just think about experiencing this suffering, confused human life again and again. It doesn't give you the opportunity to practice Dharma as you wish.

Even if you die while practicing Dharma, while using yourself as a servant of other sentient beings, it's extremely worthwhile. It's much sadder if you die while following the selfish attitude. That is extremely sad. There is then no happiness at the time of death and no happiness after death. Dying with the thought of cherishing others is the skillful death of a wise person. So, why don't you bear the hardships to practice Dharma? Even if you get sick, it's really nothing to be shocked about or to dislike—you would prefer to have your hand cut off than to be killed.

Part Four

The Concluding Ritual

Dedicate, request forgiveness, and perform the two ablutions,
Request (the deities) to reside continually or to depart, depending
on the circumstances,
And having performed these actions, gather the mandala:
These are the five final practices.

18. The Completion Practices

Request

KNEEL DOWN to recite the *Request*—you are the chant leader and are making the request not only for yourself but for all sentient beings. Aware of how all sentient beings are suffering, make the request.

Offering the Tormas

If there's room, the tormas are usually put in front of the mandala. According to the Tibetan tradition there are three beautifully decorated tormas with specific shapes. The central white torma is for Chenrezig, the white one to the right as you face the altar is the landlord torma and the torma to the left—a red, triangle-shaped torma that is flat in the front and round at the back—is for the dakinis and Dharma protectors.[82]

Tormas are normally made of tsampa mixed with water and have beautiful decorations. They are round at the base but about half way up start to become more pointed and are a little like the tip of a rocket at the top. The two white tormas have two petals above and one petal down below. The decorations are usually made from butter. However, no matter what material is used, the decorations should be as beautiful as possible. The whole point of decorating the tormas is to accumulate merit. The purpose of making them in nice shapes is to create the karma to receive beautiful, perfect human bodies in future lives.

The basic point is to offer the merit field something that you would enjoy most. I think that's the best thing. If you're going to make the tormas yourself, it's good to make them as rich as possible, with sugar, butter and milk, like a rich cake. It's good to offer something that you would enjoy eating.

---

[82] See appendix 1 in *Nyung Nä*.

However, if you don't make the tormas, you can offer three cakes or three bottles of honey, peanut butter or something else that you regard as delicious. Later, instead of throwing the tormas away, you can eat them as a blessing or give them to others.

It's good to know the traditional way of arranging the altar and doing the nyung nä practice. Once you have seen how things are done you can later do the practice alone or, when you are guiding other people, explain how to do the things that people need to understand.

In Highest Yoga Tantra practice you can eat meat and onions and drink alcohol and make offerings of meat and alcohol. A little alcohol and meat are also mixed into Highest Yoga Tantra tormas because they have power to hook realizations. Depending on a person's mind, that external condition of offering such a torma together with meditation can have the power to develop realizations

However, since Action Tantra is a different level of practice, there is no mention of mixing meat and alcohol into the torma. You use just white food, the best you can find. In Action Tantra there's no mention of illusory body and clear light as paths to achieve rupakaya and dharmakaya. Since the illusory body and clear light are mentioned in Highest Yoga Tantra, there is the offering of meat and alcohol and small amounts are taken, along with meditation, to signify the illusory body and clear light, the method and wisdom of the second [completion] stage of Highest Yoga Tantra, and the means to achieve rupakaya and dharmakaya. Since the illusory body and clear light are not revealed in Action Tantra, meat and alcohol are not used. It's not that there would be some harm to Chenrezig if you offered meat and alcohol; it's just that such paths are not mentioned at this level of practice. In Highest Yoga Tantra, when you have achieved second stage realizations, meat and alcohol become a quick way to complete the practice, to develop the illusory body and clear light. You are then able to quickly cut off dual view, and that's how you can quickly achieve enlightenment.

Blessing the Tormas

First, bless the tormas. When you do, bless all three together, then offer them individually. The first torma is offered to Chenrezig and the five types of buddhas. The second torma offering is to the protectors: Six-Arm

Mahakala, Four-Arm Mahakala and other protectors. You then offer the third torma to the local landlords, the worldly protectors.

As you recite OM PADMANTAKRIT HUM PHAT and sprinkle the water, think that the drops of water are transformed into innumerable Hayagriva deities, who chase away all the interferers abiding in the tormas. (Whenever you sprinkle vase water, you are dispelling interferers.)

With the mantra of emptiness, OM SVABHAVA SHUDDHA SARVA DHARMA SVABHAVA SHUDDHO HAM, which has a very deep meaning,[83] then purify the tormas in emptiness: the ordinary appearance of truly existent tormas is purified in emptiness. While it is empty, the syllable BHRUM appears. The BHRUM then transforms into a large and extensive jewel container. Inside it is a white syllable OM, of the nature of light, which becomes a great ocean of uncontaminated transcendental wisdom nectar, which is the torma. (*Uncontaminated* means undefiled.)

Think of a very large ocean of nectar, then bless it by reciting OM AH HUM three times.

Offering the Torma to the Great Compassionate One and his Retinue

Then offer the central torma to Chenrezig and the five types of buddhas.

Praises to the Dharma Protectors

Next recite the praises to Six-Arm Mahakala and Four-Arm Mahakala and the prayer to Pälden Lhamo that requests the four actions, *Praise to Pälden Lhamo: Requesting the Four Activities*. Mahakala, Pälden Lhamo and Kalarupa are protectors particularly related to Tibetans. Besides Mahakala and Pälden Lhamo, protectors particularly connected to His Holiness the Dalai Lama, there are other protectors connected to the whole Tibetan government.

Protectors help you to succeed in your practice, in your extensive works for sentient beings and for the teaching of Buddha. Each time you do the protector prayers, especially these days, make strong requests to Mahakala and all the other protectors, and think that they immediately accept to grant your requests.

---

[83] See appendix 1 in *Universal Love*.

Six-Arm Mahakala is a protector who, on the order of Chenrezig, is living in the pledge to protect whoever practices bodhicitta. Mahakala looks after any Dharma practitioner who practices bodhicitta, especially thought training, and Chenrezig yoga. Six-Arm Mahakala is actually a wrathful manifestation of Chenrezig. In essence, Mahakala is the great compassion of the holy mind of Chenrezig, but manifests in wrathful aspect to subdue the minds of us sentient beings.

In previous times, Panchen Losang Chökyi Gyältsän, the lama who compiled *Lama Chöpa*, did a Mahakala retreat in order to prevent hindrances to actualizing the lam-rim. He planned to do the retreat for a month or so, but after five days he had generated the loving compassionate thought of bodhicitta in his mind, so he stopped his retreat. Initially he planned to do the retreat just to prevent hindrances, not to actualize the path. He didn't expect that. So practicing Mahakala can make a big difference to your practice of bodhicitta and Mahayana thought training. Your bodhicitta practice becomes successful because Mahakala especially protects practitioners of Chenrezig yoga.

Torma Offering to the Dharma Protectors and the Dakas and Dakinis

Think in particular that you're offering the torma to all the protectors whose initiation you have received. Visualize them all there in front of you. When you make the torma offering to Six-Arm Mahakala and the other protectors, think that they instantly appear in front of you and are very pleased by your torma offering.

The final prayer was written by the Seventh Dalai Lama to encourage all those different protectors to look after the teachings and Dharma practitioners and to make one's own Dharma practice successful.

Torma Offering to the Local Deities

Next comes the torma offering to the local landlords, who are spirits situated in certain areas in each country. Landlords, ordinary worldly gods who are not beyond samsara, have much power to harm and also to help. Besides giving the torma to the landlord of the particular area where you are, you are giving it to all the many landlords who abide in this world, including the spirit of Tarko, whose story is mentioned in the nyung nä text.

Since landlords can harm or help, we give them a torma and ask them to help and not interfere, as expressed in the request—to help protect the teachings, make Dharma practice successful and make the lives of the holy beings long.

Offering an Ablution

Next we offer a bath to the merit field, which is one of the five completion practices.[84] Doing this practice is a substitute for the guru yoga practice of actually offering the guru a bath and is done to purify your negativities and accumulate merit. If you are living with your guru, the main practice of offering a bath is to actually perform the service of washing your guru's holy body, offering ornaments and so forth. Visualizing offering a bath is a substitute for that, and even visualizing offering a bath collects a lot of merit and brings great purification.

Correctly following the virtuous friend has two divisions: following with thought and following with action. Following with action then has three further divisions, one of which is offering service to the guru. As part of guru yoga practice, you visualize a bathing house and then visualize offering service by offering a bath to the beings of the merit field. The practice is done for the disciple's own profit, to accumulate merit and to purify obscurations.

The practice of offering a bath to the merit field also purifies mental pollution, which causes dullness in your mind, so that you sleep a lot and can't meditate.

Remember the story of the arhat Small Path (Lamchungpa; Skt: Chudapanthaka),[85] who couldn't memorize even the two syllables *si* and *dam* at the same time. When he learned *si*, he forgot *dam*; when he learned *dam*, he forgot *si*. Buddha then gave him the job of cleaning the monks' shoes outside the temple and asked the monks to say, "Avoid dust, avoid stains," after he had cleaned their shoes. (This could refer to renouncing true suffering and the true cause of suffering; it could also refer to the two obscurations.) Because the monks continuously recited "Avoid dust, avoid

---

[84] The five completion practices are dedication, requesting forgiveness, performing the two ablutions, requesting the deities to reside or depart and gathering the mandala.
[85] See *Liberation*, pp. 106–12.

stains" in the ear of this young child as they passed back and forth through the door, he then became able to memorize.

Small Path was then given the job of cleaning the grounds outside the temple. He then realized the meaning of "Avoid dust, avoid stains" and actualized true path, the wisdom directly perceiving emptiness. He became an arhat in that life. When he was a child he was so ignorant that he couldn't memorize even two syllables, but because of Buddha's perfect power to guide sentient beings he knew exactly how to skillfully guide Small Path so that he was able to become an arhat in that life. His realizing the path started by cleaning the monks' shoes. Buddha told him to clean the dust from the monks' shoes because the Sangha are powerful objects, so serving them by cleaning their shoes accumulated much merit and purified much negative karma.

The practice of offering a bath affects the mind in a similar way.

When offering a bath, gather a reflection of the merit field in a mirror and physically offer the bath to that reflection. Before you invoke the merit field, use a peacock feather, a pointed piece of metal or a small branch to take water from the action vase and draw four lines (a grid with two sets of two lines) on the mirror to represent the four beams of the bathing house. Then mark the squares with five drops of water to signify the five types of buddhas.[86]

Next capture the reflection of the merit field in the mirror. Also pour some water into a basin to represent the bathing pool. Then place the mirror in the basin and do the visualization of offering a bath. Even though you offer a bath to the reflection of the merit field, you can still visualize that the actual living beings are there.

At the beginning, visualize the bathing house as beautiful as possible, as described in the prayer:

> The bath house has an extremely sweet fragrance,
> A crystal floor, and beautiful sparkling jeweled pillars.
> The roof is covered by a canopy
> Decorated with shining pearls.

---

[86] See appendix 7 in *Nyung Nä*.

The bathing house is an extremely beautiful celestial mansion, with four doors and four golden steps that come down into the pool, similar to those of a hotel swimming pool. It's like a swimming pool inside a house. The bathing house is fragrantly scented. It has a radiant crystal base and you can see many different jewels on the bottom of the pool. There are beautifully decorated, radiant jewel pillars. There's also a canopy of pearl decorations between the ceiling and the walls.

Outside the bathing house, all the robes of the monks and the divine garments of the deities in the merit field are hung on the branches of trees or placed on platforms or tables. Then, like people entering a swimming pool, all the beings enter the bathing pool.[87]

Then from your heart transform goddesses carrying vases. Transform three goddesses for each holy being in the merit field, each with her own job. One offering goddess takes water from the pool and offers a bath to the holy body, another dries off the water and the third offers robes or divine dress and ornaments.

The sequence of offering a bath follows the verses of the prayer. You offer a bath first to Chenrezig, Compassion Buddha; second to the gurus and deities; third to the buddhas and bodhisattvas; fourth to the Hearers and Self-Conquerors; fifth to the dakas and dakinis; and sixth to the Dharma protectors. Also offer music as you offer the bath.

After that, you can offer a bath to the local protectors of the Himalayan regions, the five long-life dakinis and the twelve *tenma*.[88] Especially, you should offer a bath to purify all the local nagas and landlords. The bath offering becomes healing for them, healing their sicknesses and resolving whatever other problems they have. Think that all the pollutions and other undesirable things they have received from people have been purified. They enjoy the bath very much and are satisfied.

Of course, the holy beings in the merit field have nothing to clean, nothing to purify; the bath offering is mainly a method to purify us, to clean away the two obscurations. By offering them a bath we purify ourselves.

---

[87] In one commentary, Rinpoche says "the holy beings are above the water on thrones."
[88] Guardian goddesses who protect Tibet.

Drying the Holy Bodies

There are different ways of drying off the water with OM HUM TRAM HRIH AH. You can think that all the water is drawn to five different points[89] on the holy bodies of the merit field, which the goddesses dry with OM, HUM, TRAM, HRIH and AH.

Offering Divine Garments

Offer divine garments and ornaments or robes in accordance with what is appropriate, such as robes to the ordained lineage lamas. Offer Dromtönpa, a lay lineage lama, a blue animal-skin chuba.

When you offer garments, don't use just any old piece of cloth. Use a clean, beautiful scarf. In that way you create more merit. As you recite the verse, hold up the scarf and offer that as the divine dress.

Offering Ornaments

When you offer ornaments, if you have a nice jewel mala, hold it there in the folded scarf. You collect more merit if you offer that to the merit field.

Everything that you offer generates great bliss in the holy minds of the merit field. That's the main point.

Offering a Vase

When you finish offering the vase, pour a drop of water on the ground, thinking that it purifies the sentient beings of the six realms and that they generate bodhicitta in their minds.

Offering a Crown

At the end, before the merit field returns to its natural abode, it's very good to do the offering of a crown to Buddha and then dedicate for the teachings

---

[89] In *Liberation*, p. 168, Pabongka Rinpoche lists them as forehead, throat, heart and two shoulders.

to last a long time and for all sentient beings to achieve the ten powers of a buddha, or enlightenment. It's very important to do that at the end.

The two verses for offering a crown are:

> With most excellent light radiating forth to the ten directions,
> Splendor of good fortune ablaze everywhere,
> This crown ornament of precious gold dust,
> I offer to the crown of the Shakya King.
> Thereby, may the precious teachings spread to the ten directions
>
> And may the world be pervaded by supreme happiness!
> By [the teachings] becoming the crown ornament of transmigrators, including gods,
> May all attain the level of one endowed with the ten powers.

Request

Then hold the mirror up and the merit field returns to its natural abode. At that time, recite the request:

> Out of your loving compassion for myself and migrating beings,
> O *bhagavan*, please remain
> Through the force of your miraculous manifestations
> For as long as we continue to make offerings.

Then pour the water in the basin back into the action vase. When you do this, hold the stick so that the water drips down it into the vase. This is much easier than trying to pour directly from the container; it might then spill out.

Visualize that the water goes into channels that go to the six realms, purifying the negative karma and defilements of all the sentient beings in each realm. All the old robes and divine garments of the merit field left hanging in the trees are given as relics, as objects of devotion, to the beings in the six realms.

Because the water has been used to offer a bath to the merit field, it's very blessed, so, as Pabongka Dechen Nyingpo advised, you can take one drop for purification and for the blessing.

The bathing house then becomes empty right there.

Dedication

>Due to the merits accumulated by me,
>May I quickly achieve enlightenment in this world.
>May I reveal the Dharma in order to benefit the transmigratory beings
>And to quickly liberate the sentient beings who are intoxicated by suffering.
>
>In all my lifetimes, may I and all sentient beings
>Be born with good caste, clear wisdom, great compassion
>And great devotion to our gurus and without pride.
>And may we abide in the samaya of Chenrezig.
>
>In all lifetimes, to benefit other sentient beings,
>May I and all other sentient beings
>Become only like you, Guru Chenrezig,
>And like your retinue, your life span, your pure realm and your holy name.
>
>Due to having praised and made requests to you,
>May I and all other sentient beings have no disease, spirit harms, poverty and quarrels;
>And may the Dharma and auspicious things increase in the place where we are.
>
>May the precious mind of bodhicitta
>Be born in those in whom it has not been generated;
>May that which has been generated not decline,
>But increase more and more.

Dedicate in this way for yourself and for all sentient beings.

Purifying Errors with the Hundred-Syllable Mantra of Padmasattva

As I explained earlier, the reason you ring the bell during the Padmasattva mantra is not as an offering but to remind you to meditate on emptiness. The most powerful way to purify any mistake you have made is to meditate on emptiness. Recite the hundred-syllable mantra and also ring the bell, because the bell signifies wisdom, the wisdom realizing emptiness. The sound of the bell is telling you that everything is empty from its own side, that everything does not exist from its own side. While ringing the bell and reciting the Padmasattva mantra, remember that the negative karmas and obscurations accumulated through imperfect concentration and various other mistakes you have made are all empty. Remember the emptiness of all the negative karmas and obscurations.

Concentrate deeply on the emptiness of the three circles: subject, action, object. Looking at your negative karmas and obscurations as empty is extremely powerful. One or two seconds of meditation on emptiness is very powerful, like an atomic bomb. That one or two seconds of concentration purifies inconceivable obscurations.

Inner Ablution: Taking the Vase Nectar

Arya Great Compassionate One with his retinue descends in front of you. White nectar flows from their holy bodies, washing all the outside and inside of your body and purifying all diseases, spirit harms, negative karmas and obscurations accumulated with your three doors—your body, speech and mind—and even all the imprints left by negative karma. Nothing, not even the slightest mental stain, is left on your mental continuum. Generate strong faith in this. How much you are able to purify depends on how much faith you are able to generate. The purification comes from your own mind; it depends on your own mind.

The nectar should be taken in three sips. The first sip purifies all your disturbing-thought obscurations, which interfere with achieving liberation. The second sip purifies all your subtle obscurations, which mainly interfere with achieving omniscience. The third sip causes you to actualize the dharmakaya within you.

On the fasting day, don't drink the water from the vase but just put a little from your hand on your head three times, with the same meditation.

Arising as the Commitment Being

If you have visualized yourself as Thousand-Arm Chenrezig, all the faces and arms absorb back to the root face and arms, and you become one-face, two-arm Chenrezig.

Dedication

> *Ge wa di yi nyur du dag*
> *Thug je chhen po drub gyur nä*
> *Dro wa chig kyang ma lü pa*
> *De yi sa la gö par shog*

> Due to the merits of the three times accumulated by me, by all the buddhas, bodhisattvas and all other beings, may I quickly achieve the Great Compassionate One and lead every sentient being to the Great Compassionate One's enlightenment.

If you do this dedication with awareness of emptiness it becomes a pure dedication, unstained by the concept of true existence. Meditating intensively on emptiness, looking at everything as empty, dedicate the merits, sealing them with emptiness.

To make this dedication more effective for your mind, you can recite it in one of the following ways:

> Due to all the past, present and future merits accumulated by me and by all the buddhas, bodhisattvas and all other beings, which are merely imputed by the mind, may the I, who is merely imputed by the mind, achieve the Great Compassionate One, who is merely imputed by the mind, and lead every sentient being, who is merely imputed by the mind, to the Great Compassionate One's enlightenment, which is merely imputed by the mind.

Due to all the past, present and future merits accumulated by me and by all the buddhas, bodhisattvas and all other beings, which are empty from their own side, may the I, who is empty from its own side, achieve Chenrezig's enlightenment, which is empty from its own side, and lead all sentient beings, who are empty from their own side, to that Chenrezig enlightenment, which is empty from its own side.

Due to all the past, present and future merits accumulated by me and by all the buddhas, bodhisattvas and all other beings, which exist but which are empty, may the I, who exists but who is empty, achieve Chenrezig's enlightenment, which exists but which is empty, and lead all sentient beings, who exist but who are empty, to that Chenrezig enlightenment, which exists but which is empty, by myself alone, who exists but who is empty.

If we dedicate in this way, sealing our dedication with emptiness, the merits not only become inexhaustible, so that no matter how much we use them they never finish, but they cannot be destroyed by anger and heresy.

Requesting to Reside or Depart

A. When the Basis of the Front Generation is a Drawn Mandala, Request the Deities to Reside Continually

If you have a Chenrezig statue or mandala, visualize that the merit field absorbs into the statue or mandala.

You can think that the Chenrezig, five types of buddhas and mandala you have visualized in front of you absorb into all the buddha statues and holy objects in the retreat room, as well as into the picture of the Chenrezig mandala inside the mandala house, thus blessing, or consecrating, them. This becomes the same as consecrating the holy objects.

> By abiding with these holy objects for the benefit of sentient beings, please grant health, long life, wealth, control and all the sublime realizations.

OM SUPRATISHTHA VAJRA YE SVAHA

Request the deities to abide with the statues and other holy objects to benefit sentient beings. In the prayer, *control* means control over wind and mind. If you have control over your body and mind, they then become serviceable, so that you can use them in the path to enlightenment, the common path of sutra and the particular path of tantra. You also ask for your mind to be enriched with all scriptural understanding and realizations.

C. When the Basis of the Front Generation is Heaps of Substances, Request the Deities to Depart

If you don't have a Chenrezig mandala but just a heap of grains, say the following prayer:

> OM You have done the works for sentient beings
> And granted the realizations.
> Although you are going back to the land of buddhas,
> I request you to please come back again.
> OM VAJRA MUH

The transcendental wisdom beings return to the natural abode. The samaya beings then absorb into you.

Now you are one-face, two-arm Chenrezig, marked with the three syllables OM, AH and HUM at your three places. Then do the virtuous practices of the break-time.

VERSES OF AUSPICIOUSNESS

The dedication prayer written by E Khachö Tändar, *Prayer of Abiding in the Retreat*, describes the practice of nyung nä and its benefits. It is followed by the auspicious prayer written by Panchen Losang Chökyi Gyältsän.

Prayer of Abiding in the Retreat

In the fourth verse, . . . *the charming voice of Brahma* means a buddha's holy speech. There's a reason it's expressed in this way, but it means a buddha's holy speech.

If you're finding the nyung nä practice very hard, don't think, "I shouldn't have done this nyung nä." When you face difficulties, don't reject nyung nä practice because it will create the karma for you to be unable to do nyung näs in the future. It will become an obstacle so that you won't get the opportunity to do nyung näs for many future lives.

If you're experiencing difficulties and such thoughts come, remember the three lower realms. Remember especially the hell and preta sufferings and think, "Compared to their suffering, what I'm experiencing is great pleasure. This is great pleasure compared to even the lightest hell suffering." It's very good to read the sections on hell and preta sufferings in lam-rim texts, especially when there's a danger that you will break the precepts because of hunger, thirst and so forth. Remember that if you follow the three poisonous minds you will fall down into the lower realms and experience those sufferings that you don't even want to hear about now.

Expression of Auspiciousness of Abiding in the Retreat

In this prayer, Panchen Losang Chökyi Gyältsän requests Chenrezig for all the auspicious things that happened to Bhikshuni Lakshmi and the many Indian and Tibetan yogis, the direct and indirect lineage gurus, who achieved Chenrezig, to happen to us. He also requests for help in ceasing all our inauspicious things and in increasing happiness and realizations and in completing the realizations.

Think that this prayer is related to you, that Panchen Losang Chökyi Gyältsän is praying for you.

DEDICATIONS

Our being able to accumulate so much merit doing nyung näs is all basically due to His Holiness the Dalai Lama, the present holder and preserver of the whole Buddhadharma, His Holiness Serkong Tsenshab Rinpoche, who gave much inspiration to do nyung näs by giving the oral transmissions and a whole commentary on nyung nä, Kirti Tsenshab Rinpoche and Lama Yeshe.

The tradition of doing nyung näs was established in past times in Lawudo, where we did the first nyung nä. When I returned to the Lawudo Cave, the same people who used to be benefactors of the Lawudo Lama asked me to start doing nyung näs. However, it's basically due to the kindness of Lama Yeshe, who was incomparably kinder than all the buddhas of the three times, that we have been able to accumulate so much merit by doing nyung nä practice.

You can dedicate the merits in the following ways:

> Due to all these merits, may the wishes of His Holiness the Dalai Lama and all the other holy beings be accomplished and may they have stable lives until samsara ends.
>
> In particular, may Tenzin Ösel Hita have a stable life until samsara ends and be able to benefit all sentient beings like Guru Shakyamuni Buddha, Lama Tsongkhapa and Lama Yeshe, by becoming a holder of the entire teaching.
>
> May all the students of all the FPMT centers be able to actualize the complete path of Lama Tsongkhapa in this life and be able to spread it to all sentient beings. In this way, may all the rest of the sentient beings quickly achieve enlightenment.
>
> May all sentient beings receive and experience all the merit and happiness that I have accumulated. Whatever suffering sentient beings have, may I receive and experience it.
>
> Due to all these merits, just by any sentient being hearing me, touching me, talking about me, remembering me or thinking of me, may all their sufferings be pacified and may they achieve all happiness.

Lama Tsongkhapa dedication prayers

> *Mä jung nam thar tsang mäi thrim dang dän*
> *Lab chhen gyäl sä chö päi nying tob chhe*
> *De tong chhog gi rim nyi näl jor gyi*
> *Lo zang gyäl wäi tän dag jäl war shog*

> May I and all sentient beings be able to meet the pure wisdom teaching of the Victorious One, which is living in pure morality, having the brave attitude to do the extensive bodhisattva deeds and actualizing the yoga of the two stages, the essence of which is the transcendental wisdom of nondual bliss and voidness.
>
> May I and all sentient beings be able to meet this pure complete teaching of Lama Tsongkhapa, the unification of sutra and tantra, right this second.

In relation to the teaching of Lama Tsongkhapa, this verse mentions the yoga of the two stages, the sublime realization of bliss-voidness. Why is bliss-voidness mentioned separately, in addition to mention of the two stages? Even though the two stages contain all the realizations of tantra, if we have realization of bliss-voidness it means that there's enlightenment in this life. If we don't have this realization, there's no enlightenment in this life. I think that this is why this essence of the Highest Yoga Tantra path is mentioned.

If you are living in pure moral conduct and have strong bodhicitta, renouncing the self and cherishing others, you have met Lama Tsongkhapa's teaching. And if you have the realization of bliss-voidness, you have met Lama Tsongkhapa's tantric teaching.

We pray to meet Lama Tsongkhapa's teaching: *Lo zang gyäl wäi tän dag jäl war shog*, "May I be able to meet the pure wisdom teaching of the Victorious One," which means Lama Tsongkhapa. It is extremely important to pray to meet Lama Tsongkhapa's teaching in this life, where *meet* means to have all these pure realizations in this life.

We can also pray to be born wherever Lama Tsongkhapa is, in whichever pure realm:

> Guru Losang Dragpa, wherever you are, whether in Tushita, Sukhavati or another pure realm, may I, all the people around me and all sentient beings be born in this pure realm.

With this verse, you can think of your parents, relatives, friends and enemies, those who are close to you and with whom you have a good connection and those with whom you have a bad connection.

Author's Colophon

This text was composed by the Seventh Dalai Lama, Kelzang Gyatso, in his room at the Potala Palace of the Arya Compassionate One.

The Seventh Dalai Lama says that Nagarjuna composed a nyung nä practice, as did Bhikshuni Lakshmi, and that writings by other learned, highly attained beings of the nyung nä were also relied upon. While this sadhana composed by Kelzang Gyatso, the Seventh Dalai Lama, is based on those Indian scriptures, it is mainly based on the more common method of achievement composed by Gyalwa Gendun Gyatso, the second Dalai Lama.

Author's Dedication

You can also dedicate the merits with the three verses of dedication composed by Gyalwa Kelzang Gyatso, which come at the very end of the nyung nä sadhana.

> Due to all the past, present and future merits collected by me and the merits of the three times collected by all other sentient beings, including the bodhisattvas, and by the buddhas:
>
> With even a portion of the stream of the four rivers
> Of the three miracles that come from
> The Kailash Mountain of pristine white compassion,
> Arya Avalokiteshvara cleanses the stains of all living beings.
>
> Due to the virtue of arranging a ceremony of divine approximation of that protector,
> According to the custom of the pure lineage of the (Bhikshuni) Lakshmi tradition,
> May previously accumulated negativities, obscurations and imprints be purified,
> And may there be dominion over the state of the inseparable three kayas.

May all sentient beings, who have been my mother and father,
And who brought me benefit as to a dear child during countless rebirths,
Always be befriended by Avalokiteshvara
And swiftly contact the abode of supreme bliss.

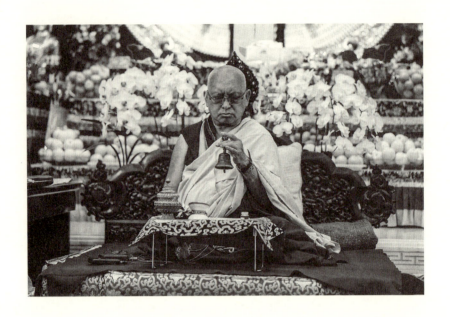

Part Five

Additional Instructions

19. Additional Advice

THE YOGA OF SLEEPING

WHEN YOU GO to bed, do so with the divine pride that you are Chenrezig. You have accumulated as much virtue as possible with your body, speech and mind during the day, and then when you go to sleep, you, Chenrezig, gradually melt into white light and absorb into the syllable HRIH at your heart. The HRIH then gradually melts into light and then disappears, like a cloud disappearing in the sky. Then, with your mind abiding in clear light emptiness, try to fall asleep.

If that is not possible, try to fall asleep by having devotion to the guru-deity, Guru Chenrezig, or by generating the special virtuous thought of compassion or bodhicitta for sentient beings. In this way your sleep becomes virtuous and meaningful. You make that part of your life meaningful.

THE FINAL MORNING

In Solu Khumbu there lived a highly realized ascetic lama called Khari Rinpoche, an incarnation of one of the Kadampa geshes. In his nunnery-monastery, near the river down below the Lawudo Cave, Khari Rinpoche established much practice of Chenrezig retreat.

According to Khari Rinpoche's advice, on the third morning of a nyung nä, the final session would start in the early morning, at three o'clock, and vase water was given as soon as the people came into the gompa. People could then speak. (After the vase water is taken, the speech is released.) Food and drink were then immediately served. Each person was given a handful of crushed brown sugar mixed with water to drink. Perhaps this was to give energy to those who had stomach pain from fasting for a long time, but the monks and nuns said that they couldn't drink it because it made them vomit. People were then served tea and thugpa, Tibetan soup.

Khari Rinpoche did this because many people found the practice too difficult when the fast was broken later and became discouraged from doing nyung näs in the future. Serving the tea and food at three o'clock allowed people to quickly recover from their thirst, hunger, exhaustion, pain or whatever other problem they were having. Khari Rinpoche served food at three o'clock mainly with the aim that many people would then do nyung nä retreat again and again.

Generally, food is served when the light starts. In some monasteries, food is served on the third morning only when the whole practice is finished—after the vase water has been blessed and the water passed around. However, food can be offered when the light starts in the eastern sky, whether or not the vase water has been given.

The session on the third morning is also shorter. If you're not planning to take the Restoring and Purifying Ordination, just do the offering of your body to the buddhas and bodhisattvas. You don't need to do prostrations to the Thirty-five Buddhas or to repeat the Thirty-five Buddhas' names as many times, and you do the *Praise to Chenrezig* only about seven times. You have a choice about doing prostrations to the Thirty-five Buddhas and how many times you do them, but the *Praise to Chenrezig* has to be recited. You usually recite it at least twenty-one times but in this final morning session it can be recited seven times. That's what is advised.

Even the mantras can be recited for half a mala or just a few times. Not reciting a full round of the mala doesn't make your life more profitable, but it's a personal choice.

If you are going to start another nyung nä immediately, the last session is very short. Have a breakfast of light soup and then start the next nyung nä. This is what you do when you do many nyung näs one after another: do a short session early on the third morning, have soup and then start the next nyung nä retreat.

There is a lighter way to do the practice. On the second morning, when you take the Eight Mahayana Precepts, make a vow to keep silence and not to eat or drink. At that time, you can make the decision not to drink until you get up the following morning instead of until sunrise. If you have made the particular vow not to drink until sunrise the next day, it's not so comfortable if you drink earlier than that. Therefore, when you take the Eight Mahayana Precepts, you can make the decision not to have a drink until you get up the following day. In that way, when the session starts the next day, you can have a drink. Then, at dawn, when the stars are no longer bright and the sky is whitish in the east, which is the very beginning of the day, you can start the session. If you're going to do another nyung nä right away, either between the two nyung nä sessions or at dawn, you can have soup. That's the lighter way to do the practice.

In the strict way of doing it, you don't drink the vase water until the whole session is finished, until the very end of the practice. You liberate the speech and then have tea after that. It depends on where you are, but by that time it's usually after dawn.

According to the Western way of calculating, the new day starts from midnight, but according to the Dharma, the beginning of the day is defined by a whitish color appearing in the sky in the east. The very beginning of the day is when there is a change of color to white in the east, even if the rest of the sky is dark. If the weather is clear and you look at the eastern sky in the early morning before the sun rises, you will see a whitish color there. That is the beginning of the dawn time. The time from dawn until the sun rises is divided into three periods. Even while the rest of the sky is dark, there are two or three changes of color in the east. When the whitish color starts in the east, it is the very beginning of the day. That is the time of sunrise on this continent, and the time referred to when we say, "until sunrise tomorrow." You can't wait until the place where you are gets sunlight, as sometimes you might be somewhere that is surrounded by mountains and gets sunlight for only half the day. If you then had to wait until that time, it would become ridiculous. *Until sunrise tomorrow* refers to the sun rising on this continent, with the start of the white color in the east, and that is the beginning of the day.

The Yoga of Eating

Offer tea or food by thinking of it as nectar. Buddhas see as nectar even that which appears to us as simple ordinary water. Because buddhas have ceased all faults of the mind and completed the collection of merit, they see everything as pure. As Chenrezig sees tea or food as nectar, offer to Chenrezig that great enjoyment of nectar, the nature of which is extraordinary bliss and the function of which is to give extraordinary bliss.

When you eat or drink with this Chenrezig practice, visualize the syllable HRIH, which signifies the holy mind of Chenrezig, at your heart, then make offering to that. Think that the HRIH at your heart is the whole merit field—all the gurus, Buddha, Dharma, Sangha—then offer the tea or food. In this way all your eating and drinking also become virtue.

If there's some food that you don't like, it's especially good to offer it. Because you're giving it to somebody else and not taking it for yourself, there's then no problem. It's a psychological thing. That way you can accept the food, and also there's unbelievable benefit from each offering of food or drink.

You can use the praise from the nyung nä text as an offering prayer by simply changing "I prostrate" to "I make offering":

> OM AH HUM (3X)
> *Chhag tong khor lö gyur wäi gyäl po tong*
> Your thousand arms signify a thousand wheel-turning kings,
> *Chän tong käl pa zang pöi sang gyä tong*
> Your thousand eyes signify the thousand buddhas of the fortunate eon,
> *Gang la gang dül de la der tön pai*
> You manifest whatever is necessary to subdue those to be subdued:
> *Tsün pa chän rä zig la chhö par bül*
> To you, Compassionate-Eyed One, I make offering.

Or you can recite the usual offering prayer:

> *La ma sang gyä la ma chhö*
> The guru is Buddha, the guru is Dharma,
> *De zhin la ma ge dün te*
> The guru is Sangha also.
> *Kün gyi je po la ma te*
> The guru is the creator of all (happiness).
> *La ma nam la chhö par bül*
> To all gurus, I make this offering.

With such guru yoga practice, every single enjoyment in daily life becomes a means to accumulate inconceivable merit, the greatest merit, because the guru is the highest object of merit, higher than all the buddhas. The guru is the most dangerous, most powerful object. Doing a tiny good thing in relation to the guru brings the greatest positive result. Doing a small bad thing, such as showing a little disrespect, however, brings the heaviest negative result. Therefore, if you offer sense enjoyments with guru yoga meditation in your daily life, you accumulate the most extensive, greatest merit from all those enjoyments. This especially happens if you can remember the guru during those times.

Since we are trying to achieve enlightenment for the sake of all sentient beings, as much as possible we should do everything with a motivation of bodhicitta so that the action becomes a cause of enlightenment. To make offering before we eat or drink is also part of the refuge practice. There are common and specific precepts that come with taking refuge in Buddha, Dharma and Sangha, and one of the common precepts is to offer everything that we eat and drink, even a candy. Doing these practices in our daily life is very important. It's Guru Shakyamuni Buddha's skillful means of enabling us to incidentally accumulate merit by making our actions in daily life become good karma.

Otherwise our eating is the same as that of a dog or a cat. First of all, our having a human body should make a difference; and second, because we listen to Dharma we then have to practice it.

Another offering prayer you can use is:

> *Dag sog khor chä tshe rab tham chä du*
> May we and all those around us, in all future lives,
> *Kön chhog sum dang nam yang mi dräl zhing*
> Never be separated from the Guru-Three Rare Sublime Ones,
> *Kön chhog sum po gyün du chhö pa la*
> Always be able to make offerings to the Guru-Three Rare Sublime Ones,
> *Kön chhog sum gyi jin lab jug par shog*
> And receive the blessings of the Guru-Three Rare Sublime Ones.

This is an excellent prayer, a perfect prayer, with nothing missing. It's a short but very rich prayer that is done for you; for the people who gave you food, clothing or other help; for all those sentient beings who suffered or died for your food or drink; and for all the rest of the sentient beings. It's the best prayer because, from your side, you're doing something to repay the kindness of others.

And receive the blessings of the Guru-Three Rare Sublime Ones means the realizations of the whole path, from guru devotion up to enlightenment. Developing all these realizations depends on creating the cause for them, merit. You accumulate merit in two main ways: on the basis of the field of sentient beings and in relation to the holy objects of Guru, Buddha, Dharma and Sangha. You need to always create merit, not only in this life but in all lifetimes. You, the benefactors and all sentient beings need to accumulate merit by making offerings to the Guru-Three Rare Sublime Ones all the time. The practice of making offerings to the Guru-Three Rare Sublime Ones is extremely important. If you want to develop your mind, this is what you should practice. You should study, understand and practice the ways of accumulating merit by making offerings.

To be able to do this, you first need to meet the Guru-Three Rare Sublime Ones. If you don't meet them, you will have no opportunity to do this practice, to accumulate merit in dependence upon holy objects. And it won't happen if you meet a wrong path and a wrong object of refuge, who cannot guide you away from disturbing thoughts but only makes your disturbing thoughts increase. A wrong object of refuge cannot guide you away from the lower realms, and everything you do will then become a cause of suffering.

Therefore, it's extremely important to pray to meet the Three Rare Sublime Ones. Those who don't meet the Three Rare Sublime Ones but ignorantly follow wrong objects of refuge with blind faith experience much suffering and always create the causes of suffering. Everything depends on meeting the Three Rare Sublime Ones. Receiving the blessings of the Three Rare Sublime Ones depends on creating the cause by making offerings to the Three Rare Sublime Ones. Being able to always practice making offerings to the Three Rare Sublime Ones depends on meeting the Three Rare Sublime Ones.

The yoga of washing

In the morning, even on the day of complete fasting, you can still wash your mouth. That is part of the practice of keeping clean.

I don't know how it happened, but one student in New Zealand was somehow told that you shouldn't wash your mouth. She then tried to clean her mouth with toilet paper. She thought it was terrible and checked with a Kagyü lama, who told her it wasn't right. She thought that I had taught her non-Buddhist things.

Mantra recitation

During a nyung nä (and maybe also when you do any other retreat), if you have bad dreams at night, if you did the mantra recitations without controlling your sense doors, while possessed by interferers or experiencing disease, carelessly, while having an upset body or mind, or past the proper time, in the daytime you should recite one hundred times the mantra of the lord of the race of the deity. The *mantra of the lord of the race* looks as if it should be the mantra of Amitabha, but in the text it says to recite any of the essence mantras of Chenrezig, the lord of the Lotus race. (Normally, mantras should not be recited during sunrise or sunset or at 12 o'clock. It doesn't mean not to recite prayers at those times; it refers mainly to the recitation of mantra.) Here, in the nyung nä practice, you should recite any of the essence mantras of Chenrezig one hundred times in the daytime.

In any case what's being recited is the Chenrezig mantra, either the long or short one. The long mantra of Eleven-Face Chenrezig contains the heart mantra. Here it might mean OM MANI PADME HUM. Otherwise, you would be reciting the same mantra.

You can then count the mantras you recite. Without reciting this mantra one hundred times in the daytime, even if you continuously recite the mantra, you cannot count those mantras as part of the retreat. You must recite one hundred times the mantra of the lord of the race related to that deity when something like that happens. After doing that, you can then count the mantras of the deity as part of the nyung nä or other retreat.

Shortening sessions

You can use the long nyung nä sadhana but shorten it in accordance with how much time you have and how you want to do the practice. Where there are offering verses followed by offering mantras, for example, you can just do the mantras and leave out the verses. And when you are visualizing Chenrezig, you can recite the elaborate description for the self-generation, and for the front generation you can just say, "Chenrezig, with one thousand eyes and one thousand arms." As long as you visualize the general aspect, it's fine to abbreviate in that way. As long as the main body of the practice is done, you can abbreviate the elaborate descriptions.

Apart from the final session on the third morning, when you can recite it seven or fewer times, you have to recite *Praise to Chenrezig* twenty-one times. You must do this, even if you're doing a short nyung nä session. Some people did not clearly understand this and were doing very few of the praises. It then becomes a very easy nyung nä.

While *Praise to Chenrezig* has to be recited at least twenty-one times, you have a choice about doing prostrations to the Thirty-five Buddhas and how many times you do them. There's no exact number of prostrations to the Thirty-five Buddhas. If you have no time, you can leave out the prostrations to the Thirty-five Buddhas, or do far fewer. But it's best to at least recite the names of the Thirty-five Buddhas, because reciting each name one time purifies many thousands of eons of different negative karmas.

You can also abbreviate the recitation of the mantras. In a nyung nä, you can recite one mala of OM MANI PADME HUM in the first session. In the next session you can recite the long mantra, or if you're short of time you can recite the long mantra once or three times and then recite the essence mantra, TADYATHA OM DHARA DHARA DHIRI DHIRI DHURU DHURU ITTI VATTE CHALE CHALE PRACHALE PRACHALE KUSUME KUSUME VARE ILI MILI CHITI JVALAM APANAYE SVAHA. His Holiness Song Rinpoche said that reciting the essence mantra is the same as reciting OM MANI PADME HUM 100,000 times.

CHENREZIG GREAT INITIATION

If you haven't received a Chenrezig great initiation, it's very good to receive one so that you become fully qualified to do the nyung nä practice. Actually, I create the cause of hell by revealing secrets to those whose minds haven't been ripened by initiation. Explaining to those who have taken a Chenrezig great initiation or a Highest Yoga Tantra initiation is fine, however. If someone has taken a Highest Yoga Tantra initiation, there's no doubt that explaining to them is not revealing secrets, unless they've lost faith in tantra after having taken the initiation.

His Holiness the Dalai Lama says that nowadays in the West many people have misconceptions about what tantra means because they see statues of Highest Yoga Tantra aspects, with the male and female deity embraced. Many people think that Buddhist tantric practice is the same as Hindu tantra (though His Holiness did not say this). They see tantric practice as simply having sex, as if there's no difference from ordinary life. Therefore, His Holiness thought that rather than letting such wrong conceptions spread, it's important to explain the meaning of tantra. It's better to do that than to allow people to have negative ideas about tantra. I think that whether a person sees tantric aspects as bad or good depends on their mind, on their wisdom and their interests.

If you have received a Highest Yoga Tantra initiation but not a lower tantra great initiation, all of the profound meditation instructions can still be explained. But they cannot be explained to someone who hasn't received even a lower tantra great initiation. Even if someone has a lot of faith, it's still not comfortable to reveal those meditations to them. It's generally strict. Most of the meditations cannot be taught, especially those explaining the transcendental wisdom of nondual clarity and profundity and the ways of generating yourself as the deity. For those you need to have received a vase initiation of lower tantra.

However, a mixture of people usually do nyung näs, with some new people and other people who have received initiation and also done nyung näs in the past. Explaining the meditations helps those who have received initiation have a clear idea of the way to meditate so that the practice is then more enjoyable and more effective, becoming a remedy to samsara and a cause of enlightenment.

Tsog offering

If you wish to offer tsog at the end of a nyung nä, you can do Gyalwa Gyatso tsog offering. The Gyalwa Gyatso tsog offering written by Lama Yeshe can be used to offer tsog to Chenrezig.

Appendixes

1. The Benefits of Cleaning

THE PRACTICE OF CLEANING has many benefits. This is not simply cleaning, but cleaning with the idea that the place you are cleaning is the abode of all the buddhas and bodhisattvas of the ten directions. As long as your mind is thinking this, it doesn't matter whether you are cleaning a temple, a meditation room, an office, a kitchen or somewhere else. The benefits are related to cleaning with that understanding.

The first result of making a place clean is that you receive a beautiful body. If you have a beautiful body, other sentient beings want to see you and respect you, so you can then benefit them. It is a way to benefit others more.

Second, you will have a beautiful, sweet voice.

You will have thin delusions, which means less ignorance, anger and attachment.

When you have cleaned a place, other sentient beings also enjoy it and are made happy. While you basically clean with the idea that you are cleaning the home of the buddhas and bodhisattvas, you also clean for the sake of sentient beings, as having a nice, clean place makes others happy. As a result of that, in the future you will be able to be in beautiful places where there is no dirt or ugliness.

You will be able to become ordained as Sangha.

You will have great wealth.

You will be born in the deva or human realm.

You will quickly achieve enlightenment.

Visualize all the dirt and garbage you clean up as your delusions and those of all sentient beings and the vacuum cleaner, broom or anything else you are using to clean as the complete path to enlightenment, the path of method and wisdom, which cleans away all your delusions and those of all sentient beings. The path of method and wisdom removes all obscurations. In this way your cleaning becomes Dharma practice.

It is advised that you visualize throwing all the garbage, all the delusions, into the mouth of Yama, the Lord of Death, where they are transformed into nectar that completely satisfies Yama. Yama then closes his mouth and goes down under the earth. Think that Yama, the Lord of Death, is completely satisfied and will never come back. This becomes a method for prolonging your life.

2. The Meaning of *Son of the Essence*

I TRANSLATE THE Tibetan term *rig kyi bu* as "son of the essence" or "son of the race" rather than "son of the caste," which is its literal meaning. This term often comes in sutra texts, such as *The Heart Sutra*, and some people translate it as "son of the family" and in other ways. The term also comes at the end of the Vajrasattva purification practice, where Vajrasattva says, "Son of the essence (*rig kyi bu*), all your obscurations and broken vows are completely purified."

If *rig* is translated literally as "caste," the meaning is not clear, as it gives more of an idea of a physical, or blood, relationship. The actual meaning is similar to caste, though. Take the example of a king's son, a prince. He is not yet a king but he is going to be a king: he is of the king's caste.

Why do I translate *rig kyi bu* as "son of the essence" or "son of the race"? Here *essence* refers to the essence of all the buddhas and *race* refers to the Mahayana race, which is entered by generating bodhicitta. It's talking about the son who has the essence of a buddha and is going to become a buddha. It's talking about the essence of mind: the buddha-essence, or buddha-nature. The relationship between the buddhas and us has nothing to do with a physical, or blood, relationship; it has to do with the nature of mind. The teachings normally talk about how every sentient being has buddha-nature—I've just used a different word, *essence*. There is the essence of buddha in the mind of every sentient being. Even flies and lice have buddha-nature. The mind of every sentient being is empty of self-existence, of inherent existence. That is the absolute nature of the mind of sentient beings. That absolute nature is not mixed, not one, with the obscurations; it is just temporarily obscured by certain obscurations.

This absolute nature of mind that each being has is the clear light nature of mind, which itself is the buddha-essence, or buddha-nature. But when a text says that we have buddha-nature, we shouldn't think that the nature of our present mind is already the nature of a buddha's holy mind, dharmakaya. We shouldn't think that our mind is actually a buddha's holy mind, that we are already enlightened. But the absolute nature of our mind, the clear-light nature, can be called the buddha-essence, or buddha-nature. Why? Simply because the clear light is not one with the obscurations.

There is the potential to achieve enlightenment in the mind of every sentient being. That potential is the clear-light nature of the mind, which is not one with the obscurations. Because the mind is not one with the obscurations but temporarily obscured, it can be purified. That absolute nature of the mind gives the possibility of achieving enlightenment. Every sentient being can achieve enlightenment because of that nature of mind.

By following the path, we purify our obscurations, and the absolute nature of our mind then becomes dharmakaya. For instance, after all our obscurations have been purified by following the path, we become Chenrezig, and the absolute nature of our mind becomes the *svabhavikakaya* (the holy body of self-nature of Chenrezig) and our mind becomes dharmakaya (the transcendental wisdom of Chenrezig's holy mind).

3. The Meaning of *Yidam*

THE TIBETAN TERM *yidam* has very profound meaning. It is sometimes translated into English as "personal deity," but I think that sounds a little strange, as if other people can't achieve that deity. *Yi* means mind; *dam* means seal, or bond, and can also mean promise. "Mind seal," or "mind bound," captures the meaning. I think *mind-seal* might be a better translation. It's similar to sealing a parcel so that it doesn't split open.

If you point to what the yidam (or deity, or buddha) is, in fact, it is the dharmakaya, the holy mind of the buddhas, the transcendental wisdom of nondual bliss and voidness. That is what we are going to achieve. Our mind becoming oneness with that, becoming that, is what we mean by achieving the yidam. Becoming the buddha, becoming the guru, achieving the guru—it all has the same meaning, even though there are these different terms.

The way to achieve that oneness is, from now on, day and night, all the time, to meditate on your own mind being oneness with the holy mind of Chenrezig (or whichever other deity you are trying to achieve). You continuously meditate on your own mind being oneness with that particular deity's holy mind, the dharmakaya. Your yidam is the particular deity, the particular aspect of buddha, that you meditate on as always being one with your own mind.

Through this method of meditating on being oneness with your yidam, your obscurations become thinner and thinner, then in that way you become closer to the holy mind of the deity. If you are meditating on Chenrezig, you then become closer to the holy mind of Chenrezig. As your obscurations get thinner, you get closer to Chenrezig. The qualities of realization also get more and more developed. Meditating on being one with Chenrezig itself is the path that leads to Chenrezig enlightenment, that enables your present mind to meet Chenrezig's holy mind. When it becomes oneness, your mind then meets Chenrezig's holy mind. At that time you have really met Chenrezig. Before, while you are following the path, it's possible for you to see Chenrezig, but as something separate. At that time, however, your mind meets Chenrezig's holy mind, the dharmakaya.

So, your yidam is the particular deity, the particular buddha, that you meditate on as always being one with your own mind.

4. Karma Stories

WE NEED TO UNDERSTAND that karma is definite to bring its own result. Any nonvirtue that is done will definitely bring its own result of suffering. As long as nothing is done, which means as long as the negative karma is not purified by generating the remedy of the path, which removes the imprints of delusions and negative karmas, or not purified with the remedy of the four powers, it will definitely bring its own result of suffering. And virtuous karma, as long as there is no obstacle to it, will definitely bring its own result of happiness. That karma is definite to bring its own result is the first law of karma to understand.

Happiness has to come from Dharma, from virtue. Any happiness of this life, including success in business, comes from Dharma. The main cause is Dharma, actions done with a motivation of non-ignorance, non-anger or non-attachment. All happiness comes from Dharma. And all difficulties, all undesirable things, come from nonvirtue, from ignorance, anger or attachment. Of course, the root is the ignorance not understanding the ultimate nature of the I, the self.

Happiness doesn't come from negative karma, from nonvirtuous thoughts and nonvirtuous actions. A person might become wealthy and have some physical comfort and enjoyments for a short time by cheating other people or by stealing their possessions, but of course, that pleasure doesn't come from stealing. That pleasure needs to come from the good karma of the person. I don't know about the conditions, but the main cause of that physical comfort is that person's own good karma. People in the world might think it came through stealing, but it's not like that. The main cause is that person's own good karma.

One cause would be having made charity to other sentient beings, but not through political charity. There are white and black Dharma politics.

Charity can be done with the self-cherishing thought, for your own happiness. You could help somebody because you want to have a good reputation, to become famous, to have other people say good things about you. This kind of charity might help others to get food or children to go to school, but your making charity does not necessarily become good karma. Even though other people benefit from it, it doesn't necessarily create good karma if you did the charity with attachment, because you wanted to achieve a good reputation. If you're making charity with attachment to the happiness of this life, even though what you're doing helps others, solving some problems of hunger and so forth, it doesn't become good karma; it doesn't become virtue. If your motivation is the eight worldly dharmas, attachment to this life's happiness, it doesn't become good karma; it becomes negative karma.

The happiness or physical comfort that a person experiences comes from Dharma, from past good karma, such as having made charity to others with a good heart, with non-ignorance, non-anger or non-attachment (which means no attachment to this life, but it can even be non-attachment to future life samsara). The wealth or physical comfort came from Dharma, from good karma. The stealing can be a condition but not the main cause of that.

By stealing, the person is creating negative karma, so then they will have to experience the suffering result of rebirth in the lower realms. And later, when born as a human being due to another good karma, they will also have to experience the three suffering results of stealing. The possessed result, which has to do with the place, means they will be born where there's a lot of poverty. They will experience poverty and be unable to obtain the means of living or they will have to share their resources with other people. They will live in a place where there's a lot of drought and other obstacles. Some years ago in Africa, one country didn't have any water. Drinking water was flown into that country, but when the plane landed there, the water had become filthy and smelly. Before, it was pure, drinkable water, but by the time the plane arrived in that place, the water had become undrinkable. That was the result of their karma. In other cases, even though somebody tries to help by bringing food from far away, local leaders steal the food and the people who are actually suffering from starvation get very little. It will be like that until from their side, they practice compassion for others; until they collect merit, good karma, the cause of all success.

The second law of karma is that karma is expandable.

The third law of karma is that karma that has been created is never lost. No matter how long it takes—even eons or hundreds of eons—the result of karma will be experienced; whether great or small, karma is never lost. Even though it might not be experienced immediately, after some time, when the conditions come together, that karma will be experienced. It is mentioned in the sutras that even if it takes hundreds of eons, when it is the right time and the conditions are gathered, karma will be experienced.

Take, for example, Nagarjuna, the great pandit who propagated the Mahayana teachings, especially the right view of the Prasangika school. Nagarjuna was a highly attained being with very high realizations. One day somebody came to beg for his head. Nagarjuna wanted to make charity of his head to that person, but no weapon could cut off his head because he had achieved the immortal vajra holy body. With his clairvoyance, however, Nagarjuna discovered that the only thing that could cut his neck was a blade of grass. The reason was that many lifetimes ago he had accidentally cut off an ant's head when he was cutting grass. He didn't kill the ant on purpose. Because of this karma from many lifetimes ago, when he became the highly attained being Nagarjuna, nothing but a blade of grass could cut off his head.

When he discovered this karma, Nagarjuna then cut off his head with a blade of grass and gave it to the person who had come to beg for it.

The killing of the ant happened incidentally while he was cutting grass. Even things that are not done intentionally create negative karma. It is still possible to experience the result of even things that happened incidentally and many lifetimes ago. No matter how small a negative karma is, it doesn't get lost.

We should relate this example to our own life; not only to this life but to our many past lives. We have created so many negative karmas. When we think of such stories about negative karma that was not even purposely created, it is scary to think about karma. It is frightening to examine karma, because karma is related not only to this life but to beginningless rebirths. There are many things we have already finished experiencing, but there are so many other things we have not yet finished experiencing.

Also, I heard a story about why Muslims have historically been opposed to Buddhism, destroying Buddhist temples, statues and many other things in India three times. For example, three times they cut down the bodhi tree under which Buddha became enlightened. Similar things happened in Indonesia, where is it hard to find an intact statue from ancient times. Most of the old statues are broken, including the ones inside the large stupa at Borobudur. Inside the many small stupas are statues of Buddha and the five types of buddhas. They have now been repaired, but when I checked there were many with broken fingers and other damage. There are huge statues, two stories high, but they also have broken fingers and other damage. One place, called Thousand Buddhas, had a thousand beautiful stone buddhas, but they were completely destroyed.

There is a story as to why Muslims have done this in particular to Buddhism. In ancient times, Buddhist monasteries in India had very strict discipline. One monk couldn't follow the monastic discipline, and when he did something opposite to the vows, the monastery punished him severely. That monk got very angry with Buddhism and made many prayers that Buddhism, wherever it spread, be harmed and destroyed. Later, after many lifetimes, he was born as a Muslim with this wrong view, then gave much harm to the Buddhist religion.

What is called "karma" is very powerful. As a result of one person getting angry with Buddhism and making many wrong prayers for Buddhism to be harmed out of that anger, for centuries there was so much harm to Buddhism, with Muslims particularly destroying the Buddhist teachings many times. It shows how powerful prayer is. When you do prayers in the wrong way, it can be very powerful. We should use this example to encourage ourselves to do as many positive prayers as possible every day. Doing correct prayers also has much power. Again, that prayers work, bringing results for many lifetimes, up to enlightenment, has to do with karma. Enlightenment, with the infinite qualities of a buddha's holy body, holy speech and holy mind, comes from positive prayers done out of bodhicitta, the thought to benefit others.

It has to do with the power of mind. That monk who didn't keep his vows got angry when he was punished by the monastery, and all the prayers he did resulted in Buddhism being destroyed for many centuries. That came from the power of his mind. It came from one person's intention, and that intention is karma. In a similar way, if you always generate a positive intention, it has incredible results; you experience happiness from life to life for hundreds and thousands of lives, and then ultimate happiness.

In ancient India in the time of King Salgyal (Skt: Prasenajit), one of his ministers disliked a woman called Sagama and slandered her to the king. Sagama was a great-grandmother, and by counting her sons, grandsons and great-grandsons, she had thirty-two male descendants. King Salgyal killed all thirty-two of them by cutting off their heads. The king then made Sagama carry all thirty-two heads back to her home.[90]

Why did Sagama have to experience such a karma? In another lifetime, thirty-two thieves came to her house with a cow they had stolen. They then killed the cow by cutting off its head. They had a big party and shared the meat with Sagama, who rejoiced in what had happened and enjoyed the meat. That was the karma. Simply rejoicing in that way was why she experienced the incredible result of having to carry all the heads of her male descendants. She wasn't involved in killing the cow, but she rejoiced in the cow being killed. The karma was very small, but the result was unbelievable.

There is another story about a bhikshuni called Utpalavarna.[91] Her husband was killed by a snake and of her two children, one was drowned in a river and the other was eaten by wolves. Her house was also burned down. She then met a man whose wife had died. One day this man got drunk, came back home and killed their son. He then forced her to eat her son's flesh. She then escaped from him and married someone else. That husband died, and the country had a custom that when the husband died the wife was buried alive with him. Some countries had this kind of custom in ancient times. Such customs are very bad and were probably created because of one person's attachment.

So, she was buried in the ground with her husband's body. That night thieves came and dug her out of the grave. She then married the leader of the thieves. That man died, and she was again buried. I think that happened one or two times.

The reason Utpala experienced all these problems, one after the other, was that a long time before, when she was in a king's harem, she killed the queen's son and swore many times that she did not kill him. It was all a result of that.

However, after all these experiences, she became a nun.

---

[90] See *Liberation*, p. 390, for a slightly different version of this story.
[91] Ibid, p. 391.

As far as positive karma is concerned, even making a small offering to Sangha accumulates great merit. For example, the life-story of Buddha mentions that all the wealth that King Kaushika had came from the one karma of making offering to Sangha. A long time ago, as a beggar in one of his past lives, with devotion he made an offering of a medicinal drink to four monks. Simply from that karma he was able to be a king with incredible wealth.

King Mabhvata had control over all four human continents. Why this king had such incredible power is that in one of his past lives he offered a handful of beans to Buddha Vipashyin. I think four beans dropped into Buddha Vipashyin's begging bowl and one dropped on his crown. Because of that he was able to become king of even the deva realm. This shows how karma is expandable—the result from a small action can be unbelievable.

From his birth, a Brahmin called Suvarnavasu had golden coins coming unceasingly from his hand. The coins could fill up a whole house. He was born like this because in one of his past lives he put one golden coin inside a clay pot and offered it to Buddha Kashyapa.[92]

So, karma is expandable in such ways.

Finally, the fourth law of karma is that without having created the karma, we can't experience its result.

---

[92] Ibid, p. 392.

Bibliography

Bardor Tulku Rinpoche. *Rest for the Fortunate: The Extraordinary Practice of Nyungne: Its History, Meaning, and Benefits*. Translated by Lama Yeshe Gyamtso. Kingston: Rinchen Publications, 2004.

Bokar Rinpoche. *Chenrezig Lord of Love: Principles and Methods of Deity Meditation*. Edited by Dan Jorgensen. San Francisco: ClearPoint Press, 1991.

Cleary, Thomas (trans). *The Flower Ornament Scripture: A Translation of the Avatamsaka Sutra*. Boston: Shambhala Publications, 1993.

FPMT. *FPMT Retreat Prayer Book: Prayers and Practices for Retreat*. Portland: FPMT, 2016.

Gyatso, Losang Kelzang, the Seventh Dalai Lama. *Nyung Nä: A Nyung Nä Ritual Sadhana of the Eleven-Faced Great Compassionate One in the Pälmo Tradition*. Portland: FPMT, 2015.

Dalai Lama, H.H. the, Tsong-ka-pa and Jeffrey Hopkins. *Deity Yoga: In Action and Performance Tantra*. Translated and edited by Jeffrey Hopkins. Ithaca: Snow Lion Publications, 1987.

Khyentse, Dilgo & Padampa Sangye. *The Hundred Verses of Advice: Tibetan Buddhist Teachings on What Matters Most*. Translated by the Padmakara Translation Group. Boston: Shambhala Publications, 2005.

Nagarjuna. *Nagarjuna's Letter: Nagarjuna's Letter to a Friend*. Commentary by Rendawa, translated by Geshe Lobsang Tharchin and Artemus B. Engle. Dharamsala: Library of Tibetan Works and Archives, 1995.

Pabongka Rinpoche. *Liberation in the Palm of Your Hand*. Translated by Michael Richards. Boston: Wisdom Publications, 2006.

Roerich, George N. *The Blue Annals: The Stages of the Appearance of the Doctrine and Preachers in the Land of Tibet*. New Delhi: Motilal Banarsidass, 1996.

Shantideva. *A Guide to the Bodhisattva's Way of Life*. Translated by Stephen Batchelor. Dharamsala: Library of Tibetan Works and Archives, 2007.

Wangchen Rinpoche. *Buddhist Fasting Practice: The Nyungne Method of Thousand-Armed Chenrezig*. Ithaca, NY: Snow Lion Publications, 2009.

Yeshe, Lama Thubten. *Universal Love: The Yoga Method of Buddha Maitreya*. Edited by Nicholas Ribush. Boston: Lama Yeshe Wisdom Archive, 2008.

Zopa Rinpoche, Lama. *The Direct and Unmistaken Method: The Practice and Benefits of the Eight Mahayana Precepts.* Portland: FPMT, Inc., 2009.

——. *How to Practice Dharma: Teachings on the Eight Worldly Dharmas.* Edited by Gordon McDougall. Boston: Lama Yeshe Wisdom Archive, 2012.

——. *The Perfect Human Rebirth: Freedom and Richness on the Path to Enlightenment.* Edited by Gordon McDougall. Boston: Lama Yeshe Wisdom Archive, 2013.

——. *Teachings from the Mani Retreat.* Edited by Ailsa Cameron. Boston: Lama Yeshe Wisdom Archive, 2001.

Suggested Further Reading

Chodron, Thubten. *Cultivating a Compassionate Heart: The Yoga Method of Chenrezig*. Ithaca: Snow Lion Publications, 2006.

Dilgo Khyentse. *The Heart Treasure of the Enlightened Ones: The Practice of View, Meditation, and Action*. Boston: Shambhala, 1992.

Gyatso, Geshe Jampa. *Purification in Tibetan Buddhism: The Practice of the Thirty-Five Confession Buddhas*. Edited by Joan Nicell. Boston: Wisdom Publications, 2016.

Yeshe, Lama Thubten. *Becoming the Compassion Buddha: Tantric Mahamudra for Everyday Life*. Edited by Robina Courtin. Boston: Wisdom Publications, 2003.

———. *Becoming Vajrasattva: The Tantric Path of Purification*. Edited by Nicholas Ribush. Boston: Wisdom Publications, 2004.

———. *Introduction to Tantra: The Transformation of Desire*. Edited by Jonathan Landaw. Boston: Wisdom Publications, 2014.

Yeshe, Lama and Lama Zopa Rinpoche. *Wisdom Energy: Basic Buddhist Teachings*. Edited by Jonathan Landaw with Alexander Berzin. Boston: Wisdom Publications, 2012.

Zopa Rinpoche, Lama. *The Door to Satisfaction: The Heart Advice of a Tibetan Buddhist Master*. Edited by Ailsa Cameron and Robina Courtin. Boston: Wisdom Publications, 2001.

———. *The Heart of the Path: Seeing the Guru as Buddha*. Edited by Ailsa Cameron. Boston: Lama Yeshe Wisdom Archive, 2009.

———. *Teachings from the Medicine Buddha Retreat*. Edited by Ailsa Cameron. Boston: Lama Yeshe Wisdom Archive, 2009.

———. *Teachings from the Vajrasattva Retreat*. Edited by Ailsa Cameron and Nicholas Ribush. Boston: Lama Yeshe Wisdom Archive, 2000.

———. *Transforming Problems into Happiness*. Boston: Wisdom Publications, 2001.

———. *Ultimate Healing: The Power of Compassion*. Edited by Ailsa Cameron. Boston: Wisdom Publications, 2001.

Lama Yeshe Wisdom Archive

The Lama Yeshe Wisdom Archive (LYWA) is the collected works of Lama Thubten Yeshe and Lama Thubten Zopa Rinpoche. Lama Zopa Rinpoche, its spiritual director, founded the Archive in 1996.

Lama Yeshe and Lama Zopa Rinpoche began teaching at Kopan Monastery, Nepal, in 1970. Since then, their teachings have been recorded and transcribed. At present we have well over 12,000 hours of digital audio and some 90,000 pages of raw transcript. Many recordings, mostly teachings by Lama Zopa Rinpoche, remain to be transcribed, and as Rinpoche continues to teach, the number of recordings in the Archive increases accordingly. Most of our transcripts have been neither checked nor edited.

Here at the LYWA we are making every effort to organize the transcription of that which has not yet been transcribed, edit that which has not yet been edited, and generally do the many other tasks detailed below.

The work of the Lama Yeshe Wisdom Archive falls into two categories: *archiving* and *dissemination*.

Archiving requires managing the recordings of teachings by Lama Yeshe and Lama Zopa Rinpoche that have already been collected, collecting recordings of teachings given but not yet sent to the Archive, and collecting recordings of Lama Zopa's on-going teachings, talks, advice and so forth as he travels the world for the benefit of all. Incoming media are then catalogued and stored safely while being kept accessible for further work.

We organize the transcription of audio, add the transcripts to the already existent database of teachings, manage this database, have transcripts checked, and make transcripts available to editors or others doing research on or practicing these teachings.

Other archiving activities include working with video and photographs of the Lamas and digitizing Archive materials.

Dissemination involves keeping up with evolving technology and making the Lamas' teachings available through various avenues including books for free distribution and sale, ebooks on a wide range of readers, lightly edited transcripts, a monthly e-letter (see below), social media, DVDs and online video, articles in *Mandala* and other magazines and on our website. Irrespective of the medium we choose, the teachings require a significant amount of work to prepare them for distribution.

This is just a summary of what we do. The Archive was established with virtually no seed funding and has developed solely through the kindness of many people, most of whom we mention and thank sincerely on our website. We are indebted to you all.

Our further development similarly depends upon the generosity of those who see the benefit and necessity of this work, and we would be extremely grateful for your help. Thus we hereby appeal to you for your kind support. If you would like to make a contribution to help us with any of the above tasks or to sponsor books for free distribution, please contact us:

Lama Yeshe Wisdom Archive
PO Box 636, Lincoln, MA 01773, USA
Telephone (781) 259-4466
info@LamaYeshe.com
LamaYeshe.com

The Lama Yeshe Wisdom Archive is a 501(c)(3) tax-deductible, nonprofit corporation dedicated to the welfare of all sentient beings and totally dependent upon your donations for its continued existence. Thank you so much for your support. You may contribute by mailing a check, bank draft or money order to our Lincoln address; by making a donation on our secure website; by mailing us your credit card number or phoning it in; or by transferring funds directly to our bank—ask us for details.

Lama Yeshe Wisdom Archive Membership

In order to raise the money we need to employ editors to make available the thousands of hours of teachings mentioned above, we have established a membership plan. Membership costs US$1,000 and its main benefit is that you will be helping make the Lamas' incredible teachings available to a worldwide audience. More direct and tangible benefits to you personally include free Lama Yeshe and Lama Zopa Rinpoche books from the Archive and Wisdom Publications, a year's subscription to *Mandala*, a year of monthly pujas by the monks and nuns at Kopan Monastery with your personal dedication, and access to an exclusive members-only section of our website containing the entire LYWA library of publications in electronic format. Please see www.LamaYeshe.com for more information.

Social Media and Monthly E-letter

Follow us on Facebook, Twitter and Google Plus and every day read gems from our online teachings, view amazing images, and keep up to date with our latest offerings. Also, each month we send out a free e-letter containing our latest news and a previously unpublished teaching by Lama Yeshe or Lama Zopa Rinpoche. See our website for links.

The Foundation for the Preservation of the Mahayana Tradition

The Foundation for the Preservation of the Mahayana Tradition (FPMT) is an international organization of Buddhist meditation study and retreat centers—both urban and rural—monasteries, publishing houses, healing centers and other related activities founded in 1975 by Lama Thubten Yeshe and Lama Thubten Zopa Rinpoche. At present, there are more than 160 FPMT centers, projects and services in over forty countries worldwide.

The FPMT has been established to facilitate the study and practice of Mahayana Buddhism in general and the Tibetan Gelug tradition, founded in the fifteenth century by the great scholar, yogi and saint, Lama Je Tsongkhapa, in particular.

Every quarter, the Foundation publishes a wonderful news journal, *Mandala*, from its International Office in the United States of America. To subscribe or view back-issues, please go to the *Mandala* website, www.mandalamagazine.org, or contact:

FPMT
1632 SE 11th Avenue, Portland, OR 97214
Telephone (503) 808-1588; Fax (503) 808-1589
info@fpmt.org
www.fpmt.org

The FPMT website also offers teachings by His Holiness the Dalai Lama, Lama Yeshe, Lama Zopa Rinpoche and many other highly respected teachers in the tradition, details about the FPMT's educational programs, an online learning center, a complete listing of FPMT centers all over the world and, especially, those in your area, a link to the excellent FPMT Store, and links to FPMT centers—where you will find details of their programs—and other interesting Buddhist and Tibetan pages.

FPMT Online Learning Center

In 2009, FPMT Education Services launched the FPMT Online Learning Center to make FPMT education programs and materials more accessible to students worldwide. While continuing to expand, the Online Learning Center currently offers the following courses:

- Meditation 101
- Buddhism in a Nutshell
- Heart Advice for Death and Dying
- Discovering Buddhism
- Basic Program
- Living in the Path
- Special Commentaries
- Courses in French and Spanish

All of the online programs provide audio and/or video teachings of the subjects, guided meditations, readings, and other support materials. Online forums for each program provide students the opportunity to discuss the subject matter and to ask questions of forum elders. Additionally, many retreats led by Lama Zopa Rinpoche are available in full via audio and/or video format.

Living in the Path is particularly unique in that it takes teachings by Lama Zopa Rinpoche and presents them in theme-related modules organized around short video clips and edited transcripts. Some modules also include guidelines for meditations, as well as for mindfulness and service practices, all of which are based on Lama Zopa Rinpoche's teachings.

Education Services is committed to creating a dynamic virtual learning environment and adding more FPMT programming and materials for you to enjoy via the Online Learning Center.

Visit us at: onlinelearning.fpmt.org

Other teachings of Lama Yeshe and Lama Zopa Rinpoche currently available

Books published by Wisdom Publications

Wisdom Energy, by Lama Yeshe and Lama Zopa Rinpoche
Introduction to Tantra, by Lama Yeshe
Transforming Problems, by Lama Zopa Rinpoche
The Door to Satisfaction, by Lama Zopa Rinpoche
Becoming Vajrasattva: The Tantric Path of Purification, by Lama Yeshe
The Bliss of Inner Fire, by Lama Yeshe
Becoming the Compassion Buddha, by Lama Yeshe
Ultimate Healing, by Lama Zopa Rinpoche
Dear Lama Zopa, by Lama Zopa Rinpoche
How to Be Happy, by Lama Zopa Rinpoche
Wholesome Fear, by Lama Zopa Rinpoche with Kathleen McDonald
When the Chocolate Runs Out, by Lama Yeshe
How to Enjoy Death, by Lama Zopa Rinpoche

About Lama Yeshe:

Reincarnation: The Boy Lama, by Vicki Mackenzie

About Lama Zopa Rinpoche:

The Lawudo Lama, by Jamyang Wangmo

You can get more information about and order the above titles at wisdompubs.org or call toll free in the USA on 1-800-272-4050.

Transcripts, practices and other materials

See the LYWA and FPMT websites for transcripts of teachings by Lama Yeshe and Lama Zopa Rinpoche and other practices written or compiled by Lama Zopa Rinpoche.

What to do with Dharma Teachings

The Buddhadharma is the true source of happiness for all sentient beings. Books like this show you how to put the teachings into practice and integrate them into your life, whereby you get the happiness you seek. Therefore, anything containing Dharma teachings, the names of your teachers or holy images is more precious than other material objects and should be treated with respect. To avoid creating the karma of not meeting the Dharma again in future lives, please do not put books (or other holy objects) on the floor or underneath other stuff, step over or sit upon them, or use them for mundane purposes such as propping up wobbly chairs or tables. They should be kept in a clean, high place, separate from worldly writings, and wrapped in cloth when being carried around. These are but a few considerations.

Should you need to get rid of Dharma materials, they should not be thrown in the rubbish but burned in a special way. Briefly: do not incinerate such materials with other trash, but alone, and as they burn, recite the mantra OM AH HUM. As the smoke rises, visualize that it pervades all of space, carrying the essence of the Dharma to all sentient beings in the six samsaric realms, purifying their minds, alleviating their suffering, and bringing them all happiness, up to and including enlightenment. Some people might find this practice a bit unusual, but it is given according to tradition. Thank you very much.

Dedication

Through the merit created by preparing, reading, thinking about and sharing this book with others, may all teachers of the Dharma live long and healthy lives, may the Dharma spread throughout the infinite reaches of space, and may all sentient beings quickly attain enlightenment.

In whichever realm, country, area or place this book may be, may there be no war, drought, famine, disease, injury, disharmony or unhappiness, may there be only great prosperity, may everything needed be easily obtained, and may all be guided by only perfectly qualified Dharma teachers, enjoy the happiness of Dharma, have love and compassion for all sentient beings, and only benefit and never harm each other.

LAMA THUBTEN ZOPA RINPOCHE was born in Thangme, Nepal, in 1945. At the age of three he was recognized as the reincarnation of the Lawudo Lama, who had lived nearby at Lawudo, within sight of Rinpoche's Thangme home. Rinpoche's own description of his early years may be found in his book, *The Door to Satisfaction*. At the age of ten, Rinpoche went to Tibet and studied and meditated at Domo Geshe Rinpoche's monastery near Pagri, until the Chinese occupation of Tibet in 1959 forced him to forsake Tibet for the safety of Bhutan. Rinpoche then went to the Tibetan refugee camp at Buxa Duar, West Bengal, India, where he met Lama Yeshe, who became his closest teacher. The Lamas went to Nepal in 1967, and over the next few years built Kopan and Lawudo Monasteries. In 1971 Lama Zopa Rinpoche gave the first of his famous annual lam-rim retreat courses, which continue at Kopan to this day. In 1974, with Lama Yeshe, Rinpoche began traveling the world to teach and establish centers of Dharma. When Lama Yeshe passed away in 1984, Rinpoche took over as spiritual head of the FPMT, which has continued to flourish under his peerless leadership. More details of Rinpoche's life and work may be found in *The Lawudo Lama* and on the LYWA and FPMT websites. In addition to many LYWA and FPMT books, Rinpoche's other published teachings include *Wisdom Energy* (with Lama Yeshe), *Transforming Problems, The Door to Satisfaction, Ultimate Healing, Dear Lama Zopa, How to Be Happy, Wholesome Fear* and many transcripts and practice booklets.

AILSA CAMERON first met Buddhism at Tushita Meditation Centre in India in 1983 and has since been involved in various activities within the FPMT, primarily in relation to the archiving, transcribing and editing of the teachings of Lama Zopa Rinpoche and Lama Yeshe. She has edited Lama Zopa Rinpoche's *Ultimate Healing* and co-edited his *Transforming Problems* and *The Door to Satisfaction* and Lama Yeshe's *The Bliss of Inner Fire* for Wisdom Publications, and several of Rinpoche's books for LYWA, including *Heart of the Path, Teachings from the Medicine Buddha Retreat, How Things Exist* and *Kadampa Teachings*. After working originally in India and Nepal, she went to Hong Kong in 1989 to help organize the electronic version of the Lama Yeshe Wisdom Archive. Ordained as a nun by His Holiness the Dalai Lama in 1987, she has been a member of the Chenrezig Nuns' Community in Australia since 1990. She is currently a full time editor with the Lama Yeshe Wisdom Archive.